# Preface

Dear Reader,

The guitar is a fantastic instrument. It has a cultured history that includes many different shapes and forms. It also has many beautiful sounds. The guitar can give you all that you could ever want in a musical instrument. This book tells you wonderful things about the guitar both old and new. It gives you a sampling of the different styles of music that are played on the instrument, shares some of the instrument's history, and tells the stories of some of its most well-known and accomplished players.

I have been a guitarist for more than 25 years. In that time, I have seen many great instruments and players alike. This new age of guitar is exciting, and it continues to grow.

With the advent of new technologies in both manufacturing and production, higher-quality guitars have become easier to build and are now more affordable. This important combination allows all players, from the beginner to the old pro, to have great instruments on which to learn, practise and play while becoming more proficient. With this book, I hope to inspire you (and hopefully your friends) to find the fun in guitar playing and to make it more enjoyable.

Like every new endeavour, it will take time to grasp, but after that, it's a fun ride. Enjoy,

*Ernie Jackson*

# THE ONLY BOOK YOU'LL EVER NEED
# Guitar

# THE ONLY BOOK
# YOU'LL EVER NEED
# Guitar

David and Charles

A DAVID & CHARLES BOOK
© F&W Media International, LTD 2011

David & Charles is an imprint of F&W Media International, LTD
Brunel House, Forde Close, Newton Abbot, TQ12 4PU, UK

F&W Media International, LTD is a subsidiary of F+W Media, Inc.
4700 East Galbraith Road, Cincinnati, OH 45236

First published in the UK in 2011

Text copyright © F+W Media Inc. 2011

The material in this book has been previously published in *The
Everything Guitar Book 2ⁿᵈ Edition*, published by Adams Media, 2007.

F+W Media Inc. has asserted the right to be identified as author of this
work in accordance with the Copyright, Designs and Patents Act, 1988.

A catalogue record for this book is available from the British Library.

ISBN-13: 978-1-4463-0138-8 paperback
ISBN-10: 1-4463-0138-9 paperback

Printed in China by RR Donnelley
for F&W Media International LTD,
Brunel House, Forde Close, Newton Abbot, TQ12 4PU, UK

10 9 8 7 6 5 4 3 2 1

Senior Acquisitions Editor: Freya Dangerfield
Assistant Editor: Felicity Barr
Project Editor: Ame Verso
Proofreader: Cheryl Brown
Senior Designer: Jodie Lystor
Senior Production Controller: Kelly Smith

David & Charles publish high quality books on a wide range of subjects.
For more great book ideas visit: **www.rubooks.co.uk**

# Contents

# Top Ten Reasons for Playing the Guitar

**1.**     It's really fun.

**2.**     It's really easy.

**3.**     Playing with others gives you more chance for social interaction.

**4.**     Going to the music shop never gets boring.

**5.**     Buying a new guitar every once in a while is far less expensive than buying a car.

**6.**     It always feels great to learn and master a new song.

**7.**     Playing the guitar gives you another reason to stand in front of the mirror for extended periods of time.

**8.**     You can carry the guitar anywhere and break out in song.

**9.**     Going to concerts and recital performances makes you a better player.

**10.**    The more you play, the better you'll get.

# Introduction

Though the guitar has been around for a long time in forms dating back to the Persian ud, its early cousin, most players today think of it as an instrument that saw its greatest evolution in the 20th century. The turn of that century was marked by the concert-hall performances of Maestro Andrés Segovia. Blues mythology tells the story of Robert Johnson (who played so movingly it was said he had sold his soul to the devil for the gift). Charlie Christian brought fluid horn-line-inspired electric jazz guitar to the masses. Riding a wave through the 1960s, a decade that changed more than the weather, the brilliant rock guitarist Jimi Hendrix defined the modern conception of what this instrument can do.

The guitar itself is a remarkable instrument. Its six strings give it a musical range of more than half what the much larger and more complex piano can achieve, and the strings can be sounded together, giving the guitar the sense of being a small orchestra. It is more intimate and in some ways more responsive to a player's mood than almost any other instrument. It has both a pure singing soprano as well as a resonant bass – not bad for a musical instrument only three feet long that can weigh less than a good haul after a day of shopping.

More than players of almost any other instrument, guitar players count more self-taught musicians among their ranks. That's because while the guitar is very difficult to play well, it is easy to play simply. Guitarists suffer from the usual string of bad jokes and stereotypes. But when it comes down to playing a good song, it's the guitar that brings people closer together.

# Chapter 1

# The Origin of the Guitar

There are many theories on the origin of the guitar. In fact, the ancient pictures, drawings and paintings of many cultures suggest a guitar, though these are actually stringed instruments of varying types. For example, Babylonian excavations in Central Asia unearthed cave carvings dating back to 1900 BC that show musicians playing together. The carvings feature stringed instruments resembling guitars as well as techniques like strumming and plucking of the strings. Similar stringed instruments like the okongo or cora, are still used in parts of Africa to this day.

# Early Guitars

Early Egyptian drawings show stringed instruments that resemble very complex lyres and harps. Ancient Rome was heavily influenced by Egyptian culture, and as a result there were many versions of these two instruments in early Western cultures. Around 400 AD, for example, the Romans brought their tanbur, also known as the cithara, to Spain.

---

**The Greeks had a stringed instrument call the kithera. Though the spelling is close to the word chitara, it is not a direct ancestor of the modern-day guitar. The kithera is closer to a lyre or harp.**

---

Varying types of stringed instruments developed in the pre-Christian Babylonian, Egyptian and Hittite cultures of the Middle East as well as in the Roman cultures in Italy, Greece and Turkey. All these instruments had certain aspects in common. Each had some sort of sound box and a long neck. Cords or strings were stretched down the neck and over the sound box. Players used one hand to strum (perhaps with a plectrum, or pick, of some sort) and the other to stop the strings at various points along the neck; as a result, they could sound a wide variety of notes, both singly and together.

## Medieval Europe

In the early Middle Ages, as the Moors passed through Egypt on their way to conquer North Africa and Spain, they brought the ud, a direct antecedent of the guitar, to Western Europe. The Moorish influence in Spain prepared the groundwork for the development of the guitar in Europe. By the 13th century, references to and pictures of guitar-like instruments begin to appear in historic documents from all over Europe.

## The Four-Course Guitar

It is possible that makers of the Roman-style cithara and the Arabic ud influenced one another. By ad1200, the four-string guitar had evolved into two types: the guitarra morisca (Moorish guitar), which had a rounded pear-shaped back, a wide fingerboard and several sound holes somewhat like a lute; and the guitarra latina (Latin guitar), which resembled a small version of the modern guitar, with one sound hole and a narrower neck. On either of these instruments, each pair of strings was called a course.

---

**The guitar has many forebears and cousins – the lute, the Middle Eastern oud, the Indian sitar, the banjo, the koto of Japan, the bouzouki of Greece, the vihuela, the yue-chin, chirar, balalaika, rehab, kayakeum, santir, ombi, vambi, nanga, shamisen … and so on.**

---

In 1487, a musical theorist named Johannes Tinctoris described an instrument he called the guiterra or the ghiterna, whose sides were 'tortoise-shaped'. Guitar historians today believe that what Tinctoris actually saw was a round-back lute. In Italy, these instruments were known as the viola da mano and chitarra.

## The Six-Course Guitar

While the guiterra was small and had four courses, the Italian chitarra was larger, with six courses. Both had thongs or cords tied at various places along the neck to make frets or squared-off divisions of the neck. These two instruments became the favourites of wandering troubadours or minstrels.

These early one-man bands had to master a variety of instruments, including pipes, whistles and flutes, plus perform songs, tell stories and provide any other form of entertainment that would earn them money and keep them from facing the displeasure of aggravated patrons.

Here's how an 11th-century Swiss poet named Amarcius described a minstrel's performance: 'When the citharist appears, after arranging for his fee, and proceeds to remove his instrument from its cover of oxhide, the people assemble from far and near, fix their eyes upon him and listen with soft murmurs as he strikes the strings with his fingers stretched far apart, strings which he himself has fashioned from sheep gut, and which he plays now tenderly, now with harsh booming sounds.'

A keen musician himself (and rumoured to be the composer of 'Greensleeves'), King Henry VIII had more than 20 guitars among his collection of musical instruments in Hampton Court Palace.

### The Lute

The lute held court as the major stringed instrument for a long while, but it had a number of drawbacks. First of all, there was no standard lute, so some were large and some smaller. Some had eight strings, while others had twelve or even more. They were difficult to balance and play, and forget about keeping one in tune!

Soon after the reign of Henry VIII, around 1550, the guitar became one of England's more popular stringed instruments. But for some time to come, rival camps of lutenists and guitarists would lose no opportunity to badmouth each other's instrument and musicianship. In 1556 in France, for example, it was reported that while the pear-shaped lute had been a popular instrument, people were playing the guitar even more.

# Compositions for the Guitar

The earliest known music for the guitar was written for a Spanish form of the instrument known as the vihuela. 'El Maestro', by the Spaniard Luis Milan, was published in 1535 for the use and enjoyment of Spanish courtiers and aristocracy. Seven books of music survive, written in tablature. This early form of music is a sort of diagram showing each string of the guitar and indicating where it should be stopped along the neck. Above the diagrams are notes indicating time values, or how long each note should be sounded. The diagrams show pieces of varying degrees of difficulty, including a series of regal dances known as pavanes.

Ten years later, Alonso Mudarra published a music book called Tres Libros de Musica en Cifras para Vihuela. This book contains several sophisticated, sometimes even dissonant, pieces that include a recurrent bass line that gives the music a syncopated, energetic feel.

By the early 17th century, there were a number of books and primers on playing the guitar, particularly in France, where the instrument had become popular. Adaptations of lute music and arrangements of dances and fantasias encouraged the use of the guitar as a member of an ensemble or as an accompaniment to songs.

**Early guitars had gut strings in courses or pairs, with a variety of tunings. A four-course guitar had ten frets and was often tuned to either F-C-E-A, G-C-E-A or C-F-A-D. The top three strings were tuned in unison, while the bass string (either F or G) was tuned in octaves, or eight notes apart.**

The music of this period was not played with the same rigid structure as classical music is today. There was room for improvisation, particularly when it came to variations of melodic phrasing and ornamentation. Advanced players, as always, could perform florid single-note passages and counterpoint and figured bass runs. Generally, however, the fashion for most guitar players of the time was to play rather basic music, mainly strummed chord patterns.

By 1600, the five-course guitar had replaced the earlier four-course and six-course guitars. The tuning also became more standardized, predominantly A-D-G-B-E. The Italian guitarist Giovanni Paolo Foscarini wrote some sophisticated new pieces for the instrument in the 1630s, while a fellow countryman, Francesco Corbetta, became one of the foremost guitar virtuosos. Corbetta travelled widely throughout Europe, popularizing the instrument.

# Many Musical Modifications

By the end of the Baroque period, two significant changes had occurred. The guitar's five courses were replaced by six single strings, and they were tuned in the modern style of E-A-D-G-B-E.

Many changes were taking place musically by this time. The modern piano made its first appearance, and the guitar began to fade from popularity. It was soon considered a more frivolous instrument of seduction and amour. A German diarist wrote, 'The flat guitar with its strum we shall happily leave to the garlic-eating Spaniards.'

---

In 1799, Fernando Ferrandiere published a method book for the six-string guitar called *The Art of the Spanish Guitar*. In that same year, Don Federico Moretti wrote the first standardized book on the six-string guitar, *The Principles of Playing the Guitar with Six Strings*. Guitar scholars believe both method books were derived from an earlier publication by guitarist Antonio Ballesteros, entitled *Obra para Guitarra del sexto orden*.

---

Romance, lasciviousness and the guitar have been fairly consistent partners for a while, not just in the modern age of heavy-metal rockers. For example, Ronsard, a famous 15th-century French poet, wrote:

*It is the ideal instrument*
*For ladies of great learning,*
*Lascivious ladies also play*
*To advertise their yearning.*

Gaspar Sanz, guitarist to the viceroy of Aragon, Spain, was as much a philosopher as a musician. His comments about the instrument and its players stand as well today as they did when he wrote the introduction to his method book on the guitar in the late 17th century: '[The guitar's] faults … lie in whoever plays it, and not in the guitar itself, for I have seen some people accomplish things on one string for which others would need the range of an organ. Everyone must make of it what he can, good or bad.'

The Napoleonic war, at the turn of the 19th century, was responsible for making the guitar popular again. The war, which raged throughout Europe, reintroduced Europeans to the guitar-based music of Spain. This period led to the work of such composers and performers as Fernando Sor, Mauro Giuliani, Matteo Carcassi and Ferdinando Carulli.

The first modern concerto for guitar and orchestra, 'Concerto No. 1 in A Major', was composed and performed by the Italian virtuoso Mauro Giuliani. Among other things, it uses the right-hand thumb for bass notes and features a strong orchestral structure, with variations on a theme, a slow second movement and finally a lively third movement.

# The Classical Guitar

Two people are responsible for the classical guitar as it is known today. The first was the brilliant guitar-maker Antonio Torres. Torres revolutionized the process of building a guitar, making a careful study of how it made its sound, where the sound came from and how he could improve it. The other was the Spanish virtuoso Francisco Tarrega.

---

**Dionisio Aguado (1784–1849), a Spanish classical guitarist and composer, invented the tripodison, a guitar accessory used to hold the guitar instead of letting it rest on the right leg. This minimized the damping effect of the guitarist's body on the guitar's back and sides.**

---

The Torres guitar, developed between the 1850s and the 1890s, had more volume than previous designs. It included a larger, deeper body and an aesthetically pleasing shape that is familiar today. Torres was the first maker to use 'fan' bracing underneath the top. He once built a guitar with a spruce top and papier-mâché back and sides to prove his theory that it was the top that produced most of the volume.

Tarrega adopted the newly designed instrument and composed and arranged hundreds of pieces for it. Ironically, Tarrega did not perform much in public. He was, however, an influential teacher, with a close circle of students and friends who acted almost like disciples in the world outside Tarrega's home and studio.

And then, at the dawn of the 20th century, there arrived a young, self-taught musician named Andrés Segovia. Before Segovia, people believed it was not possible for a solo guitarist to perform effectively to a large audience in a concert hall. Since Segovia, the world has become filled with guitarists in concert. In 1924, he made his debuts in London and Paris. He performed, transcribed, taught and discovered a tremendous amount of music for the guitar. He also encouraged many composers to write for the instrument. He managed to reawaken the public interest in the music of JS Bach, and he arranged many Bach pieces for the guitar, which he also performed and recorded.

**In addition to the modern guitar shape, Torres also created some experimental guitars. For example, to prove that it was the top and not the back or sides of the guitar that made the sound, Torres built a guitar with a papier-mâché back and sides. Torres also invented a guitar that could be assembled (without glue) and then disassembled to fit into a shoebox.**

Of Segovia's many gifts to the world, perhaps his most lasting was to make the guitar the popular instrument of the 20th century. He also standardized the way guitar fingering is notated on scores (by showing the string number written within a circle over a series of notes that could be played elsewhere on the instrument), and settled the debate among classical guitarists about nails versus fingertips (by popularizing the use of plucking the strings with the nails of the right hand). By travelling and performing throughout the world, Segovia brought respect and recognition to the instrument and left behind a vast body of work and pupils who have gone on to become maestros in their own right.

# Flamenco

There are many different styles of playing, and while the guitar was gaining legitimacy in concert halls, a parallel evolution was taking place in the bars and cafés of 19th-century Spain. Flamenco has three aspects: singing, dancing and guitar playing. It grew from the melding of Arab, Christian, Jewish and Spanish folk music and the Middle Eastern influence of seven centuries of Moorish and Arabic occupation, particularly in Andalusia, in the south of Spain, where a large population of gypsies lived.

## The Heartbeat of Spain

It was the Andalusian gypsies who turned flamenco into the heartbeat of Spain, although its roots are probably in Roman-occupied Spain. The composers Kodaly and Bartok discovered in their research into folk tunes that beautiful folksongs have a way of ending up as 'beggars' songs'. In the same way, the outcasts of Spain – the gypsies – adopted and preserved the musical traditions of the Moorish Arabs who had once ruled the land.

What remained, and became idiosyncratically gypsy, were the traditions of whip-cracking dance rhythms and the troubadour's ability to improvise, composing verses about anything and everything at the drop of a hat. In the underground jargon of 18th-century Andalusia, someone flamenco was a dazzler, a 'dude with attitude'. And the music came to be popularized by performers considered by many to be the haughtiest and most flamboyant of the gypsies.

Spain is a dancing country, and the simplest 19th-century village dance orchestra might consist of a guitar and a tambourine, with dancers wielding castanets. By the 1850s and beyond, it was also a country at war with itself. But whether royalist or revolutionary, the tradition was never to shoot a man with a guitar – at least until he was given a chance to play, anyway.

## Flamenco on the Move

The rhythmic and melodic early forms called seguidilla and rasgueado developed new and exciting forms in the café cantantes, bars with areas for performers. Gradually, guitar players developed short instrumental melodic interludes with variations called falsetas.

What had for centuries been campfire entertainment suddenly found itself on a stage attracting the attention and applause of Europe's leading writers, poets, painters and musicians – including Chopin, Liszt, George Sand, Alexandre Dumas, Edouard Manet and Jules Verne – who discovered the joys and inexpensive excitement of Spain on their 'grand tours'.

---

**The flamenco guitar sounds different from the classical guitar because instead of rosewood, cypress wood is used for the back and sides. The use of the capo (a clamp that goes around the neck and shortens the string length) also affects the tone, giving the strings a more treble sound.**

---

Ramon Montoya is considered the father of modern flamenco guitar. He was influenced by Patino, Paco Lucena and Javier Molina. Before his passing in 1949, Ramon Montoya pioneered the recording of the style and developed its traditions and techniques. In doing so, he enriched the music's vocabulary and established himself as one of the first flamenco virtuosos of the 20th century.

His real contribution, however, was to be the first person to break free of the role of accompanist and become established as a solo instrumentalist. When he performed in concert in Paris in 1936, he met with great acclaim.

It has been said that as flamenco has moved from the cafés to the nightclubs, the players have become more circus-like in the manner in which they play the guitar – wearing gloves, putting the instrument behind their heads, anything to attract and hold an audience's attention. Nevertheless, the 20th century has produced some stunning players, such as Sabicas, Carlos Montoya, Niño Ricardo, Paco de Lucia and Paco Peña.

## The Electric Guitar

In combination, the European troubadour traditions of folk music and the spiritual music of African slaves evolved into a guitar- and banjo-based music that first became ragtime and then morphed into jazz. The guitar's role was problematic, though, because it never seemed loud enough to cut through all the other instruments of the group. That was one reason for the banjo's popularity. It might not be as sophisticated a musical instrument as the guitar, but in an ensemble situation it held its own against a blaring cornet, braying trombone, squawking clarinet, the thumping of a drummer and the crash of his cymbals.

---

**George Breed, a US naval officer, received a patent in 1890 for 'an apparatus for producing musical sounds by electricity'. His patent diagram resembles a very early figure-of-eight shaped instrument with six strings activated by electricity and magnetism.**

---

In 1907, Lee DeForest invented the triode. A triode is a vacuum tube capable of amplifying weak electrical signals. This component provides an output strong enough to be fed into a loudspeaker. This invention would soon lend itself to the circuitry found in radios and old phonographs.

## More Volume

The search for more volume led Lloyd Loar, an engineer at the Gibson guitar company, to play around with electrified guitars and amplifiers. In 1924, his experiments with magnetic coils led to the development of a basic pickup, which was, in effect, a giant magnet shaped like a horseshoe that acted as a microphone for each of the strings of the guitar. The signal was then fed through a speaker with a volume control and a tone control. It was all very rudimentary stuff. Gibson didn't get the idea, though, and Loar left and formed the Vivitone Company, which produced commercial guitar pickups during the 1930s.

## The First Commercial Electric Guitar

The real breakthrough came in 1931, when Paul Barth and George Beauchamp joined forces with Adolph Rickenbacker to form the Ro-Pat-In Company (later renamed the Electro String Company). They then produced the first commercially available electric guitar, the A22 and A25 cast-aluminum lap-steel guitar, known as the Frying Pan because of its shape.

Strictly speaking, the Frying Pan wasn't really an electric version of a traditional guitar; rather, it was more of a lap-steel or Hawaiian guitar. However, in 1932 Ro-Pat-In produced the 'Electro', which was an arch-top, or F-hole, steel-string guitar fitted with a horseshoe magnet. Gibson finally caught on and adapted their L-50 arch-top model into the now famous ES-150 electric model, which first appeared in 1936.

The musician who was to make the electric guitar a household name, Charlie Christian, was not actually the first electric guitar player. That role fell to Eddie Durham, who played a resonator guitar in Bennie Moten's jazz group from 1929 and recorded the first electric guitar solo, 'Hittin' the Bottle', in 1935, with Jimmie Lunceford's band. He then made some historic recordings in New York in 1937 and 1938 with the Kansas City Six, a spin-off group of musicians from Count Basie's Big Band that featured Lester Young on clarinet as well as saxophone. For the first time, the guitar was easily a match in volume and single-note improvisation for Young's saxophone and clarinet as well as the trumpet of Buck Clayton.

There was one fundamental problem with the electric guitar, though: it kept feeding back. The amplified sound from the speaker would cause the body of the guitar to vibrate until a howl started that could only be stopped by turning the volume off. Guitarists found they were continually adjusting their volume levels to stop their instruments from feeding back. The answer was to create an instrument that didn't vibrate in sympathy with its amplified sound.

## The Solid-Bodied Guitar

There's no definitive agreement about who produced the first solid-bodied guitar. Guitarist Les Paul created a 'Log' guitar, using a Gibson neck on a flat piece of wood. He went to Gibson to get it into production, but Gibson, once again, was not impressed and turned him down.

At the same time, country guitarist Merle Travis was working with engineer Paul Bigsby, and they produced about a dozen solid-body guitar prototypes. However, the man who made the first commercially available solid-body guitar was Leo Fender, the owner of an electrical repair shop. In 1946, he founded the Fender Electrical Instrument Company to produce Hawaiian guitars and amplifiers. Encouraged by an employee, George Fullerton, Fender designed and eventually marketed a line of solid-body guitars called the Fender Broadcaster in 1950. The Gretsch drum company manufactured drums called Broadcaster, however, and told Fender he couldn't use that name. So Fender changed the name of his guitar to the Telecaster. The rest is history.

The solid-bodied electric guitar paved the way for the popularization of urban blues and an R&B boom in the 1950s, with such great musicians as Howlin' Wolf, Muddy Waters, BB King and so forth. These musicians in turn influenced a generation of young rock-and-roll players in 1960s Britain, including Eric Clapton, Jeff Beck, Robert Fripp and Jimmy Page.

# And Beyond ...

Perhaps the most revolutionary advance of the last 20 years has been the development of MIDI, or musical instrument digital interface, a computer protocol that allows computers, synthesizers and other equipment to talk to each other. While electronic music has been primarily a computer- and keyboard-oriented process, the guitar synthesizer is coming into its own. In the past it has had some problems with delay and tracking (which deals with how quickly, in effect, you can play one note after the other), but that seems to be disappearing with each new generation of equipment.

An example of the new guitar is the SynthAxe, developed in the UK in 1984. This guitar synthesizer is played via an innovative fretboard touch system. The neck acts as a MIDI controller, allowing the player to produce a full range of synthesized and sampled sounds.

Other guitarists have experimented with adding extra strings to the existing six, ranging from seven to 42 or more. But one thing seems constant: all of the players of the experimental guitars end up going back to the traditional, simple six-string guitar, regardless of what else they play.

Where the guitar goes from here is anyone's guess, but one thing is certain. Somewhere in the background of just about any music you like, you're likely to hear the twang and strum of a simple six-string guitar.

## History of the Guitar at a Glance

| | |
|---|---|
| 1700BC | Rumour has it that Hermes, the Greek messenger of the gods, invents the seven-string lyre, the forerunner of the guitar. Meanwhile, at about the same time in Egypt, pictures of a guitar-like instrument are being painted on the walls of tombs. |
| 500bc | The cithara develops from the lyre. |
| 1265 | Juan Gil of Zamora mentions the early guitar in *Ars Musica*. |
| 1283–1350 | The guitarra latina and guitarra moresca are mentioned multiple times in the poems of the Archpriest of Hita. |
| 1306 | A 'gitarer' is played at the Feast of Westminster in England. |
| 1381 | Three Englishmen are sent to prison for making a disturbance with 'giternes'. |
| 1404 | *Der mynnen regein*, by Eberhard Von Cersne, makes reference to a quinterne. |
| 1487 | Johannes Tinctoris describes the guitarra as an instrument invented by the Catalans. |
| 1535 | 'El Maestro', by Luis Milan, is published and contains the earliest known vihuela music, including courtly dances known as pavanes. |
| 1551–1555 | Nine books of tablature are published by Adrian Le Roy. These include the first pieces for five-course guitar. The addition of the fifth course is attributed to Vicente Espinel. |
| 1552 | Guillaume Morlaye's book of songs and dances for the guyterne is published in Paris. |
| 1674 | *The Guitarre Royal*, by Francesco Corbetta, is published. Dedicated to Louis XIV of France, it increases the guitar's popularity. |
| 1770–1800 | The instrument's five courses (doubled strings) are replaced by single strings and a sixth string is added to the guitar. |

## History of the Guitar at a Glance

| | |
|---|---|
| 1800–1850 | Fernando Sor, Mauro Giuliani, Matteo Carcassi, Ferdinando Carulli and Dioniso Aguado all perform, teach, write and publish their compositions. The guitar begins to enjoy wide popularity. |
| 1833 | Christian Frederick Martin arrives in New York and founds the Martin guitar-manufacturing company. |
| 1850–1892 | Guitar maker Antonio Torres develops the larger, more resonant instrument known today as the guitar. |
| 1902 | The Gibson Mandolin-Guitar Manufacturing Company is founded in Kalamazoo, Michigan, and quickly becomes one of the most famous guitar manufacturers in the world. |
| 1916 | Segovia performs at Ateneo, the most important concert hall in Madrid. Previously, it was thought that the guitar did not have the volume for this type of venue. |
| 1931 | The Electro String Company is founded, and the A22 and A25 cast-aluminum lap-steel guitars, known as 'Frying Pans' because of their shape, become the first commercially produced electric guitars. |
| 1950 | The Fender Solid Body Telecaster first appears. |
| 1960 | The guitar is finally accepted as a serious musical instrument for study at the Royal College of Music in London. |
| 1960s | Jimi Hendrix falls off stage by mistake and breaks his guitar trying to throw it back on stage. It becomes part of his stage act and starts a trend. |
| 1969 | The Alembic Company is founded by Ron and Susan Wickersham. |
| 1974 | The 'Chapman Stick' is finalized by Emmett Chapman. |
| 1982 | The Roland Guitar Synthesizer becomes commercially available. |

# Chapter 2

# Tuning, Care and Maintenance of Your Guitar

Though the basic anatomy of the guitar is simple – a nylon or steel string is attached at high tension and is plucked to produce a variety of pitches – the instrument needs constant care to be played at its prime efficiency. This chapter introduces you to the standard components of the electric and acoustic guitar as well as the most common maintenance techniques, such as selecting and changing strings, tuning your guitar and performing basic repairs.

# Guitar Anatomy and Design

Guitars come in a variety of shapes, sizes and types, but there are certain things they all have in common. A guitar has three basic parts: a body, a neck and the headstock (also referred to as a tuning head). You can learn how to maintain your instrument by understanding the various components better.

## Body

There are basically two types of guitar bodies: hollow body and solid body. The hollow body of an acoustic guitar (shown in Figure 2-1) is what produces the instrument's sound. The body of the acoustic guitar is composed of the top, sides and back. The top, or 'face', of the instrument lies just below the strings. The sound hole is the round hole in the centre of the top, from which the sound of the instrument emanates. The sides are the narrow pieces between the front and the back, which is the large surface parallel to the top. Generally, the back and sides of the instrument are made out of the same kind of wood, while on the majority of instruments the top is a finer, thinner piece of wood (or laminate, in the case of less expensive guitars). The top is the part of the guitar that most defines the overall sound.

Some acoustic guitars have a piece of plastic called a pick guard glued to the top just below the sound hole. As the name implies, the pick guard is designed to protect the top of the instrument from damage you might inflict with your pick.

In a purely electric guitar (shown in Figure 2-2), the body is made of a solid piece of wood to avoid feedback, the screeching that results from resonance when the sound of a guitar is amplified. Below are some commonly used woods in electric guitars:

- **Maple** Curly, flamed and bird's-eye are various types of maple wood used in guitars. This is a bright-sounding wood.
- **Mahogany** This hardwood provides a warmer, rounder tone than maple. It is usually found in Gibson Les Paul guitars.
- **Alder** This wood is most commonly found in guitars with an overall sonic balance. It is usually favoured by players with a broad range of playing styles.
- **Swamp ash** This is a lightweight American wood with a bright and distinct tone.

An electric solid body also houses the electronic pickups (which convert the motion of the strings into an electronic signal that can be sent through an amplifier of some kind), and volume and tone controls (which vary the loudness and bass and treble frequencies of the signal). There is also a socket called an output jack, into which you insert a special plug, or jack. The other end of the jack goes into a corresponding socket in an amplifier.

**FIGURE 2-1:**

ACOUSTIC GUITAR

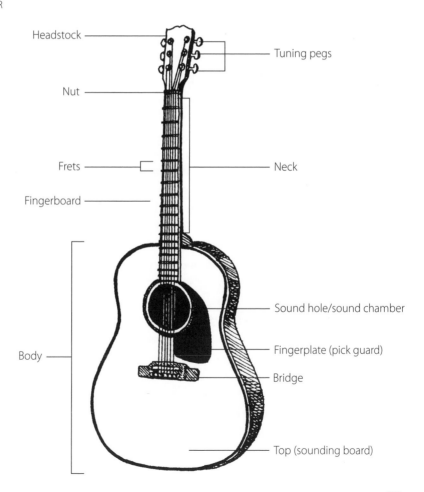

In addition, the body has a bridge, made from either wood or metal, which anchors the strings. There are also strap pins or posts, which you can use to attach a shoulder strap.

## Neck

The neck is usually fixed to the body with bolts or glue, though it might also be formed along with the body in one piece. It often has a metal truss rod running through it to strengthen it and help adjust for any slight warping or twisting. The neck is faced with a flat piece of wood (usually mahogany or ebony) called the fingerboard or fretboard. The fingerboard is divided into sections called frets. These sections are marked off by pieces of wire set into the wood, called fretwire. By stopping a string in between the fretwires – that is, 'in the middle of the fret' – you determine the different pitches or notes you can make on each string. The strings run from the bridge, along the neck and across the nut – a piece of wood, plastic or metal at the top of the neck with slight grooves for each of the six strings – to the tuning pegs.

---

**How does an acoustic guitar work?**
When a guitar string is plucked, it produces vibration. This vibration is transmitted through the bridge into the body of the instrument, causing the inside of the body to resonate, which in turn causes the front and the back of the body to vibrate. Compressed waves of sound are then created inside the body and are projected out of the sound hole.

---

The neck of a guitar also provides a primary 'tonal colour' for the sound of the instrument. Different types of wood give the guitar a distinctive sound. Maple, which is a hard wood, produces a bright, clear sound. Mahogany, which is softer than maple, produces a warmer sound. Another component of the guitar neck is the different types of neck joints. Most guitars have a bolt-on neck. Screws connect the neck to the body – usually found in Fender Stratocasters or Telecasters. A neck-through design means that the neck continues all the way from the headstock to the strap pin at the bottom of the instrument. In this design, the body is actually made up of small wings that are glued to both sides of the neck. A set-in neck glues the neck and body together. This design is usually found in Gibson Les Paul guitars.

**FIGURE 2-2:**

ELECTRIC GUITAR

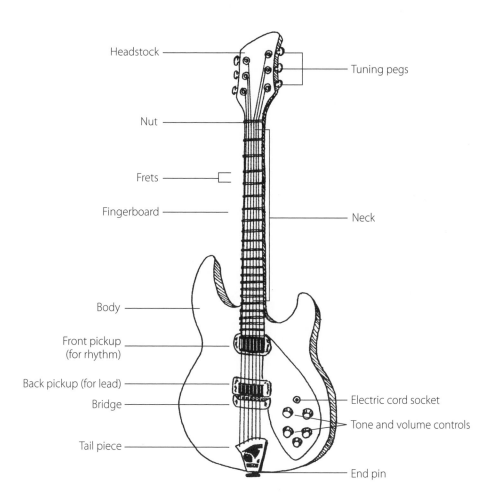

Headstock

Tuning pegs

Nut

Frets

Fingerboard

Neck

Body

Front pickup
(for rhythm)

Back pickup (for lead)

Bridge

Electric cord socket

Tone and volume controls

Tail piece

End pin

## Headstock

The headstock holds the tuning pegs (also called tuning machines, machine heads or tuning gears) that the strings are attached to. In a six-string guitar there are six tuning pegs. Each tuning peg has a knob that you can turn with your fingers. The knob tightens or loosens the string tension and thus puts each string into 'tune'. A headstock that is flat (Figure 2-3) or tilts back (Figure 2-4) determines the effect on tone. Flat headstocks are the continuation of the guitar neck. Tilt-back headstocks are broken up into two types: integral and spliced. The integral tilt-back headstock design uses one large piece of continuous wood. A spliced headstock consists of a separate piece of wood glued on to the end of the neck.

Headstocks may have their tuning arranged with three tuning pegs on each side (like a Gibson Les Paul), or with six in-line pegs (like a Fender Stratocaster).

**FIGURE 2-3:** FLAT
HEADSTOCK

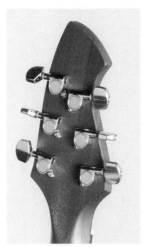

**FIGURE 2-4:**
TILT-BACK HEADSTOCK

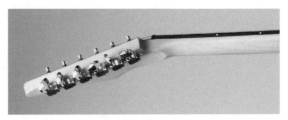

# Names of the Strings

Every fret on every string of the guitar produces a note, and every note has a name, which is represented by a letter. The names of each of the notes on your instrument are important; you'll need to know where to find them in order to read music or to communicate with other musicians. Going from the sixth string (thickest) to the first string (thinnest), the strings are named E, A, D, G, B and E. The sixth string and the first string are the same note, two octaves apart.

Because you're going to need to know the names of your strings for so many reasons, take the time to learn them now. To help you memorize them, try this little phrase: 'Every Adult Dog Growls, Barks and Eats'.

Try playing each of the strings in order while saying the names out loud as an exercise. Then test yourself by pointing to a string at random and saying the name of that string as quickly as possible.

# Tuning Your Guitar

Before you play your guitar you'll have to get it in tune. Most beginners are a little confused by this process when they start, but it becomes second nature fairly fast, and it's essential to sounding good on the guitar.

**The best way to tune your guitar is to use a 'chromatic tuner', which is an electronic device that listens to the pitch of each string, tells you what note it is, and then advises you with a visual display whether you need to tune the string higher or lower to get it in perfect tune.**

If you aren't using a chromatic tuner you'll need a 'reference pitch' from another source. This could come from another guitar or a piano, in which case an E would be a good pitch to tune to since you can tune your bottom and top strings straight off. Or it could come from a 'tuning fork', which is a piece of metal shaped like a wishbone – you strike the double end against your hand to make it vibrate, and then touch the single end against the body of your guitar or against your ear to hear the note.

If you use a tuning fork, the note it produces will probably be an A (also marked 440 on the fork, which is the number of 'cycles per second' of that note), so you would use it to tune your fifth string, and then tune the rest of your guitar around that string.

Assuming you've got your sixth string in tune, let's move on to learning how to tune the rest of the strings. If you play the fifth fret of your sixth (E) string, the resulting note will be an A, which is the pitch your fifth string is supposed to be. If you play the fifth fret of your fifth (A) string, the resulting note will be D, which is the pitch your fourth string is supposed to be. The only time this pattern changes is when you tune the second (B) string to the third (G) string – in that case you play the fourth fret of the G string to hear the B you need to tune the second string. Give it a try!

### How often should I tune my guitar?
You should tune your guitar every single time you pick it up. Guitars (particularly cheaper ones) tend to go out of tune quickly. Make sure it's in tune when you begin to play it and check the tuning frequently while you're practising, as the very act of playing the guitar can cause it to go out of tune.

### Here are some steps to tune your guitar:
1. Make sure your sixth string is in tune.
2. Play the sixth string, fifth fret (A), then tune your open fifth string (A) until they sound the same.
3. Play the fifth string, fifth fret (D), then tune your open fourth string (D) until they sound the same.
4. Play the fourth string, fifth fret (G), then tune your open third string (G) until they sound the same.
5. Play the third string, fourth fret (B), then tune your open second string (B) until they sound the same.
6. Play the second string, fifth fret (E), then tune your open first string (E) until they sound the same. Then double-check your first string against your sixth string – they should be the same.

# String Essentials

Strings don't last forever. In fact, depending on how much you play and practise, you might have to change your strings as often as once a week. In general, however, once every eight to twelve weeks is about average. If a string breaks, it's probably time to change the whole set rather than to replace just the one that broke. Strings lose their stretch and vibrancy over time because of salt from sweaty fingers and rust. You can also find a variety of problems with bridges and nuts and so forth, which we'll get into later on.

You can extend the life of your strings by cleaning them after each session. To get rid of the grunge under the string, some players 'snap' each string by pulling it back slightly, as if the string were on a bow, and then snapping it back to the fingerboard. Strings come in a variety of gauges or thicknesses. The thicknesses are described in fractions of an inch. Choosing a gauge of string is very much a personal decision. In general, the lighter the string gauge, the easier it is to bend and hold down the strings for lead playing. The thicker the gauge, the better the volume, the longer the sustain and the easier it is to keep the guitar in tune. A thicker gauge is also easier for rhythm playing. These are the common gauges:

| | |
|---|---|
| Ultra-light | .008 (first string) to .038 (sixth string) |
| Extra-light | .009 (first string) to .046 (sixth string) |
| Regular | .010 (first string) to .050 (sixth string) |
| Light | .011 (first string) to .052 (sixth string) |
| Medium | .013 (first string) to .056 (sixth string) |
| Heavy | .014 (first string) to .060 (sixth string) |

Strings come in three different types: nylon, usually for Spanish or classical-style guitars; bronze, used for acoustic steel-strung instruments because they have little electrical quality; and steel strings, used for electric and acoustic instruments. You should never put steel or bronze strings on guitars that use nylon strings. This will ruin the instrument quickly because of the increased tension these strings put on the neck.

With the exception of the first and second strings (and sometimes also the third), which are plain metal, steel strings are made up of a thread or core of wire around which another piece of wire is tightly wound. There are three types of winding:

- **Flatwound** Most commonly used on arch-top guitars, these strings consist of a flat ribbon of steel wound around a core of wire. Flatwound strings don't squeak the way other strings can when you move your fingers along them.
- **Roundwound** Most electric steel strings are roundwound, in which a piece of steel is wound around a steel core. They have a brighter tone than flatwound strings, and often last longer.
- **Groundwound** These are conventional roundwound strings that have been ground down to create a partially flat surface.

# Changing Strings

Guitars are pretty rugged instruments. Changing strings regularly will improve the guitar's sound, help keep strings from breaking at the wrong moment and help identify possible maintenance problems. (You may discover a rattling tuning peg or a gouged bridge or nut.) Old strings tend to sound dull and lifeless and they become brittle with age. This makes them feel tougher to fret and harder to keep in tune.

### Removing the Old Strings

An old wives' tale has it that replacing strings one at a time is better for the guitar because it maintains tension on the neck. Not true. Funny as it may sound, guitar necks have 'memory' and guitars themselves are made of sterner stuff. However, replacing strings one at a time can be more convenient. (A string winder, as shown in Figure 2-5, makes the job of winding new strings easier.)

It can be tedious to turn your tuning pegs while putting on new strings. Save yourself time by buying a string winder, which fits over the tuning peg and allows you to turn it far more quickly.

A potential problem with taking all the strings off at the same time is that on guitars with a movable bridge, the bridge will move. This isn't something you want to happen because resituating a bridge can be a pain. And if the bridge is not positioned properly, it can affect the tuning of the strings and the feel of the neck as you play. A good compromise is to replace the strings three at a time. Replace the bass strings first, putting them in rough tune with the old treble strings, and then replace the treble strings, putting them in tune with the new bass strings. Then you can adjust the tuning of all six new strings.

You can unwind the strings using the tuning peg to lessen the tension, or you can try a more radical approach and use wire cutters to snip the strings near the tuning peg. Once you have the old strings off the guitar, throw them away.

**FIGURE 2-5:**

TYPICAL STRING
WINDER

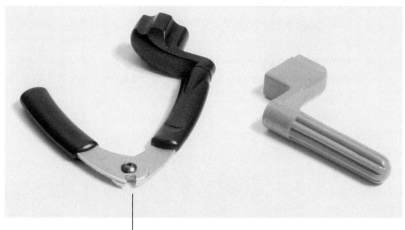

String cutter

## Guitar Bridges

The bridge is what holds the strings in place at the end of the guitar. There are various types on different guitars. Here are the most common:

- **Pin bridge** Found on steel-string acoustics; pins anchor the strings at the end of the bridge.
- **Fixed thread-under bridge** Primarily found on classical guitars (shown in Figure 2-6).
- **Through-body bridge** Found on Strat-style and Tele-style guitars; strings go in the back of the guitar, through the body and up into a metal bridge.
- **Tailpiece bridge** Also known as a 'stop' tailpiece; found on Les Paul-style guitars.
- **Tremolo-style bridge** Some guitars have 'whammy bars' that allow you to give the guitar a vibrato sound. The strings are attached to a metal block that pivots back and forth, making the strings vibrate when the whammy bar is moved.

It is important to know what kind of bridge your instrument has so you can change strings properly and keep your instrument in tune.

**FIGURE 2-6:** NYLON STRINGS ATTACHED TO A FIXED THREAD-UNDER BRIDGE

## Classical Guitars

Classical guitars have fixed bridges, which allows you to replace the strings all at once if you like. Nylon strings aren't as springy as steel and attaching the strings to the bridge can be tricky at first.

Pass the string through the hole in the bridge, leaving about an inch and a half sticking out the back. Loop the short end back up and wrap it behind the long end and then under itself. Pull it taut by tugging on the long end of the string. You may have to practise this a few times. Don't cut the string until everything is in place and in tune.

Thread the long end through the hole in the tuning peg at the head. (Figure 2-6 shows the order of the strings on the head.) Bring the end of the string over the roller (or capstan) in front of the hole and under itself. Make sure that the string sits in the small groove on the nut. Then take up some of the slack of the string and tighten the tuning peg by winding the bass strings from right to left (anticlockwise), and treble strings from left to right (clockwise). As it picks up the slack of the string, the tuning peg will tighten and lock itself in place. While the string tightens, start tuning it and stretching it by pulling on it at various times. Once the guitar string is in place and in tune, snip away the excess string, leaving a couple of inches at the tuning peg, and an inch or less at the bridge.

## Steel-Strung Acoustic Guitars

Steel-strung acoustic and electric guitars have a moveable bridge, so when you change the strings you want to be careful not to dislodge it. It's a good idea to change the strings one at a time, or three at a time, but not all at the same time in order to keep the bridge anchored in its best position.

Acoustic guitars often have pin bridges that anchor the end of the string by popping the string into a hole and keeping it in place with a pin. First, loosen the string tension at the tuning peg. Then ease out the bridge pin.

Bridge pins can stick sometimes, so carefully use needle-nose pliers to ease the pin out of its hole. Some of the newer string winders have a notch by the end of their tuning-peg holder that is used specifically for this purpose. Be careful not to dig into the wood. Once the pin is out, you can remove the string.

Place the end of the new string that has a little brass ring into the bridge-pin hole. Then wedge the bridge pin back into the hole, locking the ring and the string in place. You'll notice that the pin has a slot. Make sure the slot faces forwards, that is, towards the tuning pegs.

Now pass the string over the bridge post, making sure each string fits snugly into the groove on the bridge and on the nut. Thread the loose end through the hole in the tuning-peg post. If you want, you can kink the string a little to help keep it in place. Take up the slack on the string and then turn the tuning peg clockwise for the treble strings and anticlockwise for the bass strings, tuning the string as the tension increases.

After all the strings are attached, retune the guitar carefully, bringing all the strings up to concert pitch. Be careful: you don't want to break a string. The best technique is to turn the tuning peg a couple of times, then check the tuning until you get the string in tune. When the string is in tune, clip the end off at the tuning peg, leaving about an inch of extra wire protruding.

**New strings need to be constantly checked and then 'played in' before they settle into the correct tuning. When they're put on correctly, new strings will make your guitar sound brighter and make it easier to play.**

## Electric Guitars

With electric guitars, you attach the string to the bridge by passing one end through a hole and threading the string up to a brass ball, which keeps it in place.

Some guitars use what is called a locking-nut system, such as a Floyd Rose tremolo unit (as shown in Figure 2-7). These can make strings difficult to change. The strings are clamped into place at the bridge saddle using a special Allen key. It's a good idea to use a piece of wood or a pack of playing cards to take up the tension when a string is changed; this stops the unit from rocking back and forth. On tremolo units, when one string is changed, the tension on all the strings changes.

In order to use these bridges, you must snip off the ball end so that the string can be fitted into a small vice-like mechanism that holds the string in place. When all the strings are changed, you can remove the wood or playing cards supporting the bridge. Tune the strings as usual, using the tuning pegs then make the final adjustment on the bridge anchor using an Allen key. But be careful not to tighten the strings at the bridge too soon. If you overtighten a string, when you remove the block supporting the unit, the string may snap as the tension increases.

Remember, if you have a guitar with this kind of bridge, the spare strings need to have the ball ends removed. Get in the habit of carrying wire cutters around in your guitar case.

**FIGURE 2-7:**

FLOYD ROSE TREMOLO UNIT

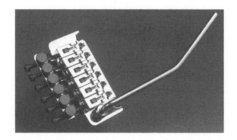

# Basic Repairs and Maintenance

The simplest thing to do to maintain your guitar is to keep it clean. Below is a list of basic, important guitar maintenance duties:

- Dust can gather anywhere on the instrument and cause problems. Use a soft cloth or feather duster, which can clean without the danger of scratching.
- Wipe down the guitar after every playing session and before you put the guitar back in its case – front, sides, back, fingerboard and back of the neck as well.
- Clean each string. The natural oils from your fingers cause the strings to corrode, a process that over time can damage the strings' ability to sound good. These oils can seep into the fingerboard and eventually injure the wood of the instrument. Hold a cloth between your thumb and index finger and run it along the length of each string.

- If the guitar has not been used for a while, first dust it and then rub down the wood with furniture polish or, better yet, guitar polish. (Some types of furniture polish contain abrasives that can damage the guitar's finish.) Never put polish directly onto the instrument, as it can damage the finish – put your cleaning solution onto a cloth first.
- Use a mild jewellery or chrome polish for the metal parts, making certain first that it's not abrasive.
- Avoid keeping your guitar in a place that's subjected to direct sunlight for long periods of time or to drastic changes in temperature and humidity. This will help keep the guitar surface from cracking.
- Depending on the weight and your strength, try to carry your guitar in a hard case. If you're just going to a gig and back, then a good padded nylon gig bag will offer some protection, but not much. A leather gig bag, though much more expensive, is a better choice.

If you do accidentally chip the surface of your guitar, take the guitar to a professional guitar repairer, who will easily fix the problem. If you decide to do it yourself, bear in mind that when you add or remove varnish, you can drastically change the wood's ability to vibrate and thus also alter the guitar's sound.

**Be careful! Don't ever touch the pickups of an electric guitar with anything other than a dry brush or cloth. Pickups are electrical and liquid can cause a short circuit. Also, you run the risk of upsetting the pickup's sensitive magnetic field.**

When travelling, keep your guitar inside the car if you can. In the boot or on the roof rack, a guitar can be subjected to extremes of heat and cold. If you have to put your guitar in the boot, try to put it as close to the passenger compartment as possible. If you're hit from behind, it will stand a better chance of surviving the impact.

# Alterations and Setting Up the Guitar

Don't fiddle with the things described in this section until you're comfortable with the idea that you know what you're doing and why you're doing it. In most cases, if you're consistently unhappy with the way your instrument plays or sounds, you'll be better off taking your guitar to a professional repairer, who may even be able to fix these things while you wait. Professional repair people often spend time watching the musician play and talking about what the guitarist thinks is right or wrong about the instrument before deciding the best way to set up the guitar. Remember, you're paying the expert to do an expert's job.

**Fret wire can wear out and grooves will appear where the strings have worn away the nickel. Eventually the frets will start to buzz. Take your guitar to a professional repairer, who will replace the fret wire with the best gauge of fret wire for your guitar. A 'fret job' can add a new lease of life to an old guitar.**

### Adjusting the Bridge

By adjusting the bridge, you can alter the action of your guitar. The action describes the height of the strings above the fingerboard. The higher the action, the more strength you need to use to fret a note. High action can be useful for rhythm playing, when you are principally playing chords all the time. Blues players who use slides often use a high action so the bottleneck doesn't scrape against the frets.

The lower the action, the easier it is to fret the note. This can be useful for fast, single-note lead-guitar playing. Ideally, you want to set the action as low as you can without getting fret buzzing. This is really a trial-and-error process. (Bear in mind that the thickness or gauge of string you use can make a difference in playability as well.) Before you make any adjustments to the action, make sure you are using a new set of strings. Old strings can affect the action and intonation.

On most electric guitars, each string has an adjustable saddle on the bridge. Either the saddle has a screw that will adjust the whole bridge saddle in one go, or each string has an individual screw that can be raised or lowered. Sometimes it's necessary to adjust the whole bridge saddle by filing it down. This should not be done by anyone other than a professional repairer.

By changing the action, you are also affecting the intonation of the guitar. When you raise or lower the action, you alter the tension and distance between the bridge and the nut. This affects the way the strings play in tune. The distance between the nut and the twelfth fret must be identical to the distance between the twelfth fret and the bridge saddle. If it isn't, the guitar won't play in tune. The easiest way to test this is to play the string open and then play the note or the harmonic at the twelfth fret. The notes played should be identical, though the fretted note or harmonic will be an octave higher. If the note at the twelfth fret is sharp, the string is too short and must be lengthened by moving the saddle back and away from the nut. If the note is flat, then move the saddle towards the nut.

## Adjusting the Neck

Temperature changes, humidity and age can cause guitars to swell and contract. This in turn can affect the set-up of the guitar. For example, a slight bow in the neck can cause fret buzz or make it difficult to get a clean note at a particular fret or series of frets. You can sometimes adjust the neck by manipulating the truss rod. The truss rod runs down the centre of the neck just under the fingerboard. Not all guitars have them (such as classical guitars), and even some that do won't allow you to adjust them. Usually you can see whether the truss rod can be adjusted because there is a plate at the headstock near the nut. Once removed, you will see a rod (or sometimes two) that has an adjustable screw or nut end. If you have a new guitar, it probably came with a truss rod wrench.

If your guitar bows out between the seventh and twelfth frets, you'll see a large gap between the strings and fretboard that makes playing the string at this point very hard. Tighten the truss rod, as you face it, by turning the nut clockwise a quarter turn. Give the instrument a few moments after each turn to settle into its new position.

If the frets buzz and the neck bows inwards at the same place, you can loosen the truss rod by turning the nut anticlockwise a quarter turn at a time (as you face the guitar). Again allow the instrument to settle after each quarter-turn adjustment.

If you can't fix the problem within a few turns, stop. Overtightening or over-loosening the truss rod can ruin a guitar and make it permanently unplayable. Seek professional advice.

## Loose Connections

If you hear a rattle, try strumming the instrument and touching various potential culprits with your free hand until you touch the correct object and the rattling stops. For example, a rattle might come from a loose screw in a tuning peg or a loose nut on a jack socket. It's a good idea to gather a small toolkit of screwdrivers, pliers, wrenches and such that will fit the various sizes of screws and nuts on your guitar.

## Tuning Pegs

Tuning pegs, tuning machines or machine heads (all different names for the same thing) are easily replaced if gears get worn or a part breaks off. If more than one tuning peg is giving you trouble, it's probably a good idea to replace the whole set.

The tuning pegs screw into the wood of the head, so take off the string, unscrew the tuning peg, take the peg to a guitar shop and try to get a matching peg. Then screw the new peg into place in the same position as before.

## Strap Pins

These are little buttons that you use to attach a strap to the guitar. They usually have normal screw bodies that can sometimes work themselves loose. If tightening the pin with a screwdriver doesn't work, dab a little wood or carpenter's glue on the end and put it back. If you still have trouble, seek the advice of a professional.

If you have a more active playing style and find that the strap comes off more often than not while you are playing, you may want to consider using strap locks. These specially designed strap buttons will not come undone unless they are specifically released.

## Electrical Problems

Dust and other grunge can affect the electrics of your guitar. If your volume or tone controls start to crackle when you turn them, or you're getting a weak or inconsistent signal, you may have dust or something else on the control. Turn the knobs vigorously back and forth to see if you can work out the dirt. If that doesn't work, try spraying the controls inside with aimed blasts from a pressurized can of air. If all else fails, go to a professional, who will give your controls a thorough clean.

The crackle can also indicate a loose wire in the jack plug. Take off the jack plate and look for the loose connection. If you spot it, use a soldering iron to reattach the wire to its appropriate lug. If you're uncomfortable doing this, take it to a professional.

Replacing a pickup is not that difficult. Often the pickups that came with your guitar aren't as good as ones you could buy to replace them. Make sure you get a pickup that's the same size and type as the one you're replacing so that it fits into the existing holes drilled into the body.

Make sure you know which wire is supposed to be soldered to which connection. Then seat the pickup in the cavity left by the old pickup and screw it into place. Again, don't attempt this if you don't feel confident that you can do the job well.

# Chapter 3

# Basics of Physical Position

Before you begin playing the guitar, you must be
comfortable holding the instrument. Though it may
sound like a simple first step, it is an important one.
Keep in mind that playing the guitar is a physical
activity. If you have medical issues with your
shoulders, back, neck or lower abdomen, consult a
doctor who can guide you on a specific approach to
learning the guitar. One of the most common reasons
people give up playing the guitar is because of a
physical limitation.

## Leg, Shoulder and Neck Connection

It is a medical fact that sitting for a prolonged period of time in one position creates more stress in your back than when you are standing. This is because your bottom pushes tension up through your spine all the way up to your shoulders and neck. If you happen to work in an office and sit in a chair most of the day, you may have a habit of slouching forwards or down in your chair. If you are accustomed to this posture, you may have a tendency to slouch over your guitar as you hold it. These postures will overstretch your spinal ligaments and cause the discs and other structures in the spine to strain.

You will also need to think about the strength of your fingers, wrists and hands. Some medical conditions, such as carpal tunnel syndrome or arthritis, may affect your ability to play the guitar. Check with your doctor or a professional guitar instructor to see if there are any known methods of playing around any injuries or conditions you may have. You never want to injure yourself further or aggravate your medical conditions. You can also ask around among your friends and relatives to see if anyone has a guitar you could practise holding to test your body's weaknesses before you invest any of your own money in an instrument.

Remember, it is important to have fun playing the guitar! Pain is not fun. So make sure you are comfortable and feeling good about playing. This is an important first step.

## Sitting with Acoustic and Electric Guitars

Even before you sit with your guitar, you must have the proper chair. The best type of chair to sit on with a guitar is one without arms. This kind of chair will allow more freedom for unobstructed left-to-right movement. Ideally, this chair should be height adjustable with a cushioned seat. An adjustable piano bench will work as well. Make sure that the chair or bench is high enough so that you can bend your legs at a 90-degree angle at the knees with your feet flat on the floor. Your back should be straight, with your shoulders relaxed. Your arms should be resting at your sides. Ask yourself, 'Do I feel comfortable?' Hopefully, you do.

**FIGURE 3-1:**

SITTING WITH AN ELECTRIC
GUITAR

Next, with your left hand hanging naturally to the side of your body, slowly raise it to the guitar and lightly grab the neck by the top. Do your best not to lean forwards with the guitar on your lap. (Figure 3-1 shows how to sit with an electric guitar; Figure 3-2 shows how to sit with an acoustic instrument.)

Playing the guitar is a physical activity that requires muscle movement. Keep in mind that any overexertion creates tension. As tedious as it may sound, you really need to practise sitting with the guitar as well as playing it. Being comfortable is always important.

**FIGURE 3-2:**

SITTING WITH AN ACOUSTIC
GUITAR

## Standing with Guitars

The guitar should hang comfortably against your body, leaving both your arms free. If the strap is adjusted properly, the neck of the guitar should describe about a 45-degree angle when compared to the ground. The bridge should be about level with your waist and the head about level with your shoulder. Standing with an electric guitar (as shown in Figure 3-3) is vastly different from standing with an acoustic guitar (Figure 3-4) because of the different shapes and weights of the instruments. Electric guitars tend to be heavier because of their solid-body construction. Acoustic guitars can be cumbersome because of their depth.

**FIGURE 3-3:**

STANDING WITH AN
ELECTRIC GUITAR

Gravity is not your friend here. The deceiving thing about standing with a guitar is that the strap allows both hands to be independent, but the guitar is still hanging from shoulders. While it may look like there is less stress on the back, that is not always the case. It looks really cool when you see those rock stars hanging their guitars down below their knees, but the future back pain is not worth the look. After you know what you're doing, you can adjust the instrument any way you want. But for now, as a beginner, don't make your life harder than it has to be. Playing with the guitar slung too low can really strain your hands, wrists, shoulders and back.

**FIGURE 3-4:**

STANDING WITH AN
ACOUSTIC GUITAR

Whether you are sitting or standing with your guitar, using a strap is always a good idea. As there are many different guitar straps on the market, the best thing to do is to take your instrument to the shop and try some on. If you have neck or shoulder issues due to injury, again, please consult your doctor.

# Position of Left Hand on the Neck

To begin with, the best way to fret a note cleanly is to find the right amount of pressure it takes to use your fingertip to make a note sound clear. This is the key to developing a good left-hand technique. Pressing too hard will cause pain.

First, let the edge of the neck of the guitar rest in the palm of your left hand. You'll notice that your thumb and fingers automatically fall to either side of the neck. Now place the left-hand thumb in the middle of the back of the neck so that there is a nice space between the neck and your palm. You should be able to pivot your whole hand on the ball of your thumb without banging into the neck.

The best practice for thumb placement is to keep your thumb on the back of the neck so that it lies between your first and second fingers, as shown in Figure 3-5.

**FIGURE 3-5:**

THUMB PLACEMENT

**FIGURE 3-6:**

FRETTING A NOTE

When you fret a note, use the tip or pad of your finger to press the string firmly to the fingerboard, as shown in Figure 3-6.

If you position your left hand on the neck so that you can put your thumb immediately behind the place where you're pressing the string to the fretboard (as if you're trying to pinch your thumb and finger together through the neck, as shown in Figure 3-7), you'll get maximum pressure on the note and it will sound clean.

**FIGURE 3-7:**

LEFT-HAND POSITION

Place the tip of your first finger on the first string at the first fret (as illustrated in Figure 3-8). Now pluck the string with your right-hand thumb.

FIGURE 3-8

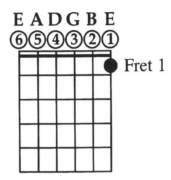

In the diagram, each vertical line represents a string. Each horizontal line represents a fretwire. The double line at the top represents the guitar nut. The black dot or number represents the finger you should use to stop that string at that fret – in this case, at the note F on the first string.

Press the string to the fretboard roughly in the middle of the fret (between the fretwires). If you press too close to a fretwire, the string may be muted; too far away and the string may buzz. To make sure you don't mute other strings, make a point of using your fingertips and keeping your fingers as close to perpendicular to the strings as possible by arching your wrist slightly (like a swan's neck). The classical guitar technique helps in this regard.

Though a lot of players allow their left-hand thumb to come over the top of the neck, it's hard for beginners to do. Remember, the more your hand is cramped up like this, the harder it is to play the note well (that is, without any buzzing sound) and the more your muscles may ache.

As soon as your hand or fingers get sore or start to hurt, stop! It will take a little time to build up the strength in your fingers. Playing a little bit often is better than playing a lot in one go.

# Right-Hand Positioning

The right hand can be used fingerstyle, which means that each finger on the right hand is used to manipulate the strings. Alternatively, you can hold a plectrum, or pick, in your right hand to strum various rhythms or pick out notes on the strings.

## Fingerstyle

The basic fingerstyle position is to use the fingernails to pluck the strings. (Initially, you may use your fingertips as well.) The fingers are held vertical to the strings with a slight arch in the wrist. The thumb plays the three bass strings, while the first finger plucks the third string, the second finger the second string, and the third finger the first string. The little finger is usually not used.

For the moment, it's probably a good idea to practise strumming all six strings first with your thumb and then using a pick. The key is to place your fingertips on the pickguard (the piece of plastic or laminate placed under the strings on the body of the guitar) to anchor your hand and then to brush your thumb across all the strings. We'll discuss more complex pick and fingerpicking techniques in Chapter 4 and Chapter 8, respectively.

## Holding a Pick

The size and thickness of guitar picks, or plectrums, vary greatly to accommodate the different playing styles and strings. In the beginning, you'll want one that has a medium size and thickness. Buy yourself two or three and experiment.

Let the pick lie flat on your first finger, and then comfortably hold it in place with your thumb as shown in Figure 3-9. You can then use it to strum the string with up-and-down motions, as shown in Figure 3-10. The movement comes from your wrist, not your fingers.

To get a feel of what to do, take your right hand and extend the fingers, thumb and first finger lightly touching at the tip. Now, with the fingertips still touching, shake your hand up and down at the wrist in a gentle, comfortable motion. This is the motion you want to use to strum the guitar strings.

**FIGURE 3-9:**

HOLDING A PICK

**FIGURE 3-10:**

USING THE PICK
TO STRUM

# How Not to Hold a Guitar

Now that you have mastered the basic positions, you'll have to choose the one that you feel most comfortable with. To avoid injury, remember to stick to proper positioning and not let your body get lazy and start to slump. Here are a few pointers on what not to do when positioning yourself for guitar playing:

- When sitting, do not lean forwards. This posture will only cause muscle pains after continuous playing.
- When standing, don't hold the guitar so low that you have to stoop low to play it. Keep it up near your chest between your neck and waist.
- Remember not to press harder on the neck than you need to produce a clear note.
- Don't hold the guitar behind your head. It looked cool on Jimi Hendrix, but it's not very practical in the end.
- Don't try to hold the guitar between your legs or on top of your head. Once again, it looks cool, but it's not practical.

Guitar tricks and strange guitar contortions may be intriguing in music videos, but they are not practical for good guitar playing and can actually cause injury to the inexperienced player. To get the most out of your guitar and optimize its sound quality, you'll need to respect the instrument (and your body) and hold it correctly.

# Chapter 4

# The Basics of Reading Guitar Music and Tablature

Learning to play the guitar is unlike learning other instruments. For example, if you were a pianist, you would most likely have learned to play the instrument through years of private study that would have included a heavy focus on sight-reading – the ability to look at a written page of music and play it immediately. However, there's nothing wrong with taking a more informal approach to learning music. Plenty of famous musicians have never learned to read music. This chapter will help you understand the basics you'll need to read guitar music.

# The Musical Alphabet

Now it's time for you learn the musical alphabet. The musical alphabet consists of seven notes, which are named for the first letters of the alphabet: A-B-C-D-E-F-G. At the end of this sequence, the notes repeat themselves. When you reach A the second time around, you're playing the same note except that it's one octave (or eight notes) higher than the A you started with.

This difference depends on the 'frequency' or number of beats per second (bps) at which a string vibrates. This frequency doubles every time you go up an octave. For example, the open A string on the guitar vibrates at a frequency of 110bps. The A one octave higher, played by fretting the twelfth fret on the A string, vibrates at a frequency of 220bps.

This note sequence can be started on any note you like (such as A-B-C-D-E-F-G-[A]; F-G-A-B-C-D-E-[F], and so on). No matter where you start, the sequence still repeats after seven notes. There are five more notes in the musical alphabet that are variations on the seven letters you are about to master.

# Basic Elements

There are two basic elements to reading and writing music: the name of the note and the length of time that note should last. Over time, these two elements were combined into one elegant system, called musical notation. A five-line 'staff' developed, and the note's position and appearance on the staff told musicians how long to hold the note before playing the next one.

The first thing you need to do is understand where notes are written and where they are placed. Look at the music staff shown in Figure 4-1. The music staff is made up of five lines with four spaces.

**FIGURE 4-1:** GUITAR STAFF LINE

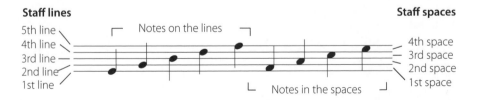

The modern staff is split into two halves, each of which is called a clef. Each clef has a particular sign at the beginning to tell you which staff you are using. These clefs are called the treble clef and the bass clef. When piano players read music, they play the treble clef with their right hand and the bass clef with their left hand.

Treble clef  Bass clef

Notes that appear below or above the clefs appear on what are called ledger lines, or individual lines where each note is written. Ledger lines are lines that extend the range of notes when needed above or below the staff lines, as shown in Figure 4-2. Ledger lines can become difficult to read as the notes get higher. In this case, the symbol 8va… is used to show that certain notes should be played one octave higher than written.

**FIGURE 4-2:**

GUITAR LEDGER LINES

Ledger lines above the staff

Ledger lines below the staff

Look at Figure 4-3. Notice that in between the treble clef and the bass clef is one note on a ledger line. That note is called middle C because it falls in the middle of the two clefs. On the guitar, it is usually played on the third fret of the fifth string.

**FIGURE 4-3:**

MIDDLE C

(treble clef)
middle C
(bass clef)

E A D G B E
⑥⑤④③②①

Those of you who are quick off the mark may have figured out a little problem when it comes to playing certain notes on the guitar. You may have noticed that you can play the same note (as it appears on the treble clef) in different places on the guitar. E, on the top space, for example, can be played on the fifth fret of the second string or on the open first string. For the moment, you'll only need to worry about reading music in the first position – that is, around the first fret.

## Note Name Identification

You'll notice that even though you are learning about the musical alphabet, you don't necessarily have to start on the note A. As you are learning about the guitar here, look at music notation as it relates to the guitar. Figure 4-4 shows the names of the notes played at various frets.

**FIGURE 4-4:** GUITAR NOTE NAMES AND FRET NUMBERS

## Guitar Tablature

Another way to write down music is to use tablature. Instead of showing the notes to be played, the way music notation does, tablature is designed for a particular instrument and shows you where to stop a particular string to play the desired note. A version of this kind of music notation was used by Renaissance and medieval lute players for years. You can show complex fingerings this way, including chords and melodies.

In guitar tablature, each of the six lines represents one of the guitar's six strings, as shown in Figure 4-5. The top line is the first string and the bottom line is the sixth string. The numbers on each line represent the fret you need to stop in order to get the desired note – a pretty good system for writing down tunes quickly.

**FIGURE 4-5:**

GUITAR

TABLATURE

# Finding the Notes on the Guitar Neck in First Position

Now that you have a basic foundation in the look of both the music and tablature staves, you should do your first exercise in first position. The purpose of this exercise is to understand the rule of finger per fret (meaning when the left hand is on the guitar, place one finger per fret so that your first finger can play any note along the first fret, the second finger can play any note on the next fret down, etc.).

The left-hand fingers are numbered as shown in Figure 4-6. The open strings are indicated by the number 0, the first finger and first fret by the number 1, the second finger and second fret by the number 2, and the third finger and third fret by the number 3.

**FIGURE 4-6:**

THE LEFT HAND,

NUMBERED

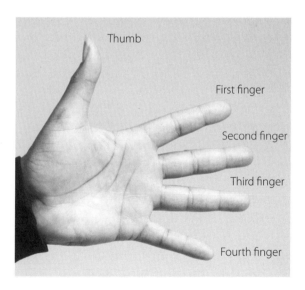

Thumb

First finger

Second finger

Third finger

Fourth finger

Here is your first exercise to try:

**FIGURE 4-7:** EXERCISE, OPEN POSITION

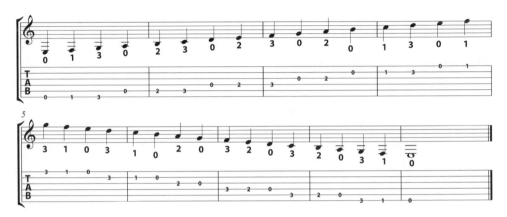

Now that you have seen where the left hand should stop each string to produce the musical alphabet in first position (as shown in Figure 4-6), the following two figures will show some notes on the fretboard with the fingerings to help you learn the musical alphabet.

(Bass Strings)

**FIGURE 4-8:**

BASS STRINGS

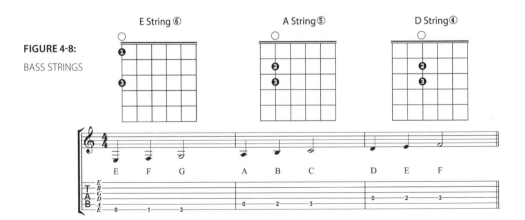

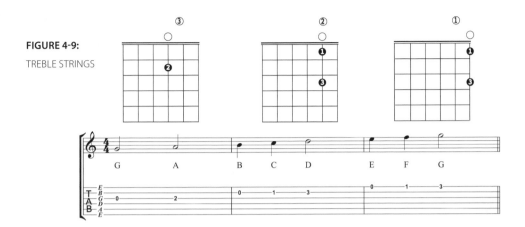

**FIGURE 4-9:**

TREBLE STRINGS

# Time and Rhythm

Having a good knowledge of 'where the beat is' and playing in time are paramount for a musician. As Duke Ellington once wrote, 'It don't mean a thing, if it ain't got that swing …'

Time breaks down into two elements: rhythm, or the 'feel' of a piece of music, and tempo, or the speed you play at. Examples of rhythm styles include swing, shuffle, waltz, bossa nova, funk, bop, bluegrass and so on. Sometimes these rhythms are also the name of the style of music. Music is often marked with a suggested tempo that may look like this: Ñ =120. The number 120 refers to the number of beats per minute (bpm) on a metronome. It denotes how fast (or slow) the piece should be played. The lower the number, the slower the piece of music. The higher the number, the faster the piece of music. In general, these are the accepted tempos (tempi, to be more precise), each of which has an Italian descriptive term, as follows:

- **Grave** Very slow (slower than 40bpm).
- **Lento** Slow (40 to 60bpm).
- **Adagio** Slow – literally, 'at ease' (60 to 75bpm).
- **Andante** Walking (75 to 100bpm).
- **Moderato** Moderate speed (100 to 120bpm).

- **Allegro** Fast – literally, 'cheerful' (120 to 160bpm).
- **Vivace** Lively (150 to 170bpm).
- **Presto** Very fast (170 to 200bpm).
- **Prestissimo** As fast as possible (200 or more bpm).

Many musicians learned to play by playing along with CDs and records or by using a simple metronome that keeps a steady tempo. If you play along with a recording, you may have to retune your guitar slightly until it is in tune with the music.

# Written Music

As you've seen, music can be written out in tablature, as shown in Figure 4-10.

**FIGURE 4-10:**

MUSIC IN

TABLATURE

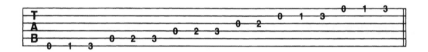

The problem is that you can't easily use this kind of chart to show how long you should sound a note. One beat? Two beats? Three beats? How can you tell? While tablature is handy, it has its limitations.

So how do you solve that problem? You split the note up into fractions that last for a certain portion of the time allotted a whole note. Because these divisions are standard and precise, the fractions retain a predictable, mathematical relationship to one another.

You'll notice that eighth notes and sixteenth notes have 'flags' attached to the stem. Flags are the little wavy lines at the top (or bottom) of the note stem. The number of flags on a stem tells you the kind of note you're playing.

| | | |
|---|---|---|
| Whole note | | = 4 beats |
| Half note | | = 2 beats |
| Quarter note | | = 1 beat |
| Eighth note | | = ½ beat |
| Sixteenth note | | = ¼ beat |

## Time Signatures

Undoubtedly you have seen a marking such as 4/4 at the front of a piece of music (or sometimes 3/4, and so on). This notation is known as the time signature. The top number (4 or 3) tells you how many beats in the bar to count. The bottom number tells you the kind of note you are counting (in this case, a quarter note). So if 4/4 (also known as 'common time') means four quarter notes to each bar, and 3/4 means three quarter notes per bar, then 2/2 would be what? You got it: two half notes to the bar. What would 6/8 be? Right – six eighth notes to the bar. And so on.

The notes in the bar have to add up to whatever the time signature says. For example, 3/4 would mean the notes must add up to three. Then a bar line like this ' | ' is drawn, and you start the next group of three. If the notes had to add up to four, then you would make sure there was a bar line every time the notes added up to four.

For example, the notes in Figure 4-11 all add up to four. The notes in Figure 4-12 add up to three.

**FIGURE 4-11**

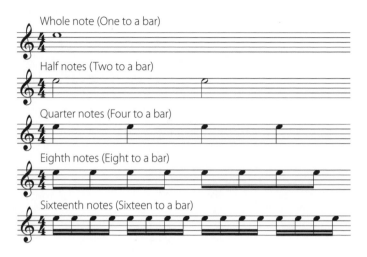

**FIGURE 4-12**

What if you don't want a note to be played? Or you want one note to last longer than usual? Each of the notes has a corresponding rest note that indicates you should wait that length of time before playing the next note, as shown in Figure 4-13. A quarter-note rest, for example, indicates that you wait, or 'rest', one beat before playing the next note. So in 4/4 time, one bar might consist of a quarter note, a quarter-note rest and two quarter notes.

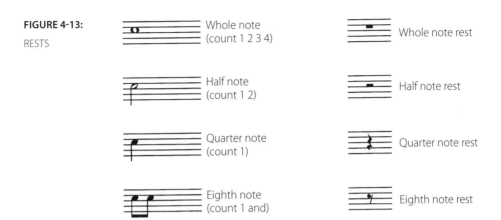

**FIGURE 4-13:**

RESTS

Writing a dot immediately after a note increases that note's duration by half as much again. For example, a dotted whole note would be four beats plus two, totaling six. A dotted half note would be two beats plus one, totaling three. A dotted quarter note would be one beat plus a half of a beat. (In this case, the next note would start on the 'off' beat.)

Another way to make a note last longer – and keep everything neatly within the bar lines – is to tie two notes together. In Figure 4-14, for example, notice you play the first note, keep your finger down and continue to count for the length of the second note that is tied to the first with a curved bar connecting the two notes. Try this exercise for yourself.

**FIGURE 4-14:**

A HALF NOTE TIED

TO A QUARTER

NOTE

**FIGURE 4-15**

## Dynamic Markings

When musicians talk about dynamics, they are basically referring to how loudly or softly you play a note or chord. Again, the dynamic markings in music have Italian names. Here they are with their symbols:

- **pp** Pianissimo (very quietly).
- **p** Piano (quiet).
- **mp** Mezzo piano (moderately quiet).
- **mf** Mezzo forte (moderately loud).
- **f** Forte (loud).
- **ff** Fortissimo (very loud).

'Staccato' means short and sharp. When you play staccato, you keep the rhythm of the piece, but you play the notes for a shorter duration than you normally would. Staccato notes are often marked with dots underneath.

The opposite of staccato is 'legato', which means slurred. Here you slur the notes together, maybe playing one note and hammering down on the next note using left-hand fingering alone.

**FIGURE 4-16:**

EXERCISE IN

COUNTING NOTES

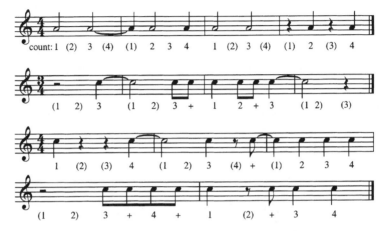

## Left- and Right-Hand Coordination

People are generally impressed by the fast Formula 1 driver, the fast track runner, and the fast-playing guitar master. The one thing all of these examples have in common is coordination. All physical skills are based on coordinated movements. Whether it's learning to walk with one foot after the other or learning to drive a car with a manual gearbox, all skill sets are a series of coordination. In guitar playing, you have to coordinate the left and right hands to the same strings at the same time. Seems easy enough. After you master that, then you have to learn to finger different notes on one string while simultaneously picking the same string and then moving through the other five strings. Whoa! Sounds like a lot, but it is more fun than daunting.

## Introduction to Picking

There are two distinct ways of hitting the string with a pick: a downstroke and an upstroke. To make a downstroke, use the tip of the pick and push down. Upstrokes are the reverse. The tip of the pick is used to pull up on the string. If you want to master using a pick, you need to become very comfortable mixing downstrokes and upstrokes. Figure 4-17 shows some exercises to help develop right-hand picking. These exercises use open strings and are written in both music notation and tablature. Things are a lot more complicated if you're left-handed and choose to use a left-handed guitar. If you get one, then just do everything in a mirror image, substituting left hand for right hand and vice versa.

**FIGURE 4-17:**

RIGHT-HAND

PICKING

EXERCISES

# Beginning Exercises

Figure 4-18 shows a left-hand fingering exercise. Notice that you should play this using each finger to a fret as shown. (Normally, you would not play the B on the fourth fret of the third string or on the open second string. But for the purposes of this exercise go ahead and do it anyway.)

**FIGURE 4-18:**

LEFT-HAND
FINGER
EXERCISES

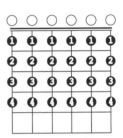

Figure 4-19 shows an exercise enabling you to practise the 'finger per fret' rule.

**FIGURE 4-19:** EACH FINGER TO A FRET

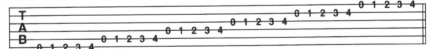

## Left- and Right-Hand Finger-Dexterity Exercise

The exercise shown in Figure 4-20 combines left- and right-hand coordination skills as well as an introduction to finger dexterity. The idea here is to practise slowly. At one point, you will have to use the little finger of your left hand. The little finger is a little weaker than the other fingers, so using it will take some getting used to. Remember, the numbers next to the notes are the fingers to be used on the left hand.

**FIG 4-20:** OCTAVE SCALE

# Practice Tips

The key to good practice habits is consistency. Ten minutes a day – every day – is better than eight hours all at once on Saturday afternoon. Your fingers have to develop a muscle memory of how to form the chords and where to go and what to do, and you have to get over the slight soreness of your fingertips until calluses build up. (A hint: if your fingertips get sore, take a break.)

# Chapter 5

# Introduction to Simple Songs

Now you're going to learn to strum some songs and play some simple melodies. To do this, you'll need to learn a few chords first. A chord is made when three or more strings are played together, usually by strumming down with a plectrum (more commonly known as a pick) or by using your thumb. Playing a chord is one of the most basic and important guitar-playing concepts, which is why it is taught before any other technique.

# Chords C and G7

The chords you are going to learn now are easy versions of basic chords. (You'll learn the more complex forms later.) The chords are C (shown in Figures 5-1 and 5-2) and G7 (shown in Figures 5-3 and 5-4). Memorize the names of the chords and the shapes they make.

**FIGURE 5-1 AND 5-2:**

BASIC C CHORD

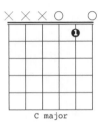

**FIGURE 5-3 AND 5-4:**

BASIC G7 CHORD

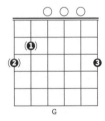

To play the C chord, put your first finger on the second string at the first fret. Press hard. Strum the first, second and third strings together to sound the C chord. Do this four times. You've now strummed four beats. When these four beats are written as shown in Figure 5-5, they make one bar (or measure) of music.

**FIGURE 5-5:**

FOUR-BEAT BAR

Strum the chord four more times. You've now strummed two bars of C.

**FIGURE 5-6**

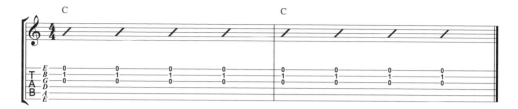

To play the chord G7, put your first finger on the first string at the first fret. Strum the first three strings together and do this four times. Play the C chord four times, and then another four times. Play G7 four times. Now play C four times.

Surprise! You've successfully played the song 'Merrily We Roll Along'. The 4/4 at the beginning means count and play four beats in every bar. (If the time signature was 3/4, what would that mean? Answer: you would play and count three beats in the bar instead of four.)

The bars are created by bar lines that look like this: ' | ' It is usual to write four bars per line and then go to another line. In 'Merrily We Roll Along', for example, as Figure 5-7A shows, the first bar is C for four beats, and the second bar is also C for four beats. The third bar is G7 for four beats, and the fourth bar is C for four beats. The next line is a repeat of the first line, so that the song has a total of eight bars altogether.

**FIGURE 5-7A:** MERRILY WE ROLL ALONG

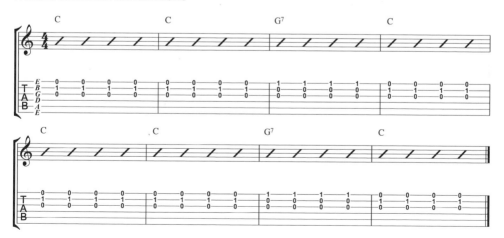

*Merrily we roll along, roll along, roll along,*
*Merrily we roll along, over the deep blue sea.*

Changing chords to play this song is going to take some practice. You may find
that your fingertips get sore. The strings will buzz if you stop them in the wrong
part of the fret or don't press hard enough. As you change chords while you
strum, it's a challenge to jump your finger smoothly from the first string to the
second string and back again. But don't get disheartened. Remember, everyone
who has ever played the guitar – from Segovia to Pat Metheny to Eric Clapton –
has had to go through this stage, and every one of them found it just as awkward
and just as frustrating as you do.

The trick again is to practise slowly and try to aim for good technique. Slightly
arch your wrist, use your fingertips and press firmly with your thumb in the middle
of the back of the neck as you press down with your fingertip to stop the string. Try
to eliminate all sounds of buzzing. Keep your other fingers out of the way.

Now try another old folk song, 'Go Tell Aunt Rhodie', shown in Figure 5-7B.

**FIGURE 5-7B:** GO TELL AUNT RHODIE

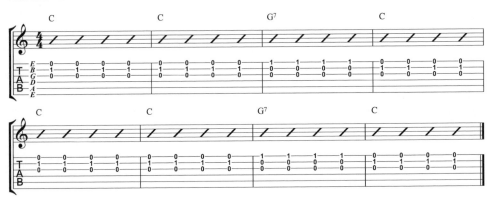

*Go tell Aunt Rhodie, go tell Aunt Rhodie,*
*Go tell Aunt Rhodie, the old grey goose is dead.*

Once you can play these two simple tunes with smooth chord changes from C to
G7, it is time to move on and learn two more important chords.

# Chords D7 and G

The next chord to learn is D7. This chord uses three fingers. Study the chord chart shown in Figures 5-8 and 5-9. Remember, the numbers represent the finger you should use on each string (third finger on second fret of first string; first finger on first fret of second string; second finger on second fret of third string).

It will probably take some practice before you make the D7 chord sound clearly. Work at it. A good exercise is first to press hard and play the chord. Next, relax your hand and lift your fingers slightly off the guitar strings but keep them in the shape of the chord. Then put your fingers back on the strings – again, pressing hard. This helps build muscle memory so that the fingers remember where they should go to form this chord.

**FIGURE 5-8 AND 5-9:** BASIC D7 CHORD

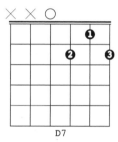

D7

When you can hold the D7 chord with all three fingers and sound the chord clearly, with no buzzing strings, it is time to move on and learn the basic G chord. The form is shown in Figures 5-10 and 5-11. If you have trouble with this, just play the note on the first string and strum the first four open strings.

**FIGURE 5-10 AND 5-11:**

BASIC G CHORD

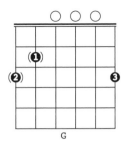

In the next song, 'Twinkle, Twinkle Little Star', shown in Figure 5-12, you'll have to move back and forth among the different chords you've learned so far.

Notice that in this song, in the second and third bars and elsewhere, you'll play two beats of C and then two beats of G. This is a hard tune to play, so practise it a lot. The whole idea is for you to get comfortable changing chords.

**FIGURE 5-12:** TWINKLE, TWINKLE LITTLE STAR

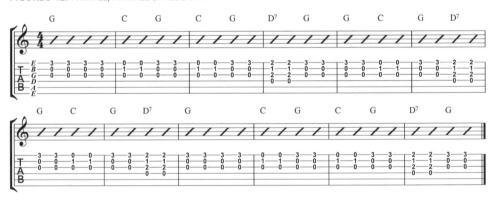

*Twinkle, twinkle little star, how I wonder what you are*
*Up above the world so high, like a diamond in the sky,*
*Twinkle, twinkle little star, how I wonder what you are.*

'Amazing Grace', shown in Figure 5-13, has a time signature of 3/4. This means you strum three beats to the bar.

**FIGURE 5-13:** AMAZING GRACE

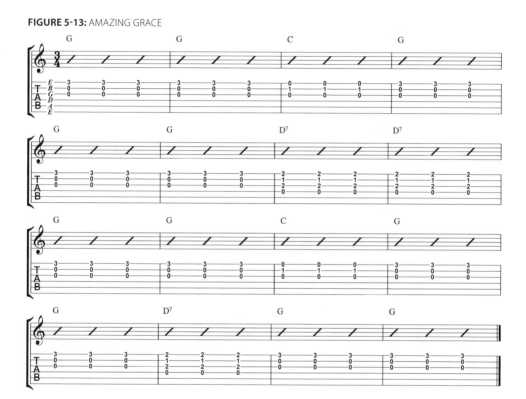

To keep notation simple, instead of writing out bars that are simply repeats of the previous bar, you can use a repeat bar sign (Figure 5-14). This sign indicates that you should repeat the previous bar. (See the way it is used in 'She'll Be Coming Round the Mountain', shown in Figure 5-22.)

**FIGURE 5-14:** REPEAT BAR SIGN

Try the fuller versions of the C, G, G7 and D7 chords (shown in Figures 5-15 to 5-18), and then go back and practise these songs.

**FIGURE 5-15
AND 5-16:**

C CHORD FULL

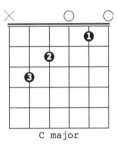

C major

**FIGURE 5-17
AND 5-18:**

G7 CHORD

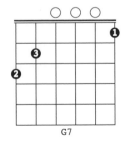

G7

# Songs on the First Two Strings

The following are the full versions of 'Merrily We Roll Along' and 'Go Tell Aunt Rhodie'. Both of these songs are played on the first two strings. Figures 5-19 and 5-20 show these songs with the melody included. Use the tablature if necessary.

**FIGURE 5-19:** MERRILY WE ROLL ALONG

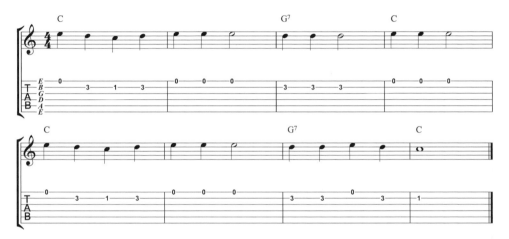

**FIGURE 5-20:** GO TELL AUNT RHODIE

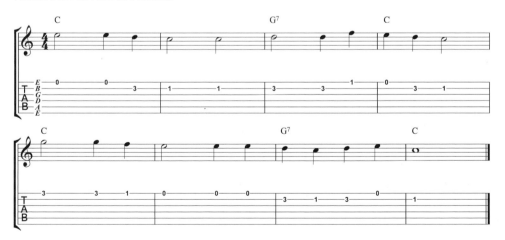

# Song on the First Three Strings

'Twinkle, Twinkle Little Star' is played on the first three strings. Figure 5-21 shows this song along with the melody.

**FIGURE 5-21:**

TWINKLE, TWINKLE LITTLE STAR (G7)

# Songs on the First Four Strings

Figures 5-22 and 5-23 show 'She'll Be Comin' Round the Mountain' and 'Amazing Grace', both played on the first four strings.

**FIGURE 5-22:**

SHE'LL BE COMIN' ROUND THE MOUNTAIN

**FIGURE 5-23:** AMAZING GRACE

# Bass Patterns on the Fifth and Sixth Strings

Just as an extra exercise, try playing 'She'll Be Coming Round the Mountain' on the fifth and sixth strings, as shown in Figure 5-24. You've just transposed the song down one whole octave – see how far you have come? Good work.

**FIGURE 5-24:**

SHE'LL BE COMIN' ROUND THE MOUNTAIN – DOWN ONE OCTAVE

# Chapter 6

# Basic Guitar Fretboard Theory

In Chapter 4, you learned that on the music staff, notes can be shown on the lines (E-G-B-D) or the spaces (D-F-A-C-E-G). You can raise or lower these notes using sharp ♯ and flat ♭ signs. (Flattening – or diminishing – a note means dropping it down a semitone or fret. Augmenting – or raising – a note means sharpening or raising it a semitone or fret.) Instead of placing lots of sharps or flats into the notation, which can look cluttered and confusing, you can instead put them at the beginning of a piece of music. This method tells you that all the notes that have a sharp or flat sign in front of them should be played that way unless a natural sign ♮ tells you otherwise.

# Key Signatures

A key signature is a series of sharps or flats at the beginning of a staff showing which notes are to be played higher or lower than the natural notes. Depending on how many sharps or flats there are at the beginning of a piece of music, you can tell which key the music is written in.

The list below shows the correspondence between sharps and flats and key signatures (shown in Figure 6-1):

- No sharps or flats = Key of C
- One sharp = Key of G
- Two sharps = Key of D
- Three sharps = Key of A
- Four sharps = Key of E
- Five sharps = Key of B
- Six sharps = Key of F♯
- One flat = Key of F
- Two flats = Key of B♭
- Three flats = Key of E♭
- Four flats = Key of A♭
- Five flats = Key of D♭
- Six flats = Key of G♭

Six flats (or altered notes) are just about as many notes as you need to remember. After this you'll learn about 'enharmonic' notes, or notes that have the same name. An example of this would be C flat, which is really B natural.

**FIGURE 6-1:**

KEY SIGNATURES

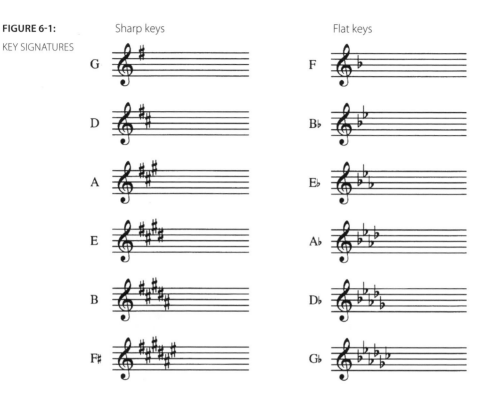

When you're comfortable with all this, try playing the tunes shown in Figures 6-2 to 6-4.

**FIGURE 6-2:**

POLLY WOLLY

DOODLE

**FIGURE 6-3:**

DRUNKEN SAILOR

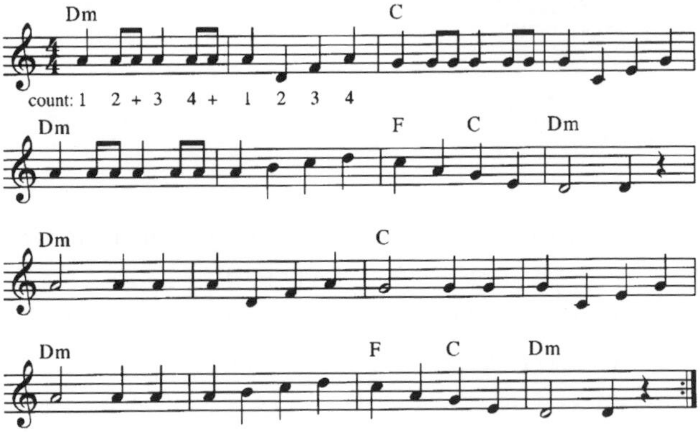

**FIGURE 6-4:**

WE WISH YOU A
MERRY CHRISTMAS

# Intervals

The distance between two notes is called an interval. The frets of a guitar are one half-step or halftone apart (same thing, different name). Well, a halftone or semitone (again, same thing, different name) is the smallest interval, or distance, between two notes – at least in Western music. This is the distance from C to C♯. (C♯ is one half-step up from C, and D♭ is enharmonically the same note, a half-step down from D.)

A whole step or whole tone (usually just called a tone), which is two semitones, would be from C to D. This would be the equivalent of jumping to a note two frets away on the guitar.

It's very helpful not only to know this information intellectually but also to see how you can apply it to your instrument. To see how intervals look in the flesh, look at your fifth string. The following examples are all counted from C, which is played at the third fret of the fifth string:

### NAMES OF INTERVALS

- The interval from C to C♯ (fourth fret, also known as D♭) is a semitone – the interval known as a minor second.
- The interval from C to D (fifth fret) is a whole tone, or two semitones – the interval known as a second.
- The interval from C to E♭ (sixth fret) is three semitones – the interval known as a minor third.
- The interval from C to E (seventh fret) is four semitones – the interval known as a major third.
- The interval from C to F (eighth fret) is five semitones – the interval known as a fourth.
- The interval from C to G♭ (ninth fret) is six semitones – the interval known as a diminished or flatted fifth. Alternatively, you can say that this interval is from C to F♯ (enharmonically the same note as G♭). In that case, this interval is called an augmented fourth.
- The interval from C to G (tenth fret) is seven semitones – the interval known as a fifth.
- The interval from C to G♯ (eleventh fret) is eight semitones – the interval known as an augmented fifth (also called a raised fifth). If you say the interval is from C to A♭ (enharmonically the same note), it is known as a minor sixth.
- The interval from C to A (twelfth fret) is nine semitones – the interval known as a major sixth.
- The interval from C to A♯ (thirteenth fret) is ten semitones – the interval known as an augmented sixth. If you say the interval is from C to B♭, the interval is called a minor seventh.
- The interval from C to B (fourteenth fret) is eleven semitones – the interval known as a major seventh.
- The interval from C to C (fifteenth fret) is twelve semitones – the interval known as an octave.

Figure 6-5 shows the intervals written as notation.

**FIGURE 6-5:** INTERVALS WRITTEN AS NOTATION

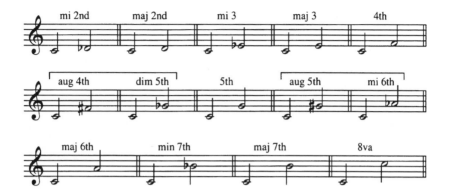

## Circle of Fifths

If you follow the key signatures carefully, you'll see that from C to G is a fifth, G to D is a fifth, D to A is a fifth, and so on through the sharp keys. Similarly, C to F is a fourth, and from F to B♭ is a fourth, and so on through the flat keys. Essentially, the pattern is a fifth in one direction, a fourth in the other. Called the circle of fifths, this pattern is illustrated in Figure 6-6.

**FIGURE 6-6:** CIRCLE OF FIFTHS

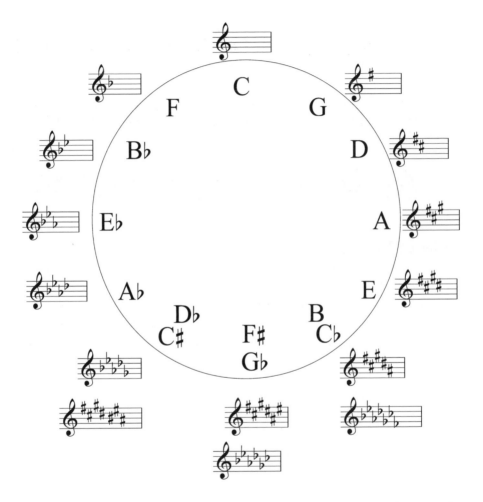

The circle of fifths is an easy but important way to learn the key of a piece of music because it tells you how many sharps or flats are in the key. C has no sharps or flats. The circle of fifths shows how when you go clockwise around the circle you go up a fifth. For example, the fifth note of the C major scale is G. The fifth note of the G major scale is D, and so on. Also notice how there are twelve notes on the circle of fifths, corresponding to twelve numbers on a clock.

How is this information helpful? Take any chord progression, for example, C major to F major. Now, suppose you'd switch that to A. In other words, you want the same exact chord progression, but you want it in A instead of C. Since F is in the position that is one turn anticlockwise of C, then all you have to do is go to A, and then go one turn anticlockwise to D. That is how easy it is to use the circle of fifths. (In guitar fretboard theory, the circle of fifths becomes easier to see when you start playing barre chords, described in Chapter 8.)

# Scales

Before you begin your journey into scales in the first position, you need to understand the major and minor scale formula. Both major scales and minor scales are created by putting together a series of tones and semitones. Depending on whether the scale is major or minor, these tones and semitones are arranged in a different sequence.

---

**Tones and semitones are commonly referred to as whole steps and half-steps on the guitar. Both of these terms are scalar arrangements of pitches. It is important to have both terms in your musical vocabulary.**

---

## Major Scale

The major scale is a set pattern of notes that ascends by whole and half-steps as follows: tone, tone, semitone, tone, tone, tone, semitone. You can start on any note and follow this pattern to derive the major scale in that key.

The following example shows how to follow this pattern to build the major scale in the key of C:

- Start with C
- From C, go up a tone (whole step) to D
- From D, go up a tone (whole step) to E
- From E, go up a semitone (half-step) to F
- From F, go up a tone (whole step) to G

- From G, go up a tone (whole step) to A
- From A, go up a tone (whole step) to B
- From B, go up a semitone (half-step) to C

## Natural or Relative Minor Scales

Each major scale has a corresponding minor scale (called the relative or natural minor). This minor scale follows the same pattern as the major scale, except that it starts with the sixth note of the major scale. In the case of the C major scale, the natural minor would start with A, as shown in Figure 6-7.

**FIGURE 6-7:** C NATURAL MINOR SCALE

C major scale

A natural minor scale
(starts on sixth of C scale)

## Harmonic Minor Scales

Besides the natural minor, there are two other types of minor scales that you can study: the harmonic minor and the melodic minor. Just as with the major scales, each of these starts with a certain note, which becomes the scale's key, and then follows a set pattern of tones and semitones. The harmonic and melodic minor scales are built slightly differently from each other. The pattern for the harmonic minor scale goes as follows: tone, semitone, tone, tone, semitone, three semitones (minor third), semitone. The A harmonic minor scale is built according to this pattern as follows:

- Start with A
- From A go up a tone (whole step) to B
- From B go up a semitone (half-step) to C
- From C go up a tone (whole step) to D
- From D go up a tone (whole step) to E

- From E go up a semitone (half-step) to F
- From F go up three semitones (minor third) to G♯
- From G♯ go up a semitone (half-step) to A

The C harmonic minor scale progresses like so: C-D-E♭-F-G-A♭-B-C. Figure 6-8 shows the C harmonic minor scale.

**FIGURE 6-8:** C HARMONIC MINOR SCALE

A harmonic minor scale

C harmonic minor scale

## Melodic Minor Scales

A melodic minor scale is more complex because it is often played in classical harmony as ascending in one form and descending in another. However, for our purposes you'll learn it the same way going up and down. The melodic minor is built on the following progression: tone, semitone, tone, tone, tone, tone, semitone.

In the key of A, the melodic minor scale looks like this: A-B-C-D-E-F♯-G♯-A.

In the key of C, the melodic minor scale looks like this: C-D-E♭-F-G-A-B-C. Figure 6-9 illustrates this scale.

**FIGURE 6-9:** MELODIC MINOR SCALES

A melodic minor scale

C melodic minor scale

# First-Position Scales

Figures 6-10 to 6-20 display the patterns for major scales played in the first position.

**FIGURE 6-10:** D MAJOR SCALE

**FIGURE 6-11:** G MAJOR SCALE

**FIGURE 6-12:** A MAJOR SCALE

**FIGURE 6-13:** E MAJOR SCALE

**FIGURE 6-14:** B MAJOR SCALE

**FIGURE 6-15:** F MAJOR SCALE

**FIGURE 6-16:** B♭ MAJOR SCALE

**FIGURE 6-17:** E♭ MAJOR SCALE

**FIGURE 6-18:** A♭ MAJOR SCALE

**FIGURE 6-19:** D♭ MAJOR SCALE

**FIGURE 6-20:** G♭ MAJOR SCALE

# Introduction to Arpeggios

An arpeggio is simply a 'broken' chord. In other words, if you play the notes that make up a chord individually, you are playing an arpeggio. For example, the C major seventh arpeggio (Cmaj7) is composed of the notes C-E-G-B; if you play those notes one by one, you are playing an arpeggio. To play these arpeggios properly, you should learn them in two octaves (an interval eight diatonic scale degrees above a note). For example, Figure 6-21 shows the Cmaj7 chord in two octaves like so: C-E-G-B-C, E-G-B-C.

**FIGURE 6-21:** C MAJOR SEVENTH ARPEGGIO IN TWO OCTAVES

The word 'arpeggio' comes from the Italian for 'to play the harp'. It refers to a chord where notes are played in succession rather than simultaneously or the sound of such a chord. Some of the instruments that use arpeggios include the guitar, bass guitar, synthesizers and various other string instruments.

Single-note arpeggio practice (meaning playing one note of a chord at a time) is a wonderful way of getting these sounds in your head. It's also a terrific basis for learning how to improvise over a chord sequence. Try the first-position exercise shown in Figure 6-22. Remember, practise slowly at first then gradually increase your speed.

FIGURE 6-22: FIRST-POSITION ARPEGGIO STUDY

# Intermediate Time and Rhythm Examples

When you are learning to play any instrument, rhythm training is essential. This training helps develop coordination and a sense of timing. One of the first skills you want to learn is how to practise along with a metronome. There are various types of metronomes on the market, so ask a salesperson to assist you in buying the best one for your needs. A simple digital metronome will do just fine.

Once you have the metronome, listen to the clicks at a slow tempo. That's all you're going to do at first – listen. It's the most important thing! Next, count out loud with the beat on the metronome: '1, 2, 3, 4' and so on. When you have the metronome groove in your head, tap along with the beat on the guitar body and count out loud again.

Once you are counting out loud and tapping with the metronome in time, it is time to put your hands on the fretboard and start some actual practice. The exercise shown in Figure 6-23 is designed to help you build your rhythm and sight-reading skills.

When you are playing this exercise, try to clap out the rhythms first and then say them out loud. Once you hear yourself speaking in time, you will like what you hear. The music will get a little more involved as you go along, but this initial first set of steps is important to your progress.

**FIGURE 6-23:** SIMPLE RHYTHM EXERCISE

# Teaching Yourself to Learn

It would be great to have a guitar teacher at the ready whenever you have a question about something, but that can get pricey. When you are teaching yourself to learn to play, take notes on your progress. Day-to-day journals of what you practised will give you the feedback you need to continue improving. It will also help to record yourself to monitor your progress. You will be very impressed with your newfound skills and will get a better idea of how to go forwards. In this digital age, you can one day put all of the recordings on to a disc in a logical order and listen to where you once were and where you are now. You will be impressed and proud of your achievement.

# Chapter 7

# Introduction to Harmony

Harmony is a vast subject. Musicians have spent their whole careers studying harmony without ever reaching the end. It can take you on a journey from the rural Delta blues of Mississippi to the songs of the Beatles; from the compositions of Frank Zappa to the jazz composition and arrangements of Duke Ellington; from the jigs and reels of Scotland and Ireland to the vast continent of classical music composition by such composers as John Dowland, Beethoven, Bach, Debussy, Stravinsky, Vaughan Williams, John Cage and many, many more.

# What Is Harmony?

At the root of all these vast and differing ways to make music are the same basic ideas: melody, rhythm and harmony. Melody is when notes follow each other to make up a tune, and rhythm is basically about how long the notes should be played and how often (see Chapter 6, in particular Figure 6-23). Now, you'll explore the third element, harmony, which is what happens when you play two or more notes together at the same time.

Most people expect music to sound a certain way, and as a result there are rules about how, when and why certain notes should go together. Even if you're a rockin' headbanger or into some other form of experimental music, to really stretch the envelope it's best that you have some understanding of the rules you're about to break.

Everything that is covered in this chapter applies equally to all the keys – to any key, in fact. But to make it easier to understand, the discussion will focus on the key of C. As you learned in Chapter 5, the key of C does not naturally have any sharps or flats (accidentals), so the variations and so forth can be seen more easily.

Figure 7-1 shows the scale of C major. Notice that the notes fall alternately on lines and spaces. For example, C is on a ledger line, D is on a space, E is on a line, F is on a space and so on.

**FIGURE 7-1:** C MAJOR SCALE

C   D   E   F   G   A   B   C

# Intermediate Interval Training

Let's revisit the concept of the distance between two notes, called the interval. You'll remember that the frets of a guitar are a half-step or halftone apart. Now you are going to apply that knowledge to the distance between strings. Look at the diagrams that follow. There are also intervals between the strings. The best way to understand the logic of intervals between strings is simply to look at them! Based on the standard guitar tuning you have been using so far, Figures 7-2 to 7-8 show how some of the intervals defined in Chapter 6 look on the guitar neck. Note that in these examples, the numbers in the white circles indicate the string number and the lines connect the two strings together. These intervals can played anywhere on the fretboard.

**FIGURE 7-2:**

MAJOR SECOND INTERVALS

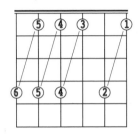 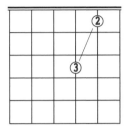

**FIGURE 7-3:**

MAJOR THIRD INTERVALS

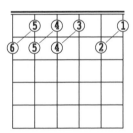 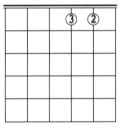

**FIGURE 7-4:**

PERFECT FOURTH

INTERVALS

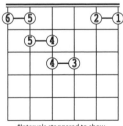 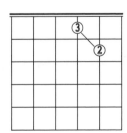

*Intervals staggered to show intervals on two sets of strings

**FIGURE 7-5:**

PERFECT FIFTH INTERVALS

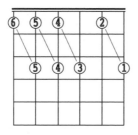
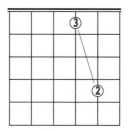

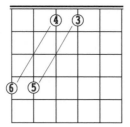
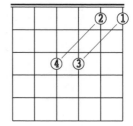

**FIGURE 7-6:**

MAJOR SIXTH

INTERVALS

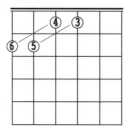
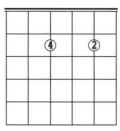
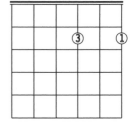

**FIGURE 7-7A:**

MAJOR SEVENTH INTERVALS

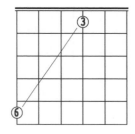
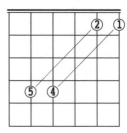

**FIGURE 7-7B:**

MAJOR SEVENTH INTERVALS

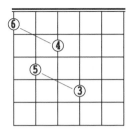
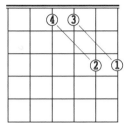

**FIGURE 7-8A AND 7-8B:**

OCTAVE INTERVALS

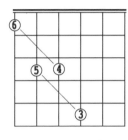
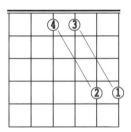

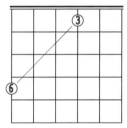
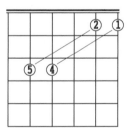

Once you are familiar with the string spacing regarding intervals, you are on your way to building chords note for note – and that's fun!

# Understanding Chord Structures

The combination of three or more notes is a chord. Three-note chords are called triads. Four-note chords are called seventh chords.

## Open String Chords

In Chapter 5 you learned the chords C, G and G7 in first position. Below are more major chords made in first position. All of these are made with open strings. These chords will be called by these names throughout the book.

**FIGURE 7-9:** D MAJOR

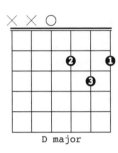

D major

**FIGURE 7-10:** A MAJOR

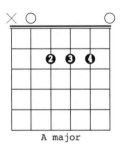

A major

**FIGURE 7-11:** E MAJOR

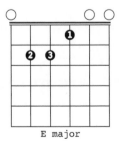

E major

**FIGURE 7-12:** B MAJOR

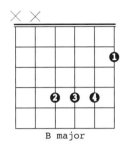

B major

Now that you're familiar with the chords, you'll learn how they are built.

## Triads

There are four types of triads: major, minor, augmented and diminished, which are built by piling major thirds and minor thirds on top of each other in different combinations. You can 'spell' the four types of triad chords this way:

| | | |
|---|---|---|
| C maj | C-E-G | maj 3rd min 3rd |
| C min | C-E♭-G | min 3rd maj 3rd |
| C aug | C-E-G♯ | maj 3rd maj 3rd |
| C dim | C-E♭-G♭ | min 3rd min 3rd |

Most chord structures are a variation on these four triads. Figure 7-13 gives you an example of how these triads can be played on the guitar.

**FIGURE 7-13:**

TRIADS

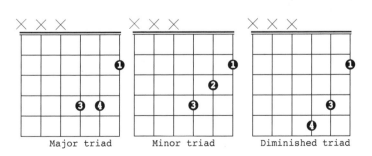

Major triad          Minor triad          Diminished triad

On the guitar, these simple chords are not always spelled this way. For example, you can mix up the order of the notes, and instead of playing C-E-G, you can play G-C-E. You can also double notes. An E maj triad is spelled E-G♯-B, for example, but it is usually played as a full chord E-B-E-G♯-B-E.

It's not really important now to know these structures inside out. Instead, learn the chord forms on the chord diagrams. Try to figure out where other triads can be played on the guitar and write them down for yourself.

## Seventh Chords

Four-note chords are called seventh chords. They generally have much more colour and they sound more interesting than triads. Furthermore, they are the basis of all standard repertoires of tunes. To make a seventh chord, add either a major third or a minor third to one of the four triad forms. Doing this, you get five basic seventh chords, with other chords being variations on these five.

In the key of C, the five are variations of these:

| | | |
|---|---|---|
| C maj7 | C-E-G-B | |
| C7 | C-E-G-B♭ | (also called a dominant 7) |
| C min7 | C-E♭-G-B♭ | |
| C min7♭5 | C-E♭-G♭-B♭ | (also written Cø7 or C half diminished) |
| C dim7 | C-E♭-G♭-A | (usually called B double flat, but here known as A, which enharmonically it is) |

As you've seen, you can make chords up by piling thirds on top of each other. Another way to look at chords is to build them from the tones of a scale (major or minor – it doesn't matter).

| | | | | | | | | |
|---|---|---|---|---|---|---|---|---|
| Here's a major scale: | C | D | E | F | G | A | B | C |
| Put numbers underneath: | 1 | 2 | 3 | 4 | 5 | 6 | 7 | 8 |
| Now use roman numerals: | I | II | III | IV | V | VI | VII | VIII |

A chord can be built by choosing every other note in the scale and then altering it if necessary:

| C major 7 | 1-3-5-7 |
|---|---|
| C7 | 1-3-5-♭7 |
| C minor 7 | 1-♭3-5-♭7 |
| C minor 7♭5 | 1-♭3-♭5-♭7 |
| C diminished | 1-♭3-♭5-♭7 |

On the piano keyboard, it's easier to play these chords as they're spelled out here. However, on the guitar that isn't the case. A C major 7 chord, for example, is often played on the guitar and spelled C-E-G-B or C-G-B-E.

If you spend some time working on understanding how chords are built, you'll soon be able to build your own. For example, if you know how to play a C major 7 chord, and suddenly you are confronted with C major 7♯5, you just need to play a C major 7 shape, figure out which note is the fifth of the chord, and raise it up a fret (semitone) to make the ♯5 part of this chord.

You learned earlier that there are five basic seventh chords. That's true, but there are seven more chords that are variations on these five. Here are the twelve:

| C major 7 | 1-3-5-7 |
|---|---|
| C7 | 1-3-5-♭7 |
| C minor 7 | 1-♭3-5-♭7 |
| C minor 7♭5 | 1-♭3-♭5-♭7 |
| C diminished 7 | 1-♭3-♭5-♭7(6) |
| C major 7♯5 | 1-3-♯5-7 |
| C major 7♭5 | 1-3-♭5-7 |
| C7♯5 | 1-3-♯5-♭7 |
| C7♭5 | 1-3-♭5-♭7 |
| C minor/major 7 | 1-♭3-5-7 (C minor major 7) |
| C6 | 1-3-5-6 |
| C minor 6 | 1-♭3-5-6 |

Think about this: a minor 6 chord, and a minor 7♭5 chord are the same thing, although they will have different root notes: C minor 6 = A minor 7♭5. (A root note is the note from which the chord is built.)

# Diatonic Chords

If you go through a major scale, building chords on every note of the scale by using every other note, you get what are called diatonic chords – all the chords that naturally occur in the key.

In the key of C, these are C major 7, D minor 7, E minor 7, F major 7, G7, A minor 7, B minor 7♭5, C major 7.

If you go through a harmonic minor scale, you get this sequence:

| C minor/ major 7 | D minor 7♭5 | E♭ major 7♯5 | F minor 7 | G7 | A♭ major 7 | B dimin- ished 7 | C minor/ major 7 |
|---|---|---|---|---|---|---|---|
| I | II | III | IV | V | VI | VII | VIII |

You've learned about chord structure – and it may seem confusing now, but when it all comes together, you'll be a chord-building master!

# Minor Chord

Up to this point you've been reading about the minor chord and its many structures, now you'll try a few chords. The minor chord has a sad or bluesy quality to it. Figures 7-14 to 7-16 show three minor chords: A minor, E minor and D minor. The song 'Drunken Sailor' (shown in Figure 7-17) uses a variety of these minor chords.

**FIGURE 7-14A AND 7-14B:**

A MINOR

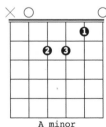

A minor

**FIGURE 7-15A
AND 7-15B:**

E MINOR

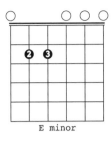

E minor

**FIGURE 7-16A
AND 7-16B:**

D MINOR

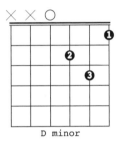

D minor

**FIGURE 7-17:** DRUNKEN SAILOR

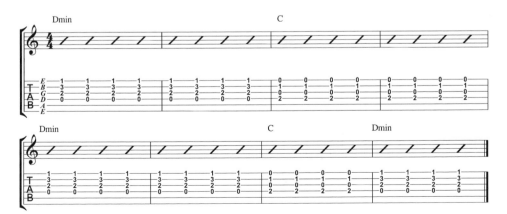

### Drunken Sailor

*What shall we do with the drunken sailor?*
*What shall we do with the drunken sailor?*
*What shall we do with the drunken sailor?*
*Earl-eye in the morning*
*Wey, Hey and up she rises,*
*Wey, Hey and up she rises,*
*Wey, Hey and up she rises,*
*Earl-eye in the morning*

Figures 7-18 and 7-19 show a couple more songs using these minor chords.

**FIGURE 7-18:** SWING LOW, SWEET CHARIOT

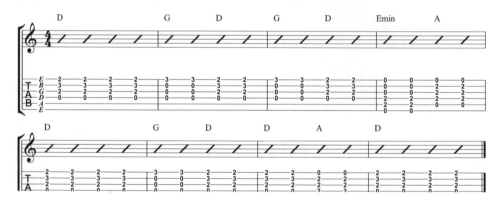

**FIGURE 7-19:** AULD LANG SYNE

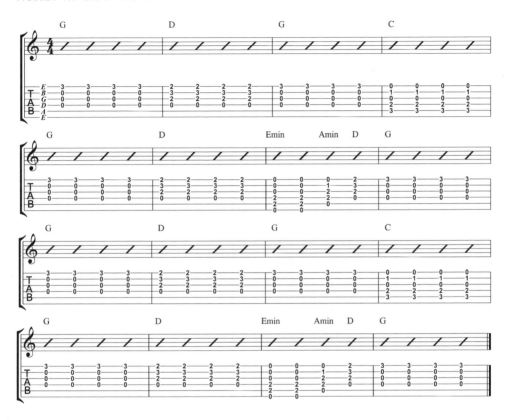

# Chord Families

Chords go together in families (or, as they are more formally called, keys). For example, a G7 chord is part of the C family, and a D7 chord is part of the G family. Play those chords and they just seem to fit naturally together. A D7 chord, for example, does not lead to a C chord nearly as well as it leads to a G chord. Try it and see.

Chords break down into three basic types:

- Major chords (like G or C), which sound happy.
- Minor chords (like Amin and Dmin), which sound sad.
- Dominant seventh chords (like G7 or D7), which sound slightly jazzy and seem to want to lead us to resolve to a major chord.

OK, now look at the E7 chord, illustrated in Figure 7-20. This chord is part of the key (family) of A, which includes A and D. Figures 7-21 and 7-22 show a couple of songs that use the E7 chord.

**FIGURE 7-20A AND 7-20B:**

E7 CHORD

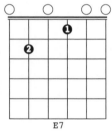

E7

**FIGURE 7-21:** KUMBAYA

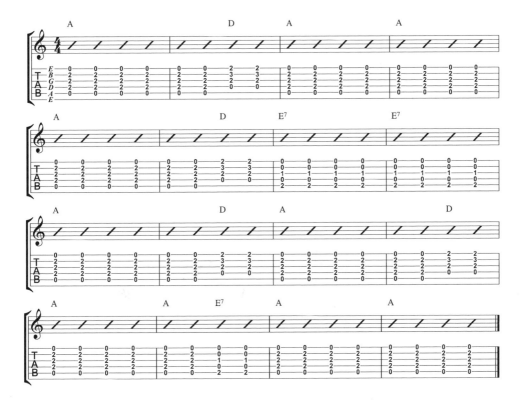

**FIGURE 7-22:** WHEN JOHNNY COMES MARCHING HOME

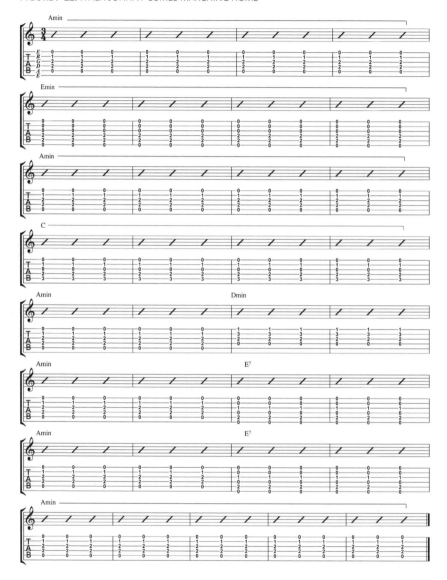

In Figures 7-23 are all the open-string chords you should learn. One of the things that makes learning chords easier is that families (keys) share the same chords or variations on them. So once you know how to play a C chord, or an E7 chord, it will be the same regardless of the sequence you find it in.

**FIGURE 7-23A**

Key (family) of G

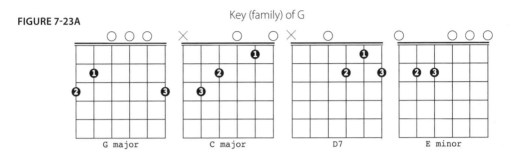

**FIGURE 7-23B**

Key (family) of A

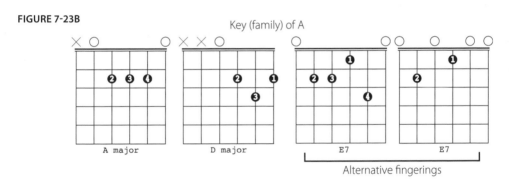

**FIGURE 7-23C**

Key (family) of C

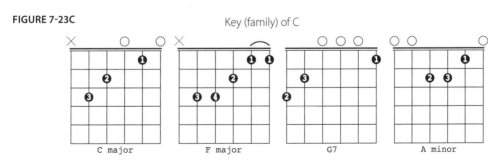

**FIGURE 7-23D**

Key (family) of D

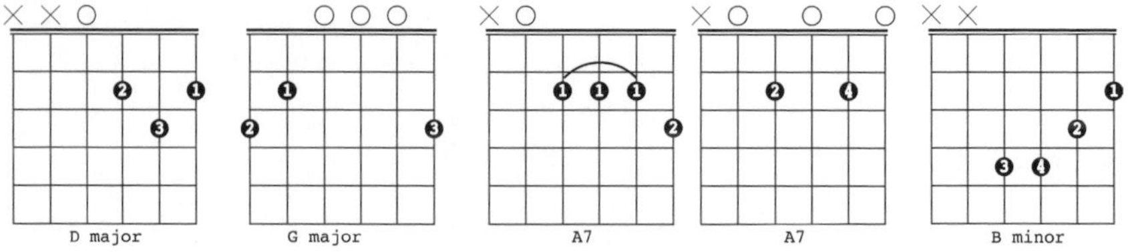

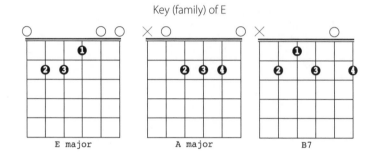

**FIGURE 7-23E**

Key (family) of E

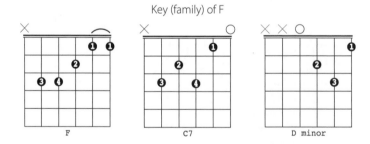

**FIGURE 7-23F**

Key (family) of F

Buy some songbooks, or look on the internet for some song sheets you can download. Make sure they have the chords to the tunes printed on them so you can practise the songs. Spend some time working on changing smoothly from one chord to another as you strum. Some of these chords involve using your first finger to stop more than one string. To do this, use the fat part of your finger. Initially, you may want to lay your second finger on top of your first finger to help you make just enough contact with the strings on the fretboard so that the strings don't buzz.

If you pay attention, you'll notice some chords in the same key are missing. That's because they can't be played with open strings. You will soon learn how to play these chords.

## Standard Progressions

Without noticing that you have been doing it, you have been playing standard chord progressions. What is meant by standard here is 'generally accepted' or 'normal'. There are standard tunes like 'Over the Rainbow', 'Moon River', and even 'Happy Birthday to You' that are created using certain chord progressions, which means that a chord naturally progresses to another chord after it's played. (A G7 chord for example, naturally progresses to a Cmaj7, partly because G is the fifth note in the scale and key of C.)

If you go back and look at the chords in the key of C shown earlier in this chapter, you'll see that each has a Roman numeral under it. There's a reason for this. Instead of saying C major 7, F major 7, G7, for example, you can just say I-IV-V. Then you can look at the notes of any major scale, and play the I, IV and V chords built on the first, fourth and fifth notes of the scale. (They would be a major 7, major 7, dominant 7 sequence of chords.)

## The Blues

To finish, you'll use a fun and usable chord progression to look at the blues. A blues sequence is really just a I-IV-V sequence. So a blues progression in B♭, say, would be B♭major7, E♭major7, F7.

Figure 7-24A shows a basic twelve-bar blues in C that uses open chords.

**FIGURE 7-24A:** BLUES PROGRESSION 1

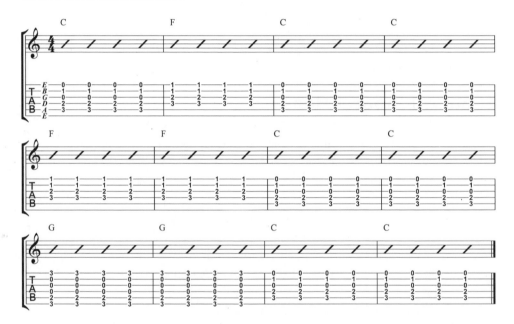

However, this is fairly bland and could do with some colour. Next, try using dominant seven chords as shown in Figure 7-24B.

**FIGURE 7-24B:** BLUES PROGRESSION 2 – DOMINANT SEVENTH CHORDS

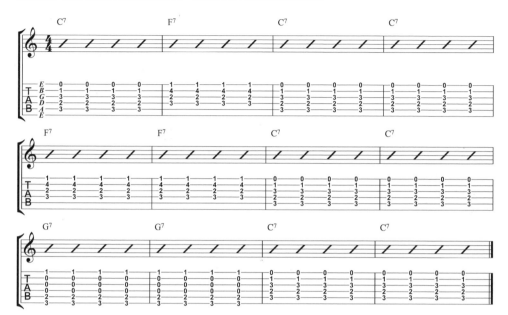

A slightly more complicated sequence is called I-VI-II-V. This sequence is the basis of most standard chord progressions. Using diatonic chords (discussed earlier in this chapter) in the key of C, this would be C major 7, A minor 7, D minor 7, G7. If you analyse songs by figuring out their key signatures, you'll discover that this I-VI-II-V sequence is used in a lot of them.

One of the things you may well discover is that the root notes in the VI-II-V-I sequence are all a fourth apart. (In key of C: A to D to G to C.) Next time you play a song, look for this pattern and this sequence. The more you practise using this cycle of fourths, the easier it becomes to play standard song progressions.

Try the jazzy blues sequence shown in Figure 7-24c.

**FIGURE 7-24C:** BLUES PROGRESSION 3 – A JAZZY BLUES SEQUENCE

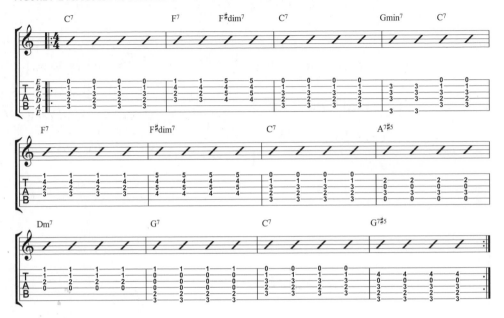

When you practise chords and scales, try to practise them in the cycle of fourths sequence. First, play a C major scale, then an F major scale, then a B♭ major scale and so on. Do your best to practise learning the logic behind the cycle of fourths and fifths based on the chords you have learned up to now.

# Chapter 8

# Intermediate Basics

This chapter will familiarize you with the basics of guitar playing, including the chromatic scale, moveable chords and barre chords. When you master the elements in this chapter you will have the keys to successful guitar playing, including some of the more difficult concepts. For example, once you understand barre chords, you will rapidly be free of the confinement of open position chords and will be able to explore the whole neck. With this chapter, you'll soon move from the realm of the newbie beginner to one of an experienced beginner.

# The Chromatic Scale

All twelve notes together make up the musical alphabet and form what is called a chromatic scale. Music is about what notes to play (melody), and how long you should play them (rhythm). You've learned about harmony (which is what happens when you play two or more notes together at the same time) in Chapter 7. Here is the complete chromatic scale, moving in half-steps from the note E:

E, F, F♯/G♭, G, G♯/A♭, A, A♯/B♭, B, C, C♯/D♭, D, D♯/E♭, (E).

Figure 8-1 shows how the chromatic scale looks written out in standard musical notation.

**FIGURE 8-1:** CHROMATIC SCALE

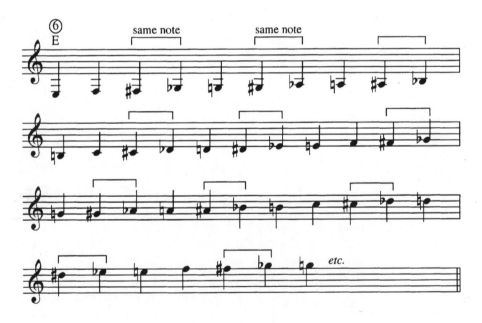

Notice that in musical notation the sharp (♯) and flat (♭) signs come in front of the note. A natural sign (♮) in front of a note means that you play that note without making it sharp or flat – as it is naturally played.

# How the Guitar Fits In

So how does the guitar fit in to all this? You may recall that each fret of the guitar is a half-step away from the next. So the guitar fretboard naturally forms a chromatic scale. Very useful.

If you play E, String 6, open, and then you play the note on every fret on the E string up to the twelfth fret, you will have played a chromatic scale starting on E. Try it.

If you play A, String 5, open, and then you play the note on every fret up to the twelfth fret, you will have played a chromatic scale starting on A.

The chromatic scale is a really important concept to understand because now you can do lots of things on the guitar fretboard, not just confine yourself to open-string chords or scales. The most important thing you can do is move the same scale shapes (also known as patterns) and chord forms up and down the neck.

Figure 8-2 shows all the notes on all the strings.

**FIGURE 8-2:** NOTES ON THE GUITAR

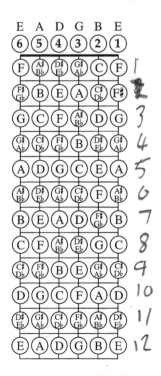

# Introduction to Moveable Pattern Logic

By now you have come a long way with major and minor scales and chords. Now you are going to learn how to do new versions of these chords and scales up and down the fretboard. Scales will be referred to as 'shapes' and chords will be referred to as 'forms'. You will begin the journey with scale shapes. These scale shapes will help you learn scale names all over the guitar neck. The first shape you will examine is the major scale with the root (beginning note) on the sixth string.

The first scale shape you'll learn is the E major, which begins on the sixth string. In Figure 8-3A, you can see that the E major scale utilizes open strings and goes up to the fifth fret on the second string. The fingerings for this scale form are next to the notes. This major scale shape begins with the root (beginning scale note name) on the sixth string.

**FIGURE 8-3A:** E MAJOR SCALE SHAPE WITH OPEN STRINGS

Next, look at the G major scale utilizing the E major scale shape (Figure 8-3B).

**FIGURE 8-3B:** G MAJOR SCALE WITH E MAJOR SCALE SHAPE

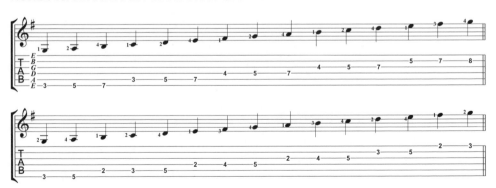

The scale shapes are identical in that they follow a major scale pattern starting on the sixth string. This G major scale is a closed pattern shape where open strings are not used. Notice the difference in where the notes are played between the two variations. The advantage to this closed system is that you can play this shape up and down the neck and know that you are always playing a major scale shape. Look at the following scale shapes as shown in Figure 8-4 and how they can be used in different keys.

**FIGURE 8-4:**

MAJOR SCALE SHAPES

These scales must look very new and strange. Play them over and over to get a better handle on them. Once you have drilled the basic concepts into your head, try incorporating the chromatic approach to the scales. The chromatic scales are shown in Figures 8-5 and 8-6.

**FIGURE 8-5:** CHROMATIC SCALE BASED ON A SIXTH-STRING MAJOR SCALE SHAPE

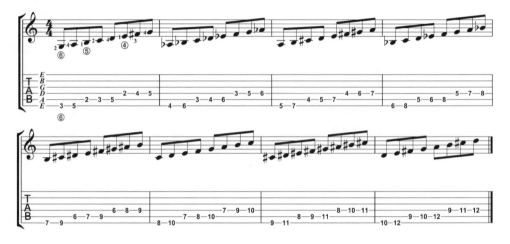

**FIGURE 8-6:** CHROMATIC SCALE BASED ON A FIFTH-STRING MAJOR SCALE SHAPE

You can now see the moveable scale pattern going up the fretboard. Figure 8-7 shows the scale sequence in C minor. You'll be learning more about sequences later. Don't worry! You'll get it – all things in time.

**FIGURE 8-7:** C MINOR SCALE SEQUENCE

# Moveable Chords

The idea that you can move one shape up and down the neck and play lots of chords at the same time is pretty amazing. These chords are called moveable chords.

You already know there are different types of chords. You've learned about major chords, minor chords and seventh chords (also called dominant seventh chords). You've probably wondered how these different types of chords get their names. For example, why E or C or G7 or A minor? Each chord has a name (or root) note. This note is usually found somewhere on one of the three bass strings.

For example, the name (root) note of E is on String 6, open as shown in Figure 8-8.

**FIGURE 8-8**

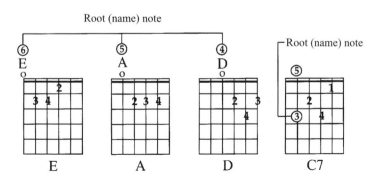

The name note or root note of A is found on String 5, open, and the name/root note of D is found – where? Right! On String 4, open.

Look at the last chord in Figure 8-8. It's a new chord, called C7. It gets its name from the note on the third fret on String 5. When you play it, you don't play String 6 or String 1, just play the inner four strings.

Using the same fingering, move that chord shape up two frets. Your third finger, on String 5, should now be at the fifth fret, and your first finger should be on String 2 at the third fret. (The other two fingers should be in the same pattern as the diagram.)

Remember, this chord gets its name from the note on String 5. Look at the chromatic scale, look at your fingers on the fretboard, and try to figure out what the name of this chord should now be. The question is, what's the name of the note on String 5 at the fifth fret?

Here's the answer. Moving a C7 chord shape from the first position (your first finger is playing a note on the first fret) to the third position (first finger is now playing a note on the third fret) means that the new chord is called D7.

'Wait a minute,' you're saying. 'Hey! Don't you play D7 a different way? In Chapter 5, you showed me a D7 chord being played this way.' (See Figure 8-9.)

**FIGURE 8-9**

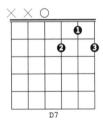

D7

You're absolutely right. In fact, you can play the same chord in different ways all over the guitar neck (more detail on this later on). Here's the thing: play the D7 chord as you originally learned it. Now play it using the new shape you've just learned. It's the same chord, but somehow it sounds subtly different. So you now have a choice of ways to play D7, depending on how the chord sounds. With a little practice, you'll find that it's much easier to change from chord to chord using moveable forms.

# Barre Chords

Barre (pronounced bar) chords are a special kind of moveable chord. You create them by using your first finger to stop all the strings across a fret, and then you play a moveable shape under it. It's quite easy with a little practice.

Practise this. Put your first finger across all six strings at the first fret. If you have trouble getting all the notes to sound clearly, put your second finger on top of your first to help press it down until the notes ring clearly. Relax. Flex your fingers. Now try it again. Move your first finger to the second fret, play the strings then relax your hand.

Repeat this at the third fret then the fourth – and so on – trying to get a clear sound from each note on the strings as you do it. Use that first finger to stop all the frets in turn as far up the neck as you can go, playing all the strings at a fret, relaxing your hand then trying again, all the time making sure that the notes on each string sound clear and don't buzz or sound muffled. Like everything else with the guitar, it gets easier with a little practice.

Now look at the notes on String 6. If the root note, or name note, for the E major chord is String 6, open, then theoretically, if you move the E chord form up one fret, you move the root note up one fret as well.

Use your first finger to bar the strings on the first fret. Use the suggested fingering to play an E chord form at the first position/fret while you bar the first fret with your first finger. This is not easy but persevere. Try to get all the notes on all the strings to sound clear when you play them. Relax your hand.

The note on the first fret of String 6 is F. That means that an E chord form, which in the open-string position is called E, in the first position (that is, at the first fret) is now called F. Move it up to the third fret and now it is called G.

Quick test – try to find and play these chords (hint: you'll find the root notes of all these chords on either String 6 or String 5):

- G♭ (major)
- F7
- C♯7
- A♭
- E♭7
- F♯

Having trouble with this exercise? Take a break, grab a guitar magazine then reread this chapter until you're comfortable with the concept and you can find these chords. It's really not that hard. Honest.

Go back through some of the earlier lessons and try playing the songs using the moveable chord shapes you've learned.

Figure 8-10 shows moveable chord types gathered together based on the location of the root note. Some of these chords have fingerings that are not that easy because they involve using more than one finger to bar more than one fret – A, for example, or D minor 7 – but with a little practice, you'll get it.

**FIGURE 8-10:**

E-SHAPE:
MAJOR

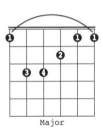

Major

E-SHAPE: DOMINANT 7

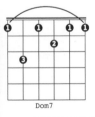
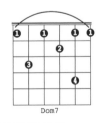

Dom7     Dom7

Alternate fingerings

E-SHAPE: MINOR

Minor

E-SHAPE: MINOR 7

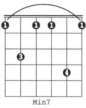
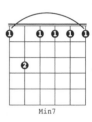

Min7        Min7

Alternate fingerings

A-SHAPE: MAJ (DOUBLE BARRED CHORD)

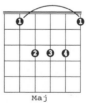
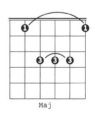

Maj        Maj

Alternate fingerings

A-SHAPE: DOMINANT 7

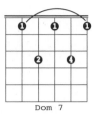

Dom 7

A-SHAPE: MINOR

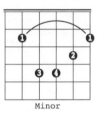

Minor

A-SHAPE: MINOR 7

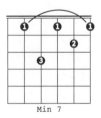

Min 7

D-SHAPE: MAJOR

 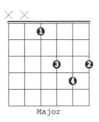

Major

D-SHAPE: DOMINANT 7

 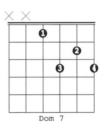

Dom 7

D-SHAPE: MINOR

 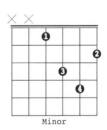

Minor

D-SHAPE: MINOR 7

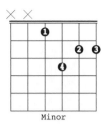

Minor

C-SHAPE: MAJOR (HALF BARREL)

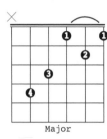

Major

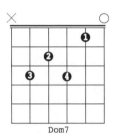

Dom7

# Moveable Chords with Muted Notes

Up until now there hasn't been much of a fuss about which strings you strum when you finger a chord. It has been enough that you get the strings to sound out clearly without buzzing while you fret the notes and play.

At the beginning of this lesson, you played a C7 chord. Remember the advice that accompanied that chord: 'don't play String 6 and String 1, just play the middle four strings.' What you did, in a way, was to mute or deaden the sound of String 6 and String 1 so that they wouldn't sound when you played the chord. That's because while the open note E is part of a C7 chord, if you move that chord shape up the neck, the note E quickly clashes with the other C7-shape chords that don't contain the note E. (Refer to Chapter 7 for a detailed explanation of harmony.)

A muted chord is one in which you must deaden (or mute) one or two strings while you play the chord. You mute the strings so that you get the correct key tones out of the chord shape every time you play it, wherever you play it. Figure 8-11 shows a moveable G chord with two strings (that is, notes) crossed out with an X: String 5 and String 1. That means you shouldn't let these strings sound when you play the chord. A fairly tall order, right? Even knowing about barre chords, haven't you just spent all this time reading over and over that you should make the notes ring out clearly? Well, the answer is yes – and no. As you get better at playing the guitar, you'll find that some things that are good to do when you're beginning are not so good to do when you become more advanced.

**FIGURE 8-11:**

MOVEABLE G CHORD

WITH MUTED STRINGS

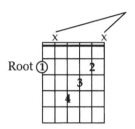

To mute a string, you need to shape your hand in such a way that these two strings are dampened or deadened when you strum a downstroke. To sound the note, you should use the tip of your finger on your left hand. To dampen or mute a note, use the fat or flat part of either the side of your finger or just under your fingertip, depending on the kind of chord you're trying to play. Now play each of the remaining notes of the chord until they sound clear. Play them individually (called an arpeggio, as discussed in Chapter 6) to make sure you have them right.

Figure 8-12 shows the five basic seventh chords in muted forms. These chords sound very colourful. If you can learn to play them well, you'll develop a great feeling of achievement.

**FIGURE 8-12:** MAJOR 7

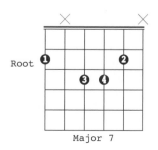

Major 7

DOMINANT 7

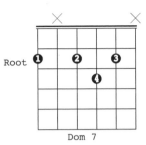

Root

Dom 7

MINOR 7

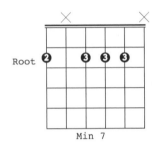

Root

Min 7

MINOR 7F5

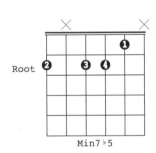

Root

Min7♭5

DIMINISHED 7

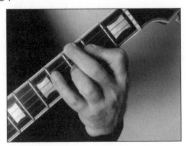

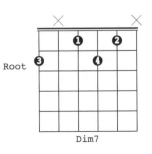

Root

Dim7

# Right-Hand Techniques

Now it's time to learn some right-hand fingerpicking techniques. The first thing you need to know are the terms used when speaking of right-hand fingerstyle techniques. Each finger is assigned a specific letter that is written on the music staff. The letters for the fingers were derived from the Spanish names for the fingers on the picking hand (see below; Spanish name is in parentheses):

- *p* = Thumb (*pulgar*).
- *i* = Index finger (*indicio*).
- *m* = Middle finger (*medio*).
- *a* = Ring finger (*anular*).

These fingerings work for both classical styles and steel-string fingerpicking styles, but were developed primarily for classical guitar. Using open strings only, play the exercise shown in Figure 8-13.

This is a very simple exercise to get your fingers used to the pattern of fingerpicking on all of the strings. The reason you'll begin this exercise on open strings is because they are the most difficult to control.

**FIGURE 8-13:** OPEN-STRING EXERCISE

For good classical technique, it's best to grow your nails slightly so that you get a nice percussive attack. You should also arch your wrist slightly so that your fingers are vertical to the strings. The difference between the hand position in folk/blues right-hand picking and classical guitar playing is one of degree. Note that while the folk/blues position seems more relaxed, it can also cause some muscle strain if you're not careful. Practise the patterns shown in Figure 8-14 for ten minutes a day. They will help you to develop better coordination and muscle memory.

**FIGURE 8-14:** OPEN-STRING EXERCISES FOR THE RIGHT HAND

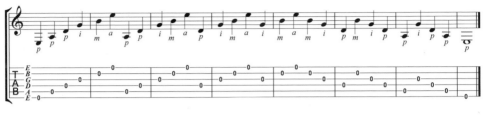

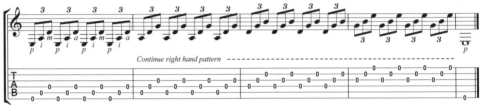

# The Basics of Classical and Folk Guitar Styles

The following musical examples are to provide a glimpse into both the classical and folk guitar genres of guitar playing. Classical may feel a little more 'formal' than folk, but it certainly wakes your hand up for better right-hand development and finger dexterity.

### Classical Guitar Examples

Figure 8-15 provides right-hand exercises in the classical style.

**FIGURE 8-15:** RIGHT-HAND EXERCISES – C TO G7

## Folk Guitar Styles

The main difference between the right-hand approaches of folk and classical styles is that folk guitarists tend to use their thumb, first and second fingers for their playing technique. You will usually see fingering notation like this:

- T = Thumb.
- 1 = First finger.
- 2 = Second finger.

The right-hand pattern will be thumb, index, thumb, middle. This is an alternating fingerpicking technique. The third finger is not used as much, as the whole folk style approach to guitar is primarily to accompany a singer. But if you don't sing, then you can have just as much fun as the next person!

Figure 8-16 provides examples of the folk style.

**FIGURE 8-16:** FOLK GUITAR STYLES

**FIGURE 8-16:** FOLK GUITAR STYLES (*continued*)

You have certainly learned some intense techniques. To see how an advanced classical or fingerstyle technique looks, have a look at 'An Andante' by Justin Holland, shown in Figure 8-17.

**FIGURE 8-17:** AN ANDANTE

**FIGURE 8-17:** AN ANDANTE (*continued*)

*Repeat first two sections
(without repeats), then
go to next section*

Variations

# Chapter 9

# Classical and Flamenco Guitarists

While the classical guitars and guitarists are very different creatures from the flamenco, the technique for playing these types of guitars is very similar. The common technique involved in playing these styles is the use of fingers instead of a plectrum or a pick. The first three fingers and the thumb are used to pluck the strings. Fingernails are used to hand pluck the strings, providing articulation and tone to the sound. As a result, both types of guitar playing require that fingernails be kept strong and even. The history of the classical and flamenco guitars and their players makes for wonderful research and study. The music is truly beautiful. The players are masters of the art.

# Fernando Sor (1778–1839)

Fernando Sor was a great composer of guitar music. He was also a violinist, organist and singer. His musical education began at a monastery, the Escolania at Montserrat. When Sor studied there, he was a student of Father Anselmo Viola. Sor's first musical education consisted of singing, harmony and counterpoint. He left the monastery at the age of 16, moved to Barcelona and joined the military academy. During the four years he stayed in the academy, he kept his musical interests alive and dedicated his life to the guitar after hearing the guitar music of Moretti.

**The Escolania Monastery at Montserrat is currently the oldest surviving music school and boys' choir left in Europe. It has documents that date back to the 13th century that establish it as a religious and musical institution made up entirely of choirboys.**

Sor lived in Spain, London, Paris and Russia. His travels exposed him to many different cultures and musicians. When France invaded Spain, he became familiar with French music and ideals. He then left Spain in 1813 and moved to France to concentrate fully on his music.

From 1815 to 1823, Fernando Sor lived in London, where he became very popular for his guitar talent as well as his vocal skills. He wrote *Cendrillon*, a ballet that was performed at the Kings Theatre in 1822. The ballet was so successful that it was performed in Paris a year later and then in Moscow, where it was met with enormous success again.

Sor stayed in Moscow from 1823 to 1826. He returned to Paris between 1827 and 1828 where he finally settled and lived the rest of his life devoted to the guitar. He published one of the most complete methods for guitar during this time.

Fernando Sor composed more than 400 pieces for the guitar. His compositions include studies, fantasies, themes and variations, and sonatas.

# Mauro Giuliani (1781–1829)

Mauro Giuliani was a master composer for the guitar. He played the violin, flute and guitar. The guitar became his primary instrument and his main devotion. He was considered a virtuoso by the age of 20.

Giuliani's1800 tour of Europe escalated his already virtuoso status in his native country of Italy. Giuliani settled in Vienna in 1806, which was becoming one of the greatest musical centres in all of Europe.

---

**Mauro Giuliani was in Vienna during the classical period. He would have heard the music of Haydn, Mozart, Gluck and Beethoven. Beethoven's *Eroica Symphony* had just debuted in 1803.**

---

While in Vienna, Giuliani was appointed chamber musician and teacher to the Austrian royal family, who frequently studied guitar with him. Giuliani's work ranged from the simplest exercises to the most technically challenging pieces. There are concertos with duets for violin and duets for flute and guitar.

# Francisco Tarrega (1852–1909)

Born Francisco de Assis Tarrega Eixea in Villareal de los Infantes, Castellón, Spain, Francisco Tarrega was without question one of the greatest classical guitarists of all time. He is considered the founder of the modern classical school. He was both a pianist and a guitarist. He attended the Madrid Conservatory and studied harmony and composition. He eventually became professor of guitar at the Barcelona and Madrid Conservatories.

It is through the dedication of Francisco Tarrega that the modern classical guitar and its practices are still utilized today. Tarrega devised the sitting position for the guitar as well as the position of the arms, legs and hands. He also insisted on the use of the footstool to raise the guitar body. The great guitar builder Antonio Torres had just perfected a new and larger classical guitar (the same as is used today), and Tarrega found that a new technique had to be developed for this amazing new instrument.

Another great contribution of Francisco Tarrega was his transcriptions of Bach, Chopin, Beethoven and other composers. His transcriptions of pianists Enrique Granados and Isaac Albeniz are considered standard classical guitar repertoire. Tarrega's students included Emilio Pujol, Miguel Llobet and Andrés Segovia.

# Vahdah Olcott-Bickford (1885–1980)

Born Ethel Lucretia Olcott in Norwalk, Ohio, Vahdah Olcott-Bickford began the study of guitar at the age of eight and eventually studied with Manuel Ferrer (1828–1904). Ferrer was a distinguished guitarist in America. Vahdah was Ferrer's last student.

Vahdah moved to New York in 1914, where she became known through her concerts and teaching of the guitar. She lived for a time with the famous Vanderbilt family at Biltmore, and tutored both Mrs Vanderbilt and her daughter, Cornelia. She also became involved with astrology, through which she gave herself the name Vahdah, by which she is commonly known.

**Vahdah Olcott-Bickford's entire musical collection estate was bequeathed to the University of California at Northridge. You can view the collection at the University of California at Northridge website (at http://library.csun.edu/igra). You can read more about Vahdah at http://library.csun.edu/igra/bios/olcott-bickford.html.**

In 1915, Vahdah met Myron Bickford (the organist, conductor, composer-musician and instrumentalist par excellence), whom she married. In 1923, Vahdah and Zarh (Myron's astrological name) moved to Los Angeles. Vahdah was instrumental in founding the American Guitar Society in Los Angeles. Her dedication to the classical guitar in America was significant to repertoire. In fact, during her life, Vahdah collected music on a grand scale. Her library of sheet music is the stuff of legends. Vahdah died at the age of 94 in 1980. She was dedicated to the guitar until the very end.

# Andrés Segovia (1893–1987)

Many musicians feel that without Segovia's efforts, the guitar would still be considered the equivalent of a honky-tonk barroom instrument. He is considered the father of the modern classical guitar.

Segovia was born in Linares, Spain, in 1893. When he was four years old, his uncle sang songs to him and pretended to strum an imaginary guitar. A local luthier (guitar maker) made an instrument for the child and although his family actively discouraged Segovia, he single-mindedly pursued his studies of the instrument. While self-taught, he adopted many of the techniques and practices of Francisco Tarrega, the influential guitar maestro of the late 19th century.

In 1909, Segovia made his debut at the age of 16 in Granada at the Centro Artistico and he performed his professional debut in Madrid in 1912. The guitar was widely believed to be incapable of proper classical expression, but Segovia stunned his critics with his skill. Starting in 1916, he began touring South America, and in 1924, he debuted in both London and Paris, becoming known as the 'ambassador of the guitar'. Segovia made his American debut in New York in 1928. He had a wide repertoire of lyrical works, which he played with great emotional expressiveness using fingernails on gut strings. He also demanded silence and concentration from his audiences.

### The Messenger

As Segovia grew older, he came to consider himself the messenger who would bring the guitar to the world concert stage so that it could take its place beside the violin and the piano. Before long, composers like Hector Villa-Lobos began to compose original pieces specifically for the guitar. Segovia himself arranged many pieces from the classical canon for the guitar – most notably JS Bach, whom he resurrected from the shadows of the musical canon and turned into a popular 20th-century composer – as well as lute and harpsichord music.

The central problem he faced during his early career was to make the guitar's sound fill a concert hall. Over the years, Segovia experimented with new woods and designs, to increase the instrument's natural amplification. The development of nylon strings gave the guitar more consistent tones and projected the sound much farther, yet were much less likely to break. During the 1940s, he adopted nylon for his strings rather than gut, starting a practice that continues to this day.

Segovia also standardized the way guitar fingering is notated on scores (by showing the string number written within a circle over a series of notes that could be played elsewhere on the instrument). He also settled the debate among classical guitarists about nails versus fingertips by popularizing the use of plucking the strings with the nails of the right hand.

---

**Segovia played a Ramirez classical guitar from 1912 until the 1930s, when he met the German luthier (guitar maker) Hermann Hauser. Hauser was so impressed with Segovia's guitar that he changed the way he built guitars. Hauser presented Segovia with a new instrument in 1937 that the maestro used until the 1960s.**

---

### Segovia's Gift

Of Segovia's many gifts to the world, perhaps his most lasting was to make the guitar the popular instrument of the 20th century. In addition to recording and performing, Segovia spent the remainder of his life and career successfully influencing the authorities at conservatories, academies and universities to include the guitar in their instruction programmes with the same emphasis as is given to the violin, cello and piano. He continued to give concerts into his 80s. His early struggles are recounted in his 1983 memoir, *Andrés Segovia: An Autobiography of the Years 1893–1920*. He died in 1987.

# Ida Presti (1924–1967)

Born Yvette Ida Montagnon, Ida Presti is considered one of the finest classical guitarists of the 20th century. She began taking piano lessons from her father at the age of five but soon switched to guitar. Ida Presti studied guitar with guitarist and luthier Mario Maccaferri, who taught her harmony and music theory. In 1932, Ida gave her first public recital at the ripe old age of eight! At the age of ten, she made her concert debut in Paris. At the age of 16, Ida played the guitar that was once owned and played by Paganini for a commemorative concert on the 100th anniversary of his death. Talk about an honour!

Ida Presti and Alexandre Lagoya were the first well-known 20th-century classical guitar duo. Presti had the unusual technique of playing using the sides rather than the tips of her fingernails.

In 1952, at the age of 27, Ida Presti met Alexander Lagoya through a friend. They were married a year later. This was Ida's second marriage. Two years after that, the Lagoya-Presti guitar duo performed their first concert. From then on, they performed exclusively as a duo. Ida Presti died tragically from an internal hemorrhage while preparing for a concert in New York in 1967.

# Narcisco Garcia Yepes (1927–1997)

Yepes was a Spanish guitarist of agility, precision and execution. He was the first to record Rodrigo's 'Concerto de Aranjuez' commercially in 1955. In 1963, he played a ten-string classical guitar of his own design, to which he had added four bass strings tuned to C, B♭, A♭, and G♭. These extra strings helped him arrange and play the piano compositions of composers such as Albeniz and Falla on the guitar, as well as fuller transcriptions of baroque music by composers such as Teleman and Scarlatti.

You can hear the best of Narcisco Yepes and ten-string guitar music on the CD entitled *Mad About Guitars*. The CD also features the talents of German ten-string guitarist Göran Söllscher.

# Julian Bream (1933–)

Born in Battersea, London in 1933, Bream is considered by many students of classical music as the premier guitar and lute virtuoso of the 20th century. He was an admirer of the Belgian gypsy jazz musician Django Reinhardt and began his musical career playing a steel-string guitar. When he heard a recording of Segovia playing 'Recuerdos de la Alhambra', he was captivated and devoted his time to studying the classical guitar.

He was largely self-taught (although helped by the Philharmonic Society of Guitarists) and he attended the Royal College of Music. There he studied piano and composition, because the guitar was not considered a 'serious' instrument at that time.

In 1945, Julian Bream won a junior exhibition award for his piano playing. His public debut was at the Cheltenham Art Gallery in 1946, and he began broadcasting for BBC Radio in the late 1940s. He also took up the lute and studied and played early music. In 1960, he founded the Julian Bream Consort, an ensemble of original instrument virtuosi that enjoyed astounding success, greatly revitalizing interest in the music of the Elizabethan era.

---

**One of the main contributions Julian Bream has brought to the classical guitar repertoire is the commissioning of works by 20th-century composers like Benjamin Britten, William Walton and Hans Werner Hense, among others. In order to hear the enormous contribution of Julian Bream, check out the 28-CD set,** *Julian Bream: The Ultimate Guitar Collection.*

---

By the 1950s, Bream had won fame for his technique and mastery of a wide range of musical styles. Like Segovia, he encouraged composers to write for the guitar. Unlike Segovia, Bream encouraged fresh, sometimes dissonant, modern material, which he nevertheless managed to perform with a striking tone and great emotionality. In the 1960s, he won two Grammy awards and an Edison award. In 1985, he was appointed Commander of the Order of the British Empire (CBE) on the Queen's Birthday Honours list.

# John Williams (1941–)

Born in Australia, Williams began learning the guitar at the age of four at the knee of his father, Len, who was also a gifted guitarist. When the family moved to London in 1952, Williams met and studied with Segovia. On Segovia's recommendation, Williams entered the Academia Musicale di Siena in Italy, where he won a scholarship to study and stayed until 1961. In 1958, at the request of his fellow students, Williams was the first student of any instrument to give a complete solo recital at the Academia Musicale. He began recording and touring, and in 1960, he was made professor of guitar at the Royal College of Music in London.

Segovia dubbed Williams 'the prince of the guitar', and his brilliant technique soon attracted worldwide attention. He and Julian Bream played and recorded a series of duets and recorded works as diverse as transcriptions of Scarlatti and Andre Previn's 'Guitar Concerto'.

While the older Bream encouraged contemporary composers to write for the instrument, he was also instrumental in a revitalization of early music. Williams, on the other hand, has been in the forefront of breaking down the barriers between classical music and popular music. He has performed with flamenco guitarists, at Ronnie Scott's Jazz Club in London, and in rock concerts playing steel-strung acoustic and electric instruments. His album *Changes* (1971) features arrangements of songs by the Beatles and Joni Mitchell, as well as a rock version of JS Bach's 'Prelude from the Suite in E Major'. The piece 'Cavatina' actually hit the UK pop charts briefly. In 1979 he formed Sky, a group that fused classical, jazz and pop ideas.

# Christopher Parkening (1947–)

One of the world's premier classical guitarists for the past 25 years, Parkening has received three Grammy nominations for best classical performance and holds an honorary doctorate in music from Montana State University, USA, where he teaches a masterclass each summer. Parkening continues to inspire and awe audiences around the world with both his technical brilliance and musicianship, performing more than 80 concerts a year.

# Sharon Isbin (1956–)

Sharon Isbin began playing the guitar at the age of nine. Her father was a professor at the University of Minnesota on sabbatical in Italy when she began her serious study with Aldo Minella. When she returned to the United States, she continued her studies with teachers Sophocles Papas and Jeffrey Vant. She also attended masterclasses given by Segovia disciple Oscar Ghilia and took additional classes from Alirio Diaz.

In order to hear the scope of Sharon Isbin's incredible use of baroque ornamentation on guitar, listen to her recordings of the Bach Lute Suites. She performs all four Bach lute suites, the first time these pieces were all recorded on guitar.

Sharon Isbin gave her first European tour at the age of 17. She has the distinction of being a triple-prize winner. In 1975, she won first prize in the international Guitar '75 competition in Toronto. In 1976, she won the top prize in the guitar division of the Munich International Competition, which was televised and broadcast internationally. In 1979, she was the winner of the Queen Sofia International Competition in Madrid. All these amazing accomplishments explain why Sharon Isbin was appointed the first professor of guitar at the Julliard Music School in New York in 1989.

## Classical Music Examples

The following music examples, Figures 9-1 to 9-5, show the diverse techniques used in playing classical guitar music.

**FIGURE 9-1:** MAURO GIULIANI STUDIES FOR GUITAR: NO. 81

**FIGURE 9-2:** MAURO GIULIANI STUDIES FOR GUITAR: NO. 97

**FIGURE 9-3:** CARCASSI GUITAR METHOD: PRELUDE IN A MAJOR

**FIGURE 9-4:** GEORGE FREDERICK HANDEL: GAVOTTE

**FIGURE 9-5:** BEETHOVEN: SONATINA IN G MAJOR

# Ramón Montoya (1880–1949)

Born into a flamenco-playing gypsy family, Montoya was influenced by Rafael Marin, who had studied with the great classical guitar master Francisco Tarrega. Montoya's playing was sophisticated. He built on existing traditions while at the same time adding new ideas and enriching the flamenco vocabulary. Early in his career, in the 1920s, he accompanied many of the major singers and dancers in the Café de La Marina in Madrid and won renown as a virtuoso player.

**Flamenco guitars have a different sound than classical guitars, due to lighter construction, cypress wood bodies and lower string action.**

Montoya's most important contribution to flamenco, however, was to break free of the role of accompanist and become a solo instrumentalist. He recorded many flamenco records, but his early recordings, such as 'Granadina', made in Paris in the 1930s, are among some of the most exciting and extraordinary.

# Carlos Montoya (1903–1993)

Like his uncle Ramón Montoya, Carlos Montoya also became a successful and influential flamenco guitarist. Born into a gypsy family in Spain, his interest in music and the guitar began at an early age. He began studying the guitar with his mother and a neighbouring barber, eventually learning from Pepe el Barbero, a guitarist and teacher.

Montoya started playing professionally at the age of 14, accompanying singers and dancers at the cafés in Madrid. Two of the dancers he played for most often were La Teresina and La Argentina.

Starting in the 1920s, he began touring Europe, Asia and North America. At the time World War II broke out in 1939, Carlos was on tour with a dancer in the United States. He decided to settle in New York, eventually becoming a US citizen.

By the end of the war, Carlos had broadened his repertoire to include not only flamenco, but also blues, jazz and folk music. He became the first flamenco guitarist to tour the world with symphonies and orchestras. He performed on television and recorded more than 40 albums, including *Suite Flamenco*, a concerto he performed with the St Louis Symphony Orchestra in 1966.

Carlos Montoya transformed flamenco from a dance accompaniment to a serious form of guitar music with a style all its own. With his own style, he adapted it to other genres of music, making himself an international star along the way. He died at the age of 89 in Wainscott, New York.

# Sabicas (1912–1990)

Born Agustin Castellon Campos, Sabicas was the son of a gypsy family in the north of Spain. A prodigy whose virtuoso style helped define modern flamenco, he left Spain in 1937 for Mexico, where he formed a company with the flamenco dancer Carmen Amaya that toured the world, making recordings.

By the mid-1950s, Sabicas moved to New York, where he concentrated on a solo career as a concert and recording artist. His dramatic style and breathtakingly accurate articulation and technique became a blueprint for subsequent generations of flamenco players. A powerful improviser, he once said he could never play the same thing twice.

## Paco Peña (1942–)

Paco Peña began his professional career at the age of 12. After touring with various groups as an accompanist, he settled in London and began a recording and concert performance career as a soloist. His television appearances in the 1960s afforded him more success. He has held an international festival of guitar in Córdoba, where he now resides. He has played concerts with John Williams, widening his popularity with the classical guitar audience.

## Paco de Lucia (1947–)

One of the leading flamenco guitarists of the late 20th century, Paco de Lucia was born in Algeciras, in the south of Spain, into a family of talented flamenco players. He began playing at the age of seven. Not only did his father encourage him to spend hours practising, but his house was also sometimes visited by Niño Ricardo, a major flamenco guitarist who had studied and played with Ramón Montoya. He later discovered the recordings of Sabicas, whose speed and clean execution had a profound influence on the development of his style.

At 14, de Lucia won first prize in a major flamenco competition. In 1962, at the age of 15, he accompanied the singing of his brother Pepe, and the two of them won the top prizes at the Jerez Concurso, a prestigious music festival. The following year he joined José Greco's dance troupe and toured the United States, meeting Sabicas and others.

Greatly inspired by a trip to Brazil, de Lucia began a series of innovative developments in flamenco guitar style based on new rhythms derived from Brazilian music and jazz. In addition to leading his own sextet, de Lucia enjoyed a long and creative partnership with the leading flamenco singer, El Camaron de la Isla.

Increasingly influenced by jazz, by the end of the 1970s de Lucia was working with John McLaughlin and Larry Coryell. In the 1980s, he and McLaughlin went on to work with Al Di Meola.

In 1991, de Lucia memorized and recorded Rodrigo's famous 'Concerto de Aranjuez', which he played with a flamenco feel. The release of 1999's Luzia heralded de Lucia's return to traditional flamenco, though he continues to play in other music forms with other musicians.

# Techniques to Play Classical and Flamenco

In order to understand classical and flamenco guitar techniques, you must be familiar with the 'lingo' used to describe those styles.

### Right-Hand Terminology

First, as you learned in Chapter 8, each finger of the right hand is indicated by a letter that stands for its Spanish name:

- *p* = Thumb (*pulgar*).
- *i* = Index finger (*indicio*).
- *m* = Middle finger (*medio*).
- *a* = Ring finger (*anular*).

The following terms describe the action of the right hand:

- **Dolce** The strings are plucked closer to the neck of the guitar, giving a softer, mellower tone.
- **Pizzicato** The thumb plucks the guitar string. The side or heel of the hand rests on the strings close to the bridge of the guitar.
- **Ponticelli** The strings are plucked close to the bridge, giving the notes a sharp treble sound.
- **Tremolo** The thumb plays a bass note, which is immediately followed by a treble note played three times, once by each finger, in this sequence: *p-a-m-i, p-a-m-i, p-a-m-i.*

### Rest Strokes and Free Strokes

The right hand hits the strings in two different ways, called the rest stroke and the free stroke. In the rest stroke (apoyando in Spanish), the finger plucks the string and rests on the next string. Only the tip end of the finger is placed on the string. This technique is primarily used for scale passages and to bring out melodies. Segovia developed scale exercises that used the rest stroke with alternating fingers.

In the free stroke (tirando in Spanish), the finger hits nothing after plucking the string. This technique is used to play chords and arpeggios. Folk guitarists and singer-songwriters also use this method when they accompany themselves.

## Left-Hand Terminology

In classical guitar, there is terminology for the left-hand technique as well:

- **Artificial harmonic** This is a type of note played by resting a left-hand finger on a string, without pressing it down, and then playing the note with the right hand. The best places on the fretboard for these sounds to be heard are on the seventh and twelfth frets.
- **Slur** This is when two or more notes are played one after the other, with only the first of the two being struck by the right hand.
- **Trill** This is an extension of the slur, with notes played in a more rapid succession.

On the left hand, each finger is indicated by a number:

- 1 = First finger.
- 2 = Second finger.
- 3 = Third finger.
- 4 = Fourth finger.

# Chapter 10

# Blues Guitarists

One of the earliest forms of original American music, blues music in its simplest form could be likened to African-American poetry set to music. The words and lyrics can address day-to-day struggles, love and call-and-response exchanges. Blues is essentially based on a twelve-bar structure, usually in 4/4 time. An early form of blues was sung by the field slaves working in the Southern states. Today, blues is a popular musical style with many variations and interpretations. Blues music is usually associated with guitar players who can also sing.

# Leadbelly (1885–1945)

Huddie William Ledbetter was born on Jeter Plantation in Mooringsport, Louisiana, in 1885 into a relatively prosperous family that farmed land, first as sharecroppers in Louisiana, then as landowners on the Texas-Louisiana border. Taught to play accordion and then guitar by his uncle Terrel Ledbetter, Leadbelly soon blossomed and began to employ his talents at local 'sukey-jump' parties and down on Shreveport's notorious Fannin Street.

After fathering a second child at age 16, Leadbelly was propelled by an outraged community to leave home. On his own, he became an itinerant minstrel and a farm labourer. He roamed around Dallas with the legendary blues singer Blind Lemon Jefferson though they parted company in 1917, when Leadbelly was jailed for assault. This was the first of many years Leadbelly spent in Southern penitentiaries.

He got his nickname, Leadbelly, in prison because of his physical toughness. He escaped from prison and returned home, but after hiding out briefly on the farm, he went to New Orleans and lived under the assumed name Walter Boyd. However, he got into a fight with a relative, Will Stafford, and Stafford was shot in the head and killed. Though Leadbelly always maintained his innocence, he was convicted of murder and assault with intent to kill and was sentenced as Walter Boyd to a long term of hard labour on the Shaw State Farm.

His musical gifts served him well in the prison camps, where he became a favourite of the guards. Legend has it that in 1925, Leadbelly pleaded for (and was given) his release in a 'please pardon me' song composed for and addressed to Governor Neff. After receiving Neff's pardon, Leadbelly returned to Mooringsport, Louisiana, but his womanizing and rough ways led to yet another conviction for assault with intent to murder. In the Louisiana state prison farm at Angola, the authorities discovered his previous conviction and considered this an aggravating factor. They turned down his written pleas for an early release.

## Discovery

In the 1930s, the Texas folklorist John Lomax was travelling through the South under a US Library of Congress grant, among other things recording the 'musical treasury locked up' in the prisons. Lomax discovered Leadbelly at Angola in July 1933. He was astounded by Leadbelly's enormous repertoire, intense vocal style and commanding physical presence. Using state-of-the-art equipment for the day, a bulky recorder that recorded onto aluminium discs and occupied most of the boot of his car, Lomax began recording Leadbelly.

**John A Lomax is internationally known as the person who spearheaded the US Library of Congress's Archive of American Folk Songs with his field-recording trips. With many obstacles in his way, he, and later his son Alan, were responsible for preserving roots music. You can read about their amazing contributions at the Library of Congress's website (http://memory.loc.gov/ammem/lohtml/lohome.html).**

Under 'double good time' measures adopted to save costs, Leadbelly was released early from prison. Lomax decided to take Leadbelly to New York, where he performed before audiences of musicologists at elite universities, inspiring fear and admiration. The mystique of his convict past and his commanding physical presence, replete with horrific scars, added to his allure. His eclectic repertoire, performed on a twelve-string guitar – which was not widely used then – was largely unknown and harked back some 30 or more years to near-forgotten rural traditions. John Lomax also negotiated a contract with Macmillan publishers to write a book that would be titled *Negro Folk Songs as Sung by Leadbelly*. It detailed Leadbelly's history and the events surrounding his discovery by Lomax, together with transcripts from his repertoire and explanations of the background of his songs and their place in American folklore.

Lomax also arranged a recording contract with the American Record Company, which had highly sophisticated recording studios and equipment. However, the commercial success of rural blues had passed some ten years earlier, with the heyday of Blind Lemon Jefferson, and the records sold poorly. This was compounded by the company's insistence that Leadbelly recorded blues rather than the folksongs that dominated his repertoire, most of which pre-dated the blues and were the chief source of his attraction for white audiences. As the stay in New York and environs wore on, the relationship between Lomax and Leadbelly deteriorated and they parted company in March 1935.

### Survival Instinct

Leadbelly survived on odd jobs and welfare. The Lomax book gained him some publicity but saw poor sales. The African-American music market had moved on and Leadbelly continued to find his principal audience among whites, especially the trade union movement and its left-wing associates. Always ready to adapt to his environment, Leadbelly added topical and protest songs to his repertoire for the first time, tackling segregation and other issues.

In early 1939, he was arrested yet again, this time for assaulting a man with a knife, and he eventually served eight months on Rikers Island. In early 1940, at the age of 51, Leadbelly was released. Moving back into the New York folk circuit, he met up with newcomers Woody Guthrie, Sonny Terry, Brownie McGhee, Pete Seeger, the Golden Gate Quartet, Burl Ives and many others who had migrated to New York and would fuel a minor folk boom during and after World War II.

He came to resent the convict image that he had acquired but found it impossible to shake off. He toured briefly in France, where jazz had become hugely popular, in early 1949. While in Paris, persistent muscle problems led to a diagnosis of Lou Gehrig's disease, amyotrophic lateral sclerosis. Six months later, on 6 December 1949, he died. In 1950, his trademark song, 'Goodnight Irene', became a nationwide number-one hit for the Weavers.

## Charlie Patton (1887–1934)

Born in Mississippi, Patton was considered one of the early innovative and influential figures in blues, ragtime, country songs and spirituals. His 'Pony Blues', recorded in 1929, became a commercial success that made him a star in blues circles. He played with a loose style that bent bar lengths and timing, though his style was nevertheless earthy and rhythmic.

Charlie Patton was one of the great blues showmen. He played often at 'jukes' (small bars) and often on street corners. One of his tricks, later adopted by rock musicians such as Jimi Hendrix, was to play the guitar behind his back.

If you listen carefully, you can hear Patton play instrumental responses to his sung phrases. He evoked sounds from the guitar in a crude percussive style, snapping strings and drumming on the instrument. He also tuned his guitar higher than normal to give it a bright, penetrating sound. By the time of his death in 1934, he had become a legendary figure in the Mississippi Delta who had influenced countless other blues musicians.

# Big Bill Broonzy (1893–1958)

Born in Scott, Mississippi, to a sharecropping family, Broonzy learned the rudiments of the fiddle before his family moved to Arkansas. By the age of 14, he was working for tips at country dances and picnics. In the early 1920s, he moved to Chicago, where, under the guidance of Papa Charlie Jackson, he learned to play blues guitar. Big Bill Broonzy's brand of blues stretched from ragtime-influenced blues to city blues backed with jazz musicians, to traditional folk blues and spirituals. He is considered the godfather of the Chicago blues scene.

Broonzy influenced many young bluesmen and he often took artists of lesser stature under his wing, helping them secure recording sessions and performance dates. His stature as a blues artist grew far beyond the Chicago scene after his performances at John Hammond's famous Spirituals to Swing concert series in 1938 and 1939 at Carnegie Hall in New York.

In 1951, Broonzy toured Europe, helping to introduce blues to France and Britain and opening the door for other American blues artists. In 1955, with help from writer Yannick Bruynoghe, he wrote his autobiography, *Big Bill's Blues*. Originally published in London, the book was one of the earliest autobiographies by a bluesman. Two years later, Broonzy was diagnosed with throat cancer. He continued to perform, often in great pain, until he died of the disease in 1958. Broonzy was inducted into Blues Foundation's Hall of Fame in 1980.

# Blind Lemon Jefferson (1897–1929)

Considering he was the most popular male blues recording artist of the 1920s, little is known about Blind Lemon Jefferson. He was born in Couchman, near Wortham, in Freestone County, Texas, in 1897. He was blind from childhood, possibly even from birth. Between 1925 and 1929, he made at least 100 recordings, including alternative versions of some songs, and issued 43 records.

He had few imitators, due to the technical complexity of his guitar playing and the distinctiveness of his high, clear voice. As a young man, Jefferson took up the guitar and became a street musician, playing in Wortham and nearby East Texas towns such as Groesbeck (mentioned in his 'Penitentiary Blues'), Buffalo and Marlin. Around 1917, he moved to Dallas, playing in the area centred on Deep Ellum, Dallas's equivalent of Memphis's Beale Street.

It was here that he met up with Leadbelly, an older and more experienced musician with a large repertoire of songs. Nonetheless, it was the younger man who had the greater command of the blues. They played together in Dallas until Leadbelly was sentenced to prison on an assault charge.

---

**Blind Lemon Jefferson played a Stella guitar, developed from twelve-string guitars (made up of six pairs of strings, with some strings tuned in unison and others an octave apart), which were common in Central and South America.**

---

In the early 1920s, Jefferson played around the South, especially the Mississippi Delta region, where there was lucrative work for an itinerant bluesman. He sold more than a million 'race records' to the emergent African-American market during the 1920s, but nevertheless died a pauper in Chicago, in mysterious circumstances, towards the end of December 1929.

# Memphis Minnie (1897–1973)

Born Lizzie Douglas in Algiers, Louisiana, Minnie was the oldest of 13 brothers and sisters. She is considered by many as one of the most influential and pioneering female blues musicians and guitarists of all time. She received her first guitar at 11 and recorded for 40 years, unheard of for any woman in show business at the time and unique among female blues artists. A flamboyant character who wore bracelets made of silver dollars, Memphis Minnie was the biggest female blues singer from the early Depression years to World War II.

After learning to play guitar and banjo as a child, Minnie ran away from home at the age of 13 to Memphis, Tennessee, playing the guitar in nightclubs and on the street as Lizzie 'Kid' Douglas. The next year, she joined the Ringling Brothers circus. She recorded her debut release in 1929 with second husband, Kansas Joe McCoy. Their song 'Bumble Bee' was a hit and success was just around the corner.

Memphis Minnie was one of the first blues artists to take up the electric guitar. She combined her Louisiana country roots music with Memphis blues and produced a unique country-blues sound. Minnie turned country blues into electric urban blues, which paved the way for Muddy Waters, Little Walter and Jimmy Rogers.

Minnie and McCoy broke up in 1935 and by 1939 she was with Little Son Joe, with whom she recorded nearly 200 records. In the 1940s, she formed a touring Vaudeville company. With musical tastes and cultures changing in the 1950s, public interest in her music declined, and in 1957 she and Little Son Joe returned to Memphis. In 1961, Joe died and Minnie suffered a stroke, which forced her to spend the rest of her life in nursing homes until her death in 1973. In 1980, Memphis Minnie was inducted into the Blues Foundation's Hall of Fame.

# Lonnie Johnson (1899–1970)

Almost unique among 20th-century musicians, Lonnie Johnson bestrides two of the most popular music forms of the early century – jazz and blues, defying categorization as belonging solely to either.

Johnson helped define the guitar's role in blues playing, and his melodic ideas and jaunty singing were on a par only with jazz's first recorded genius, the trumpeter Louis Armstrong. It's perhaps no coincidence that Johnson recorded in 1927 with Louis Armstrong's Hot Five. Armstrong may be considered the first jazz musician to step in front of a band and take an improvised solo, but Lonnie Johnson is the first guitarist to play a single-note improvised jazz chorus on the guitar. The two-guitar duets he recorded in 1928 and 1929 with jazz guitarist Eddie Lang – a musician who recorded several tracks for contractual reasons under the name of Blind Willie Dunn – are groundbreaking in their inventiveness.

For more than 40 years, Johnson played blues, jazz and ballads, his versatility stemming in part from growing up in the musically diverse Crescent City, New Orleans. His first instrument was the violin, but he developed an unaccompanied style as a guitar player that was sophisticated, fluid and melodic. He signed up with Okeh Records, and between 1925 and 1932, he cut an estimated 130 tracks.

Lonnie Johnson was a colossus who bestrode several genres of guitar, particularly blues and jazz. He often recorded using a Stella twelve-string and a regular six-string arch-top.

Johnson moved to Chicago and returned to recording in 1939. In 1947, he recorded one of his biggest hits, the ballad 'Tomorrow Night', which topped the US R&B charts for seven weeks in 1948. More hits followed, but by the late 1950s Johnson was earning a living as a hotel caretaker in Philadelphia. He was 'rediscovered' by banjo player Elmer Snowden and enjoyed a major comeback, recording a series of albums for Prestige's Bluesville subsidiary during the early 1960s. He also toured Europe with the American Folk Blues Festival.

Alas, in 1969, Johnson was hit by a car in Toronto and died a year later from the effects of the accident. His influence was massive, from Robert Johnson, whose approach to guitar playing strongly resembled his older namesake, to Elvis Presley and Jerry Lee Lewis, each of whom at different times paid tribute with versions of 'Tomorrow Night'.

# Howlin' Wolf (1910–1975)

Born Chester Arthur Burnett, this man's musical influence extends from the rockabilly singers of the 1950s and the classic rock stars of the 1960s to the grunge groups of the 1990s, plus a legion of imitators whose numbers rival the ranks of Elvis impersonators.

Born on 10 June 1910, in White Station, Mississippi, a tiny railway stop between Aberdeen and West Point in the Mississippi hill country, Chester was fascinated by music as a boy. He would often beat on pans with a stick and imitate the whistle of the trains that ran nearby. He also sang in the choir at the White Station Baptist Church, where Will Young, his stern, unforgiving uncle, preached.

When his parents separated, his father moved to the Delta and his mother left Chester with his Uncle Will, who treated him harshly. His mother spent much of her adult life as a street singer, eking out a living selling handwritten gospel songs for pennies to passers-by. She disowned her son, claiming he played 'the Devil's music'. Chester's paranoid rants about women in some of his songs can be traced to this bleak mother-son relationship.

## Becoming a Wolf

When he was 13, Chester ran away to rejoin his father and half-siblings, who lived on the Young and Morrow Plantation near Ruleville. There, Chester became fascinated by local blues musicians, especially the Delta's first great blues star, Charlie Patton, who lived on the nearby Dockery Plantation.

When his father bought Chester his first guitar in January 1928, he also convinced Patton to give Chester guitar lessons. Chester later took impromptu harmonica lessons from Sonny Boy Williamson, who was romancing his half-sister, Mary. He learned to sing by listening to the records of musicians like Blind Lemon Jefferson, Jimmie 'the Singing Brakeman' Rodgers and Lonnie Johnson. When he wasn't working on his father's farm, he travelled the Delta with musicians such as Robert Johnson, Charlie Patton, Son House and Willie Brown, playing guitar and blues harp (harmonica) simultaneously using a rack-mounted harp. From the start, Chester's voice was so huge and raw, like Charlie Patton's, that he earned the nickname Howlin' Wolf.

**Howlin' Wolf was a daunting presence. He stood six feet, six inches tall and weighed approximately 21 stone. His voice was also loud and booming, compared on one occasion to 'the sound of heavy machinery operating on a gravel road'.**

## Rising to Fame

In 1948, at the age of 38, Howlin' Wolf moved to West Memphis, Arkansas, where he put together a band that included harmonica players James Cotton and Junior Parker, and guitarists Pat Hare, Matt 'Guitar' Murphy and Willie Johnson. He also got a spot on radio station KWEM, playing blues and endorsing farm gear. In 1951, Wolf came to the attention of a young but very influential Memphis record producer, Sam Phillips, who took him into the studio and recorded 'Moanin' at Midnight' and 'How Many More Years', and leased them to Chess Records. Released in 1952, they made it to the top ten on Billboard's R&B charts. Wolf then moved to Chicago in 1953 and called the city home for the rest of his life. Phillips, who also discovered Elvis Presley, Carl Perkins, Jerry Lee Lewis, Johnny

Cash and Charlie Rich, said that losing Wolf to Chicago was his biggest career disappointment.

In his later years, Wolf continued to perform with a manic intensity, often in small clubs that other well-known bluesmen had already abandoned. He played electric guitar with his bare fingers – an oddity for a Chicago bluesman – and his eccentric, slashing style made him a favourite guitarist of Eric Clapton, Jimmy Page, Stevie Ray Vaughan and Jimi Hendrix.

## The Last Performance

In the late 1960s, Wolf suffered several heart attacks, and in 1970 he was in an car accident that destroyed his kidneys. For the rest of his life, he received dialysis treatments every three days. Despite his failing health, Howlin' Wolf stoically continued to record and perform.

In 1970, he recorded *The London Howlin' Wolf Sessions* with Eric Clapton, members of the Rolling Stones and other British rock stars. It was his bestselling album, reaching number 79 in the pop charts.

In 1973, he cut his last studio album, *Back Door Wolf*, which included the incendiary 'Coon on the Moon', the autobiographical 'Moving', and 'Can't Stay Here', a tribute to Charlie Patton. Wolf's last performance was in November 1975 at the Chicago Amphitheater. On a bill with BB King, Albert King, OV Wright, Luther Allison and many other great bluesmen, Wolf almost literally rose from his deathbed to recreate many of his old songs, performing some of his old antics – such as crawling across the stage during the song 'Crawling King Snake'. The crowd went wild and gave him a five-minute standing ovation. He exerted himself so much that when he got offstage, a team of paramedics had to revive him. Two months later, his heart gave out during an operation and he died.

He was inducted into the Blues Foundation's Hall of Fame in 1980 and the Rock and Roll Hall of Fame in 1991. His hometown of West Point, Mississippi, erected a statue in his honour in 1997 and continues to host a Howlin' Wolf music festival every summer.

# Robert Johnson (1911–1938)

Robert Johnson was born on 8 May 1911, in Hazlehurst, Mississippi, and moved with his mother to Robinsonville, a small but thriving northern Mississippi cotton community some 20 miles south of Memphis. A consummate musician, Johnson's talent was so awe-inspiring that myths grew up around him, particularly one about selling his soul to the devil at a crossroads at midnight in return for worldly success.

In Johnson's early teens, the harmonica was his main instrument. He took up the guitar during the late 1920s. He made a rack for his harp out of baling wire and string and was soon picking out appropriate accompaniments for his harp and voice. Willie Brown, a musician of some renown and ability, tried to show Johnson some things, and it was through Willie that Johnson met Charlie Patton.

Johnson farmed for a while but both his 16-year-old wife, Virginia, and their baby died in childbirth in April 1930. Less than two months later, close to the first of June, Son House came to live in Robinsonville at the request of Willie Brown. House, a precarious combination of bluesman and preacher, brought with him a kind of music whose intensity was shared by no one, not even Patton. It was raw, direct emotion and Johnson followed House and Brown wherever they went. Son House's influence can be clearly heard in Johnson's recordings of 1936 and 1937.

America was deep in the Depression at that time, but central Mississippi was fortunate in that the federal government were building roads in an attempt to provide work and an injection of cash into the economy. The Saturday-night 'juke joints' of the road gangs and lumber camps became Johnson's stage, and bluesman Ike Zinneman became his coach and mentor.

Johnson also found out that women could provide almost everything else for him. If he was going to be in any one place for a while, he developed a technique of female seduction that generally kept him well fed and cared for. As soon as he hit town, he'd find a homely woman. A few kind words and he knew he'd have a warm smile and a place to stay anytime, though his womanizing more than once got him in a scrape.

He travelled up and down the river playing in levee camps, for road gangs and in juke joints, visiting family and friends in Robinsonville and Memphis. He even roamed as far afield as Canada and New York in later years, but he always came home to Helena, Arkansas, one of the most musically active towns in the Delta.

Johnson was protective about his guitar playing and was acutely aware of other musicians 'ripping off' his 'stuff'. If someone was eyeing him too closely, he would get up in the middle of a song, make a feeble excuse and disappear for months. It all seemed very quirky, although recent research has suggested that he may have been guarding a very personal method of tuning his guitar.

Out of necessity, he developed the ability to play almost anything requested of him. In addition to the blues for which he was known, he had a repertoire that included pop tunes, hillbilly tunes, polkas, square dances, sentimental songs and ballads. Among the more common pieces he played were 'Yes, Sir, That's My Baby', 'My Blue Heaven' and 'Tumbling Tumbleweeds'.

---

**All the great musicians of the era came through Helena, Arkansas. Sonny Boy Williamson, Robert Nighthawk, Honeyboy Edwards, Howlin' Wolf and countless others performed in area nightclubs and hot spots.**

---

Pretty soon the word would go out that Robert Johnson was going to be at such-and-such a place, and the people would come. They knew they'd have a good time and hear some fine music. It was said he could hear a piece of music just once and be able to play it. He could be deep in conversation with a group of people and hear something – never stop talking – and later be able to play it and sing it perfectly. This talent amazed some very fine musicians and they never understood how he did it.

### Enter Ernie

Ernie Oertle was the American Record Company salesman and informal talent scout for the mid-South in the late 1930s, and after an audition, Oertle decided to take Johnson to San Antonio, Texas, to record.

Johnson's first session in November 1936 yielded the song for which he is most widely remembered: 'Terraplane Blues'. It was his bestseller and a fair-sized hit for Vocalion Records. He was invited back to Texas to record some more singles the following June, but nothing sold as well as 'Terraplane'. Although six of Johnson's eleven records were still in the Vocalion catalog by December 1938, he wasn't called back that spring or even the following summer. Vocalion released one final 78 in February 1939, but that was probably due to a great deal of interest in him by John Hammond.

## Johnson's Last Job

Sometime in August 1938, Johnson left Helena and swung through Robinsonville to see his people before playing a gig down in the Delta. As ever, he had become friends with a local woman – who unfortunately happened to be the wife of the man who ran the juke house at the intersection of Highways 82 and 49E, which the locals often referred to as 'Three Forks'. It was here that Johnson played his last job.

---

**Robert Johnson often played a Gibson L-1 with a pin bridge and a round (as opposed to F-shaped) sound hole. Gibson built its reputation on the arch-tops – or F holes – but began to introduce flat tops after 1926.**

---

On 13 August 1938, Three Forks offered the talents of Robert Johnson and singer and harmonica player Sonny Boy Williamson. There was a great deal of music and dancing that Saturday night, as both men sang and played their own brand of Delta blues. Williamson noticed the attraction Johnson displayed for the lady of the house, as well as the marked tension in the room. He recognized a potentially explosive situation when he saw one.

During a break in the music, Johnson and Williamson were standing together when someone brought Johnson an open bottle of whisky. As he was about to drink from it, Williamson knocked it out of his hand and it broke on the ground. He advised Johnson never to drink from an open bottle. But Johnson was angry and told Williamson never to knock whisky out of his hand.

When a second open bottle was brought to Johnson, Williamson could do no more than stand by and watch. Back on the stand, it wasn't too long before Johnson could no longer sing. Williamson took up the slack for him with his voice and harmonica, but Johnson stopped short in the middle of a number and got up and went outside. Before the night was over he displayed definite signs of poisoning. It seems the houseman's jealousy had finally got the best of him and he had laced Johnson's whisky with strychnine. Ironically, Johnson survived the poisoning but contracted pneumonia. He died on Tuesday 16 August. He was 27 years old.

He was buried in the graveyard of the Little Zion Church just north of Greenwood, Mississippi. Eleven 78rpm records were issued during Johnson's lifetime and one posthumously. Including the material that never saw issuance on 78s, there are a total of 42 recordings – the only recordings of one of the true geniuses of American music.

# Muddy Waters (1914–1983)

Born McKinley Morganfield, Muddy Waters (named by his grandmother, Della Rose) became a blues icon. Known as the 'Hoochie Coochie Man', his deep-bottom Mississippi blues voice is the sound of the Mississippi Delta personified. Influenced by the music of Son House and Robert Johnson, Muddy Waters came into his own voice with the power of a hurricane. Playing Delta juke joints up and down the Mississippi, Muddy gained more experience with new songs and playing ability.

Muddy Waters first recorded music for the US Library of Congress, which is what Son House and Robert Johnson did early in their careers. But Muddy would have to wait for his release a little longer. Playing at house parties for rent money and the like, Muddy was a travelling man. He would eventually get the recording break he was looking for in 1946, when he recorded for Columbia Records under the direction of Leonard Chess. Their contract was based on a handshake. He recorded the legendary 'I'm Your Hoochie Coochie Man' in 1954 and 'Got My Mojo Working' in 1956. Muddy Waters' influence on music in general is far-reaching. He took the Delta blues to Chicago, plugged in an electric guitar and turned it up, essentially electrifying the Chicago blues style. Plus, he added the sexual component to the music, which eventually found its way into music of Led Zeppelin. Keith Richards would eventually name his band after the Muddy Waters classic 'Rolling Stone'. Muddy Waters influenced the development of rock-and-roll with three chords being played loud and with powerful rhythms.

The album *Fathers and Sons* is a tribute to the achievements and talent of Muddy Waters, guitarist Michael Bloomfield and harmonica player Paul Butterfield. The album, produced by Chess Records, paired the blues masters with several young artists who had been influenced by them.

# Albert King (1923–1992)

Known as 'The Velvet Bulldozer', Albert King is one of the giants and 'Three Kings' of the electric blues guitar (along with BB King and Freddie King). He stood six foot four and weighed over 18 stone. He was born Albert Nelson in Indianola, Mississippi, on a cotton plantation where he worked early in his life. His father – Will Nelson – was one of his earliest influences, as he was a guitarist too.

King began his professional work as a musician with a group called In the Groove Boys, in Osceola, Arkansas. Albert King's approach to playing lead guitar solos was about getting killer tones, bending and sheer power. He took the 'less is more' road when it came to playing. His signature instrument, the Gibson Flying V (which he named 'Lucy') was played left-handed without changing the strings around. A right-handed player will bend the note by pushing the string upwards against the frets, causing the pitch to go up, Albert King did the reverse – pulling the string downwards to get the same result.

Albert King's first hit was 'I'm A Lonely Man', released in 1959. In 1961, he released 'Don't Throw Your Love on Me So Strong'. This was his first major hit, reaching number 14 in the American R&B charts. When he signed with Stax Records in 1966, he began recording his legendary album *Born Under a Bad Sign*, released in 1967. The title track of that album was written by Booker T Jones and William Bell.

Albert King's guitar playing was as intimidating as his stature. Guitarists of the time were mesmerized by it. But Eric Clapton saw something in King's solos. Clapton reworked some of King's solos (note for note) in Cream's 'Strange Brew'. He also recorded Albert King's 'Born Under a Bad Sign', which became a hit during the blues-rock era. King died on 21 December 1992 from a heart attack in Memphis, Tennessee. He has a star on the St Louis Walk of Fame.

# BB King (1925–)

BB King (along with his musical 'wife', his Gibson guitar 'Lucille') is one of the most famous electric blues guitarists in the world. Inspired early on by Blind Lemon Jefferson and Lonnie Johnson, he also drew inspiration from early jazz guitarists such as Charlie Christian. King developed a style of playing that used the guitar not just as a rhythmic accompaniment but also as a sort of 'back-up' – or accompanying voice – when he sang, playing short, riff-like single-note melodic phrases. His first hit came in 1951 with 'Three o' Clock Blues', and he went on to record many more, with big band accompaniment and jazzy phrasing.

**The Gibson 335 guitar, a symmetrical, thin-bodied instrument that became the mainstay for bluesmen such as BB King and Freddie King, first appeared in 1958. During the 1940s, BB King used a Fender Bassman amplifier with his Gibson, and the combination became the standard for blues playing and recording until the late 1980s.**

# Johnny Winter (1944–)

Born John Dawson Winter III in Beaumont, Texas, Johnny Winter is the first son of John and Edwina Winter. He and his younger brother Edgar Winter are blues legends. Interestingly, both brothers are albinos. At the age of 14, Winter had accumulated an enormous record collection from which he could draw on numerous influences. His recording career began at the age of 15. During this time, he was able to see performances by classic blues artists such as Muddy Waters, BB King and Bobby Bland.

*Rolling Stone* printed an article about the Texas blues scene and a local unsigned guitarist. In the 1968 feature, writer Larry Sepulvado described Johnny Winter as 'a 130-pound [nine-stone], cross-eyed albino with long fleecy hair, playing some of the gutsiest, fluid blues guitar you ever heard.' From that article alone, Johnny Winter would be thrown into the spotlight. In 1968, Johnny began playing in a trio with bassist Tommy Shannon and drummer Uncle John Turner. The album *Johnny Winter* was released by Columbia Records near the end of that year. Classic tracks from that release include 'Be Careful with a Fool', 'I'm Yours and

Hers', and 'When You Got a Good Friend'. In 1969, the trio performed at numerous rock festivals, including Woodstock.

In 1973, after struggling with a drug problem, Winter returned in classic form with 'Still Alive and Well'. In 1977, he produced the Muddy Waters recording, 'Hard Again'. Their partnership produced a number of Grammy-winning recordings, and Winter recorded the album *Nothing but the Blues* with members of Muddy Waters' band. In 1988, he was inducted into the Blues Foundation Hall of Fame.

# Joe Bonamassa (1977–)

Joe Bonamassa had one of those lucky early starts – his father was a guitar dealer and player, so guitars were always around the house and part of his life. 'They were like chairs or tables, in that they were just as everyday,' says Bonamassa. Joe began performing at local venues at the age of ten, and at twelve, he was asked to open for BB King. Now that is an honour! After King heard Joe play for the first time, he declared, 'This kid's potential is unbelievable. He hasn't even begun to scratch the surface. He's one of a kind.'

Joe's first band was called Bloodline, a group he put together with musician Berry Oakley Jr. They would eventually sign with EMI Records and release their self-titled debut CD, which produced two chart hits, 'Stone Cold Hearted' and 'Dixie Peach', both songs with a fusion of blues, boogie, funk and southern roadhouse rock. After their initial success, Bloodline eventually disbanded.

In 2000, Joe worked with the legendary producer Tom Dowd, who had, in the course of his 25-year career at Atlantic Records, recorded rock-and-roll royalty. Dowd worked on Joe's debut solo CD, *A New Day Yesterday*. The title song was first recorded by the group Jethro Tull in 1969.

Tom Dowd worked with Aretha Franklin, Ray Charles, Eric Clapton, Rod Stewart, John Coltrane and Ornette Coleman. He helped shape the Memphis sound and was even a member of the team who worked on the Manhattan Project. You can see his story in the documentary *The Music of Tom Dowd*.

In 2002, after returning from the road, Bonamassa hired producer Clif Magness to record 'So, It's Like That', which hit number one on the Billboard Blues Chart multiple times. When the 'So, It's Like That' tour ended, Bonamassa recorded some of his favourite blues covers with producer Bob Held and engineer Gary Tole. The result was a record and 2003 release called *Blues Deluxe*, featuring nine cover versions of blues classics along with three originals.

Joe is involved with 'Blues in the Schools', a programme developed by the Blues Foundation to help perpetuate the heritage and legacy of blues music to a new generation of fans. After being personally asked by BB King to open for his 80th Birthday Celebration Tour in the summer of 2005, Bonamassa was nominated as the youngest member of the Blues Foundation committee board in January 2006. Along with his ever-expanding vintage guitar collection, Bonamassa makes his home in Los Angeles.

# Chapter 11

# Jazz Guitarists

Jazz guitar has had more of an uphill battle than most other genres. With its need for more volume, less feedback and stepping out of the chord-accompaniment zone, jazz guitar has come a long way. It took a long time before the guitar played a decisive role in the evolution of jazz, but the musical style has since enjoyed a rich and eventful history. This was partly a result of the development of the arch-top guitar, which could compete with the volume of sound in a large ensemble. Following are some of the greats of the jazz guitar.

# Eddie Lang (1902–1933)

Eddie Lang is considered by many to be the father of jazz guitar, and he is thus the first jazz guitar virtuoso. Lang took violin lessons for 11 years but switched to guitar before he turned professional in 1924 with the Mound City Blue Blowers. His sophisticated chord patterns made him a unique accompanist. Lang was a versatile player who could back blues singers, play classical music and jam with the greatest musicians of his day. Using the pseudonym Blind Willie Dunn, Lang often teamed up with blues guitarist Lonnie Johnson. Eddie Lang led several recording dates of his own between 1927 and 1929, including a session with King Oliver and Johnson, under the name Blind Willie Dunn and His Gin Bottle Four.

Lang also worked regularly with Bing Crosby during the early 1930s and can be seen (briefly) with Crosby in the film *The Big Broadcast*. Because of his association with Bing Crosby, Lang was making between $1000 and $1200 a week in 1932 – during the Great Depression! Lang died tragically in 1932 due to a botched routine tonsillectomy, in which he lost too much blood. Bing Crosby was said to have been deeply troubled by Lang's death, not only because he had suddenly lost one of his best friends and most talented sidemen but because he had personally urged Lang to have the operation.

Eddie Lang's chord technique has influenced jazz greats like George Van Eps, Django Reinhardt and Charlie Christian.

# Django Reinhardt (1910–1953)

Django is considered the first major figure in jazz who was not American. That he was a guitarist, considered a lowly part of the rhythm section, is even more remarkable. Born of a musical gypsy family in Belgium, Reinhardt spent his childhood in a shantytown gypsy encampment outside of Paris. By the age of 12, he was playing banjo and violin in various gigs, and his first recordings, made in 1928, were with an accordionist and someone playing slide whistle.

That same year he had an accident with a candle in his caravan and was momentarily trapped in a blazing inferno. He was so badly burned that he was bedridden for 18 months, and his left hand was so injured it did not seem likely that he would ever play a musical instrument again.

What he did next was an indication of his sheer genius and willpower. He came up with a completely radical way of playing the guitar using the two uninjured fingers on his left hand, barring the guitar neck occasionally with the fused stumps of the rest of his fingers, which gave his playing a harmonically distinctive 'modern' sound. He also developed his right-hand technique, and his famous liquid chromatic runs were achieved by coordinating one shift of a left-hand finger with a down- or upstroke of his plectrum in his right hand, for each note of the phrase.

His first recordings on guitar were made in 1931 as an accompanist to a singer. Accustomed to listening to and playing the improvised forms of gypsy music, he was fascinated with American jazz and its parallels to flamenco. It's more than likely he was listening to recordings by Duke Ellington, Louis Armstrong, guitarist Lonnie Johnson, and violinist Joe Venuti and his tracks with guitarist Eddie Lang, who also recorded some classic guitar duets with Lonnie Johnson.

By 1935, after recording with Hawkins and Michel Warlop's group, Reinhardt had attracted the attention of visiting American musicians. Record dates with Hawkins, Benny Carter, Dicky Wells, Eddie South and Bill Coleman resulted in some classic recordings. In 1934, the Quintette du Hot Club de France was formed, featuring Django on lead guitar, two rhythm guitars, a bass player and violinist Stéphane Grappelli.

**That Django and Grappelli work well on disc is clearly evident. That they distrusted each other for the whole of their playing career is not. Django was a fiery, emotionally powerful and naturally inventive improviser, but he was also impetuous and unpredictable. Grappelli was his opposite – cool, elegant and the 'straw boss' of the group who made it all happen behind the scenes.**

Django had ambitions to compose for larger groups, but he was handicapped by the fact that he could neither read nor write music and was thus dependent on others to take down his musical dictation.

At the outbreak of World War II in 1939, the group was in London. Grappelli stayed in Britain while Django returned to Paris. Ironically, despite the fact that the Nazis despised it, jazz seemed to flourish after they occupied France in 1940.

Django reorganized the Hot Club de France, replacing one of the guitarists with a drummer and Grappelli with a clarinet player.

**The Selmer Maccaferri, made famous by Django Reinhardt, had a D-shaped sound hole, a flat cutaway and a two-octave fingerboard. The internal strutting was developed to enhance the volume and sustain. The guitar was launched in 1932, but by the end of the 1940s, Django was using a Stimer pickup attached to his Maccaferri, using a small combination amp to get an electric sound.**

### Coming to America

After the war, Django went to America for a series of concerts. He expected to be feted as a conquering hero, but the audiences were cool to his antics. He brought no guitar with him, for example, and people had to rush around finding one for him to play. At his first concert, with Duke Ellington's band at Carnegie Hall, he was so late that Ellington was forced to offer an embarrassed apology for Django's non-appearance. Shortly after, Django strolled on stage and began to play.

### Adopting Electric

In 1946, Reinhardt reunited with Grappelli, although he continued to play with other line-ups as well. The major change in his career was his adoption of the electric guitar.

From 1937 onwards, he had played a Selmer Maccaferri, a specially designed guitar that was louder than the normal acoustic instrument. After his American adventure, he fitted a 'Charlie Christian' bar pickup on the Maccaferri, before eventually going all-electric in 1950.

By this time Reinhardt's improvisation was being influenced by the newly emerging bebop style of Charlie Christian and Charlie Parker, with their more sophisticated and complex harmonies and rhythms. In the last couple years of his life Reinhardt went into semi-retirement in the French village of Samois-sur-Seine, spending his time fishing, painting and playing billiards. Yet he continued to play with the emerging French bebop players like pianist Martial Solal and Raymond

Fol, and alto saxophonist Hubert Fol. He recorded his last record on a purely electric instrument with this next generation of musicians.

On 16 May 1953, he finished playing at the Club St Germaine in Paris and caught the train to Avon, the station nearest to Samois. He went to a local bar for a drink and passed out. He was rushed to a hospital in Fontainebleu but soon died. Three days later he was buried in Samois, at the age of 43.

# Les Paul (1915–2009)

Born Lester Polfuss in Waukesha, Wisconsin, Les Paul was an American guitarist and guitar builder. He was one of the pioneers of the solid-bodied electric guitar. In 1941, he created his first prototype, which he called 'the log'. The log was nothing more than a common four-by-four fence post with bridge, guitar neck and pickup attached. He also invented the floating guitar bridge, electrodynamic pickups, dual pickup guitars and the 'Les Paulverizer', a machine used during performances to record sounds, play them back and electronically modify them.

He was also an innovator of recording studio technology, developing such radical trends as multi-tracking, echo delay and positional close-miking techniques. He primarily worked from his garage in California, where he recorded for Capitol Records.

---

**To this day no one knows exactly how the 'Les Paulverizer' works, but it's clear that some of the things it does still cannot be exactly duplicated with current technology.**

---

Les Paul continued to perform weekly in New York well into his 90s. He won a Grammy in 2006 for *Les Paul and Friends: American Made, World Played*. He died on 13 August 2009 at the age of 94.

# Charlie Christian (1916–1942)

Charles Christian was born on 29 July 1916 in Bonham, Texas, into a musical family. His mother played piano to silent movies, his father sang and played both trumpet and guitar, and brothers Clarence and Edward, also played professionally.

The family moved to Oklahoma City in 1918, and Christian's first instrument was the trumpet, a choice that no doubt helped formulate the horn-style, single-note guitar improvising that later made him famous.

Novelist and family friend Ralph Ellison said that at the age of 12, Christian 'would amuse and amaze us at school with his first guitar – one that he made from a cigar box … playing his own riffs. But they were based on sophisticated chords and progressions that Blind Lemon Jefferson never knew.'

Throughout Christian's early teens, he played in the family band and performed in Oklahoma City clubs. It was there that he first heard and met the great tenor saxophonist Lester Young. The meeting was a seminal moment for Christian.

'Lester Young didn't bring Charlie Christian out of some dark nowhere,' Ralph Ellison commented. '[Charlie] was already out in the light. He may only have been 12 or 13 when he was making those cigar-box guitars in manual training class, but no other cigar boxes ever made such sounds. Then he heard Lester and that, I think, was all he needed.'

By the early 1930s, Christian doubled on bass and guitar in a band fronted by his brother Eddie and was busy learning solos of Django Reinhardt and Lonnie Johnson. After briefly leading his own band, he played bass and/or guitar with a variety of well-known regional bands.

The second seminal moment in Christian's life was in 1937, when he discovered the electric guitar. The amplified electric guitar was still an experimental novelty, although electric guitarist and trombone player Eddie Durham was already playing it as a solo instrument in Jimmie Lunceford's band. The new invention made the jazz guitar solo a practical reality for the first time. With the exception of Lonnie Johnson and Eddie Lang, guitarists were part of the rhythm section, strumming chords. Now, guitarists could revel in the volume and sustain provided by an amplifier – in other words, they could produce a sound like a saxophone or trumpet.

### Christian and Goodman

Christian quickly realized the potential the electric guitar unleashed, and he soon developed a saxophone style of playing that was reminiscent of his hero, Lester Young. He got himself a Gibson ES-150 (listed in 1936 at $77.50, including a 15-foot cable), and by 1938, he was playing electric guitar in the Al Trent Sextet.

By 1939, Charlie Christian's innovative guitar style had won the admiration of many influential musicians in the jazz circuit, including pianists Teddy Wilson and Norma Teagarden. Pianist Mary Lou Williams recommended him to record producer and jazz promoter John Hammond. In August 1939, Hammond arranged for Charlie to have an audition with Benny Goodman, known at the time as 'The King of Swing', and Hammond's brother-in-law. Goodman, who was white, was not only a great clarinet player, he was also a pioneer in touring with a mixed-race swing band.

Goodman needed some convincing. As Hammond recalled, when Christian arrived in Los Angeles, Goodman was presented with a country bumpkin so to speak. Goodman gave Christian a cursory audition, asking him to comp on 'Tea for Two' without allowing him time to plug in his amp. He wasn't impressed.

**Christian had been experimenting with amplifying the guitar for several years in an effort to get a saxophone sound. Guitarist Mary Osborne recalled hearing what she thought was a tenor saxophone being played in a club in Bismarck, North Dakota, in 1934 and discovering it was Christian with a microphone attached to his guitar.**

Hammond said that he decided to convince Goodman by sneaking Christian onstage later that night during a concert at the Victor Hugo. Goodman angrily launched into 'Rose Room', a number he figured Christian wouldn't know. 'After the opening choruses Goodman pointed to Christian to take a solo,' Hammond wrote, 'and the number which ordinarily lasted three minutes stretched out to 45! Everyone got up from tables and clustered around the bandstand, and there could be no doubt that perhaps the most spectacularly original soloist ever to play with Goodman had been launched.'

Goodman was won over. Christian's presence turbo-charged the group and Goodman made the most of the guitarist's new sound. His first studio recordings with the band were in New York on 2 October 1939, in a session that included 'Rose Room', 'Flying Home', and Christian's memorable solo on 'Stardust'. By 1940, he had recorded 'Gone With What Wind', and 'Air Mail Special', which featured snappy lines reminiscent of Django Reinhardt, and he had been voted 'Top Guitarist' by *Metronome* magazine readers. While Goodman sometimes took credit for melodies actually composed by his sidemen, he nevertheless gave Christian partial credit for several classics, including 'Seven Come Eleven', 'Air Mail Special' and 'Solo Flight'.

**Charlie Christian played a Gibson ES-150. Launched in 1936, the guitar was based on the L-50 acoustic arch-top with the addition of a heavy, large bar-magnet pickup and a tone and volume control. He later switched to the newer ES-250.**

## Jam Sessions

The sextet made Christian a star in the jazz world and helped legitimize and popularize the electric guitar as a jazz instrument. Some of Christian's last recordings were made in two after-hours clubs in Harlem, in the cutting-edge hothouse environment of Minton's and of Monroe's Uptown House. They are considered by many to be the first recordings that show the 1930s swing style evolving into the fiery, harmonically, and far more rhythmically complex bebop style.

Minton's, on West 118th Street, established by a retired sax player named Henry Minton, was located in a former dining room in the Hotel Cecil. The manager was a fellow saxophonist and former bandleader, Teddy Hill, who hired a rhythm section that included Thelonious Monk and Kenny Clarke. Jam sessions would sometimes last all night.

Christian was so into the jam sessions that he bought a second amp to leave at Minton's. The band often included Kenny Kersey on piano, Kenny Clarke on drums, trumpeter Joe Guy and bassist Nick Fenton. Private recordings made by a jazz enthusiast at Minton's reveal Charlie Christian at his most inventive and experimental, as on the extended 'Swing to Bop'.

### An Early Death

In the summer of 1941, Christian developed the first signs of tuberculosis. He was forced to leave the Goodman band's tour of the Midwest and entered the Seaview Sanatorium on Staten Island. Count Basie's doctor kept an eye on him. Teddy Hill came once a week bearing fried chicken and other goodies, and well-meaning friends sneaked him whisky and dope. He began to improve but found life dull, so one night he slipped out with some friends for off-limits carousing, caught a chill and died. The date was 2 March 1942. He was 25 years old. Christian was buried in a small cemetery in Bonham. Although the exact location of his grave is not known, a marker and headstone were erected in his honour in 1994.

The amazing thing about Christian is that though he recorded for a mere three years, he managed in that short time to influence many generations of musicians. He has been cited as an influence by blues and rock musicians as well as jazz guitarists. His style may lack some of the technical virtuosity of some modern guitarists, but Christian's lively, inventive single-note playing helped popularize the electric guitar as a solo instrument and ushered in the era of Charlie Parker and bebop.

# Talmage (Tal) Farlow (1921–1998)

While working in the seminal Red Norvo Trio with vibes player Norvo and the bass player Charlie Mingus, Tal Farlow commented there were only two tempos the group played – fast and even faster.

Farlow is one of the two major influential bebop guitar players who led jazz into the 1950s after Charlie Christian, inspired by Charlie Parker. The other was his long-time friend Jimmy Raney, although Farlow is often considered the slightly more influential of the two. Farlow's large hands helped him develop sophisticated chord voicings full of space and slight dissonances, while his inventive up-tempo single-note improvisations and imaginative use of artificial harmonics quickly won him a place as a major figure in jazz.

---

**Both Barney Kessel and Tal Farlow used the Gibson ES-350, the first electric arch-top with a cutaway, which was launched in 1946.**

---

Born in North Carolina, Farlow began playing professionally at the relatively late age of 22. He apprenticed as a sign painter at the insistence of his guitar-playing father, and intermittently throughout his playing career he returned to that trade. A reticent, self-effacing man with a laconic sense of humour, he once commented that playing a jazz solo was 'pretty much the same thing as painting a sign'.

Farlow was essentially a self-taught musician, inspired by hearing Charlie Christian on the radio with Benny Goodman. He moved to New York and quickly fell under the influence of major bebop musicians like Charlie Parker and Bud Powell, whom he listened to and occasionally played music with in and around 52nd Street. He first came to prominence as a sideman with clarinetist Buddy DiFranco, but his breakthrough happened in 1949 when he joined the Red Norvo Trio (1949–1953) at the recommendation of guitarist Mundell Lowe. The trio was one of the first expressions of modern chamber jazz.

After Norvo, Farlow joined Artie Shaw's Gramercy Five and then led his own groups. He recorded several classic jazz records before marrying in 1958 and retiring from the limelight. He moved to Sea Bright, New Jersey, where he continued to play locally, teach and work as a sign painter.

In the 1970s, he came out of retirement, contracted with Concord Records, and began to tour internationally again. In his declining years, he performed and recorded under the banner of the Great Guitars, with Herb Ellis, Charlie Byrd and Barney Kessel. A 58-minute documentary, *Talmage Farlow*, was released by Lorenzo DeStefano. A compilation selected from Farlow's seven discs for Verve in the early 1950s, *Jazz Masters 41*, and *Tal*, also on Verve, are exemplary recordings of his work. He died of cancer in 1998.

# Johnny Smith (1922–)

Smith, like Tal Farlow, another guitarist with long fingers, developed a distinctive style of guitar playing that was well captured on his 1952 hit record 'Moonlight in Vermont', which also featured saxophonist Stan Getz. He worked with Benny Goodman in the early 1950s and established himself as a session musician at NBC in New York. A self-taught musician who originally played the trumpet, violin and viola before switching to the guitar, he incorporated classical phrasing and precise articulation. In the 1960s, he moved to Colorado and opened a music shop, taught, and maintained a lower profile, occasionally recording in New York.

# Barney Kessel (1923–2004)

Born in Muskogee, Oklahoma, Kessel took on Christian's mantle in the mid-1940s and carried it through to the late 1980s. An innovative guitarist, he followed and developed Charlie Christian's swing style of playing, developing the harmonic possibilities of the instrument in a way that clearly showed a guitar player could do anything a piano player could do, and sometimes better.

Kessel got his first guitar at the age of 12 and was playing gigs with all-black bands two years later. At 16 he met and jammed with Charlie Christian, whose music he knew from recordings and radio broadcasts with Benny Goodman. A year later he left for Los Angeles to make it as a musician.

He got a job in Chico Marx's band, and in the mid-1940s he was featured with Charlie Parker and Lester Young. He was also featured with Lionel Hampton in the Jazz at the Philharmonic concerts. By 1947, he had worked with a number of big bands, including Benny Goodman's and Artie Shaw's. That same year he went into the studio with Charlie Parker, and the results were some classic bebop recordings that established Kessel as an accomplished and confident musician.

---

**In 1934, Gibson introduced the large-bodied arch-top Super 400, designed to give more volume.**

---

In 1952, Kessel joined the Oscar Peterson Trio for a Jazz at the Philharmonic tour that visited 14 countries. He continued to record with Peterson and a score of other major jazz names. In the late 1950s and the 1960s, he became a major figure in the Los Angeles recording industry. His 1955 Trio record Cry Me a River, featuring singer Julie London, is a classic of its type. He also recorded a series of records called *The Poll Winners* with bass player Ray Brown and drummer Shelley Mann. The records were so-called because he and his partners consistently won jazz polls in *Down Beat*, *Esquire*, *Playboy*, *Metronome* and *Melody Maker* magazines.

He continued to play jazz and tour until 1992, when he suffered a stroke that left him unable to play any more. He eventually regained his ability to speak and move, but died of a brain tumour in May 2004.

# John L 'Wes' Montgomery (1925–1968)

Considered one of the great jazz guitarists, Wes Montgomery admitted to influences that included Charlie Christian and then later the saxophonist John Coltrane, with whom he played briefly in an unrecorded group.

Wes's development and use of octaves became both influential and a trademark, but it took Wes a long time to become an overnight success. He achieved commercial success with his Verve recordings during his last few years, only to die prematurely of a heart attack.

Like his idol, Charlie Christian, Wes came from a musical family and taught himself the guitar by learning the solos of Charlie Christian and Django Reinhardt, from whom he developed the idea of playing octaves. He tried to use a pick in the conventional style but eventually opted to use his thumb because he preferred the thick, warm sound it produced. He toured with Lionel Hampton's big band from 1948 to 1950 and can be heard on a few broadcasts from the period. Then he returned to Indianapolis, where he played in relative obscurity during much of the 1950s, working a day job and playing at clubs most nights.

He recorded with his brothers, pianist and vibraphonist Buddy and bass player Monk, from 1957 to 1959, and in 1959 he made his first album, *The Wes Montgomery Trio*, with organist Mel Rhyne.

In 1960, the release of his album, *The Incredible Jazz Guitar of Wes Montgomery*, made him famous in the jazz world. Later that year he spent some time playing with the John Coltrane Sextet.

Montgomery's Riverside dates (1959–1963) are among his most inventive jazz recordings, in small-group sessions with such sidemen as George Shearing, Tommy Flanagan, James Clay, Victor Feldman, Hank Jones, Johnny Griffin and Mel Rhyne.

From 1964 to 1966, Montgomery moved to Verve and recorded a series of orchestral dates with arranger Don Sebesky and producer Creed Taylor. These records popularized him with the general listening audience, widening his appeal from a pure jazz base. In 1967 he continued this trend, signing with Creed Taylor at A&M, where he recorded three bestselling albums that featured him playing pop melodies backed by strings and woodwind instruments.

Wes Montgomery died at the height of his success. However, his influence is still felt through many young guitarists, notably Pat Metheny.

# Jimmy Raney (1927–1995)

A definitive cool jazz guitarist and a fluid bop soloist with a quiet sound but a great deal of inner fire, Raney was influenced by Charlie Christian. His style grew to encompass not just Charlie Parker but also the Lennie Tristano school of 'cool bop'. Indeed, Raney was sometimes called the Lee Konitz of the guitar, after the famous alto player associated with Lennie Tristano.

As a soloist, Raney emphasized lines inspired by those of Lester Young. He compensated for the emotional coolness of his improvisations by employing long melodic lines, cleanly articulated. One of the true innovators on his instrument, Raney exercised a profound influence on guitarists of the 1950s.

Born in Louisville, Kentucky, Raney was influenced by his mother, who played the guitar. Raney studied with the guitarist Hayden Causey, whom he replaced in a band led by Jerry Wald. In 1944 he moved to Chicago, where he worked with pianist Lou Levy. In 1948, Raney joined Woody Herman's orchestra and recorded with Stan Getz.

After leaving Herman, Raney played with Al Haig, Buddy DiFranco, Artie Shaw (from 1949 to 1950) and Terry Gibbs, then joined Getz's quintet. It was this group that brought him to prominence as he became known for his playing on several of Getz's important albums between 1951 and 1953. He replaced Tal Farlow in the Red Norvo Trio (1953–1954) and worked at the Blue Angel, New York (1955–1960), in a trio led by the pianist Jimmy Lyon. He rejoined Getz in 1962, but remained with him until only the following year.

In the mid-1960s, Raney was active in New York as a studio musician in radio and television before returning to Louisville in 1968. He later played at clubs in New York (1972), gave a recital at Carnegie Hall with Al Haig (1974), and toured internationally with Haig and his son Doug Raney, with whom he also recorded guitar duets. In the 1980s he performed and recorded as the leader of his own groups, which included his son, although encroaching deafness hampered his ability to play in his last few years. He died in 1995.

# Jim Hall (1930–)

A cool-toned, subtle guitarist whose playing seems to be the jazz equivalent of a Japanese painting, Jim Hall has been an inspiration to guitarists – some of whom, like Bill Frisell, sound nothing like him.

Inspired (as almost all the guitarists of his generation were) by Charlie Christian and the tenor saxophonist Lester Young, Jim Hall attended the Cleveland Institute of Music and studied classical guitar in Los Angeles with Vincente Gomez. He was a founding member of the Chico Hamilton Quintet (1955) and in 1956 joined the Jimmy Giuffre Three.

After touring with Ella Fitzgerald in 1960 and sometimes forming duos with Lee Konitz, Hall joined Sonny Rollins' quartet in 1961 and recorded the classic guitar-tenor saxophone quartet *The Bridge*. Next, he co-led a quartet with Art Farmer (1962), and recorded on an occasional basis with Paul Desmond. He then became a New York studio musician.

Hall has mostly been a leader since then and has also worked on his own projects for a variety of record labels, including two classic duet albums with pianist Bill Evans. A self-titled collaboration with Pat Metheny was released in 1999.

# John McLaughlin (1942–)

John McLaughlin, also known as Mahavishnu John McLaughlin, is a jazz-fusion guitar player from Doncaster, Yorkshire. He came to prominence in the late 1960s with Miles Davis's electric group and with other well-known players such as Chick Corea and Tony Williams.

**John McLaughlin popularized both the fibreglass, round-backed Ovation as well as the Gibson EDS-1275, a double-necked guitar comprised of a six-string and a twelve-string.**

In 1969, McLaughlin recorded *Extrapolation* (with Tony Oxley and John Surman). The album showcased McLaughlin as a guitarist of great technical virtuosity, power, speed and inventiveness (such as the ability to play in odd metres). Later that year, McLaughlin moved to the United States to join Tony Williams' group Lifetime. He subsequently played with Miles Davis on his landmark albums *In a Silent Way*, *Bitches Brew* (which has a track named after him), *Big Fun* (where he is the featured soloist on 'Go Ahead John') and *A Tribute to Jack Johnson* – Davis paid tribute to him in the sleeve notes to Jack Johnson, calling McLaughlin's playing 'far in'. He returned to the Davis band for one recorded night of a week-long club date, which was released as part of the album *Live/Evil*.

His reputation as a 'first-call' session player grew, resulting in recordings as a sideman with Miroslav Vitous, Larry Coryell, Wayne Shorter, Carla Bley and others.

McLaughlin's 1970s electric band, the Mahavishnu Orchestra, featured violinist Jerry Goodman (later Jean-Luc Ponty), keyboardist Jan Hammer (later Gayle Moran/Stu Goldberg), bassist Rick Laird (later Ralphe Armstrong) and drummer Billy Cobham (later Narada Michael Walden). The band was respected for its technical virtuosity and complex fusion of eclectic jazz and rock with hints of Eastern/Indian influence.

After the Mahavishnu Orchestra split, McLaughlin worked with the far more low-key acoustic group Shakti. This group combined Indian music with elements of jazz and thus may be regarded as a pioneer of world music. McLaughlin was one of the first Westerners, if not the very first, to attain any acclaim performing Indian music to Indian audiences.

**Along with Carlos Santana, McLaughlin was a follower of the guru Sri Chinmoy, and in 1973, they collaborated on an album of devotional songs, *Love Devotion Surrender*, which included recordings of Coltrane compositions including 'A Love Supreme'.**

In the early 1980s, McLaughlin teamed up with flamenco guitarist Paco de Lucia and Larry Coryell (later replaced by Al Di Meola) as The Guitar Trio. They reunited in 1996 for a second recording session and world tour. In the early 1990s, McLaughlin toured with Trilok Gurtu and Dominique DiPiazza to support the *Que Alegria* album. Recently he toured with Remember Shakti (as well as original Shakti member Zakir Hussain, this group has featured eminent Indian musicians V Selvaganesh, U Srinivas, Shivkumar Sharma and Hariprasad Chaurasia). His recording projects have included a ballet score, *Thieves and Poets* (2003), arrangements for classical guitar ensembles of jazz standards, and a hard-bop/jazz-fusion album *Industrial Zen* (2006).

## Pat Martino (1944–)

One of the most original of the jazz-based guitarists to emerge in the 1960s, Martino began playing professionally when he was 15. He worked early on with groups led by Willis Jackson, Red Holloway and a series of organists, including Don Patterson, Jimmy Smith, Jack McDuff, Richard 'Groove' Holmes and Jimmy McGriff. After playing with John Handy (1966), he absorbed the influences of avant-garde jazz, rock, pop and world music into his advanced hard-bop style. His debut album *El Hombre* (1967) exploded onto the scene.

Martino made a remarkable comeback after brain surgery in 1980 to correct an aneurysm that caused him to completely forget how to play. It took years but he regained his ability, partly by listening to his records. He did not resume playing until 1984, making his recording comeback with 1987's *The Return*.

## Joe Pass (1929–1994)

A hard-hitting bebop guitarist early on in his career, Pass became known as a great solo performer. His outstanding technique, recorded in the *Virtuoso* series of records on the Pablo label, gave him the deserved popular fame and renown that had eluded him in his earlier career.

Hailing from Philadelphia (and influenced by the troubled but virtuoso jazz guitarist Billy Bean), Pass began playing in a few swing bands and was with Charlie Barnet for a time in 1947. After serving in the military, Pass became a drug addict, spending nearly a decade in and out of prison.

While Pass was recovering along with other musicians at the Synanon Halfway House, the Santa Monica city council decided to disband the house. In order to make money to establish the halfway house outside the city limits, the recovering addicts borrowed instruments to record a series of original jazz tunes. *Sounds of Synanon* (1962) brought Pass instant recognition as a new jazz talent. He followed this record with his first as a leader, *Catch Me*, and then the seminal *For Django*, before going on to record several other albums for Pacific Jazz and World Pacific.

In 1974, Pass signed with Norman Granz's Pablo label and issued Virtuoso, the first of his solo guitar recordings. The record got great attention. After that he recorded both unaccompanied and with small groups, including artists Neils Hennig, Osted Pedersen, Sarah Vaughan, Ella Fitzgerald, Duke Ellington, Oscar Peterson, Milt Jackson and Dizzy Gillespie, until his death from cancer.

# George Benson (1943–)

Born in Pittsburgh, Pennsylvania, Benson began performing as a young teenager, singing in nightclubs and cutting several records for RCA. In 1960, Benson formed a rock band, but he soon became more interested in jazz, awed by performers like Charlie Parker and Charlie Christian. After a stint in Brother Jack McDuff's Band, Benson formed his own jazz group in 1965, recording several albums for Columbia and appearing on Miles Davis's *Miles in the Sky*. In 1967, Benson moved to Verve and then to producer Creed Taylor's own CTI label for much of the 1970s. In the late 1970s, Benson recorded with Warner Bros., focusing on his soulful Nat King Cole-inspired singing. Beginning with the top-ten 1976 album *Breezin'* and its hit single 'This Masquerade', Benson began producing a series of pop albums, working with producer Quincy Jones on what was to be Benson's biggest album yet, *Give Me the Night* (1980).

Following a similar career path to Wes Montgomery, Benson lost touch with hardcore jazz fans, but he found himself becoming more popular and commercially successful with a broader audience. By the 1980s, Benson's vocal talent was better known than his amazing guitar playing. However, by the early 1990s, he began to re-emphasize his jazz guitar ability.

Benson continues to perform regularly and his most recent album Songs and Stories, was released in 2009. In 2010, he toured America, Europe and the Pacific Rim.

# Emily Remler (1957–1990)

Born in New York, Emily began to play the guitar at the age of ten and she continued to excel in her musical studies at the Berklee School of Music in Boston, Massachusetts, from 1976 to 1979. Emily Remler was a jazz guitarist who came onto the scene in the 1980s. She worked in blues and jazz clubs in New Orleans before beginning her recording career in 1981 with support from guitar great Herb Ellis.

In addition to her recording career as a bandleader and composer, Emily played in blues groups, on Broadway and with artists as diverse as Larry Coryell, with whom she recorded an album entitled *Together*, and the singer Rosemary Clooney. She played in the pit in the Los Angeles version of the show *Sophisticated Ladies* for a three-month stint between 1981 and 1982.

Remler was equally adept at playing with and without a pick in such diverse styles as bop, jazz-rock and Latin music; her playing incorporated smooth and fluid eighth-note passages, doublings at the octave in the style of Wes Montgomery and blues phrasing. She recorded seven albums of bop, jazz standards and fusion guitar before dying of heart failure at the age of 32 while on tour in Australia. You can see Emily's amazing playing style in the Hot Licks instructional videos *Advanced Jazz and Latin Improvisation with Emily Remler* and *Bebop and Swing Guitar with Emily Remler* (1986).

# Al Di Meola (1954–)

Al Di Meola is five-times winner of the 'Best Jazz Guitarist' award in *Guitar Player* magazine's reader poll. Di Meola is known for his technical mastery and extremely fast, complex guitar solos and compositions. He has a unique fondness for Mediterranean cultures and acoustic genres like flamenco. These influences can be heard on 'Mediterranean Sundance' and 'Lady of Rome, Sister of Brazil' from the *Elegant Gypsy* album (1977). He was very influential among rock and jazz guitarists alike.

Di Meola continued to explore Latin music within the jazz-fusion genre with albums like *Casino* and *Splendido Hotel*. His acoustic technique is ferocious. His touch on numbers like 'Señor Mouse' and 'Fantasia Suite for Two Guitars' from the Casino album, and on the bestselling live album with John McLaughlin and Paco de Lucia, *Friday Night in San Francisco*, are the stuff of legend.

When Di Meola began his training with jazz guitarist Robert Aslanian, he was taught to focus on reading, picking technique and technical proficiency. Di Meola listened to rock as well as jazz. In fact, one of Al's influences was the 1960s surf group The Ventures. In 1971, he enrolled in the Berklee College of Music in Boston. In 1974, he joined Chick Corea's band, Return to Forever, and played with the band until a major line-up shift in 1976. He has collaborated with numerous artists and continues to perform in intimate concert venues.

In 1979, guitarist Larry Coryell formed The Guitar Trio with jazz-fusion guitarist John McLaughlin and flamenco guitarist Paco de Lucia. The three toured Europe briefly, eventually releasing a video recorded at Royal Albert Hall in London entitled *Meeting of Spirits*. In early 1980, Larry Coryell was replaced by Al Di Meola.

Di Meola often closes his shows with an energetic rendition of one of his most challenging (to play, that is) pieces, 'Race with Devil on Spanish Highway', from the *Elegant Gypsy* album. Even though this particular composition is nearly 30 years old, Al's technical command is undeniable. His scale runs are still blindingly fast and the energy is always at a high level. Because of his early recordings, Di Meola indirectly became the pioneer of shred guitar in the 1980s, influencing guitarists such as Yngwie Malmsteen, Steve Vai and Paul Gilbert.

# Chapter 12

# Country Guitarists

Country music was originally known as 'old-time music' and began in America's southern Appalachian Mountains with musicians playing and recording fiddle tunes. The origins of country music can be found in the recordings of Jimmie Rodgers ('the Singing Brakeman') and the Carter family. The fiddle, mandolin and banjo were the dominant instruments in the early days, but the guitar gradually became more accepted by string band musicians in the early 1900s. There are many heroes of country guitar; here are some of the most influential.

# Maybelle Carter (1909–1978)

'Mother' Maybelle Carter was born Maybelle Addington in Nickelsville, Virginia. Maybelle married Ezra J Carter on 13 March 1926. They had three daughters: Helen, Valerie June (better known as the legendary June Carter Cash) and Anita.

Maybelle Carter was one-third of country music's original first family, the Carters. Maybelle played guitar, autoharp and banjo in the group. The unique sound for the group came from her innovative use of bass tunings and her 'scratch' style of guitar playing, in which she used her thumb to play melody on the bass and middle strings, and her index finger to complete the rhythm – completely opposite from today's fingerstyle playing technique. Maybelle played this style on all of the Carter family's most famous recordings from 1928 to 1943.

'Maybelle Carter played a Gibson L-5 arch-top, which was first produced in 1922. The instrument was revolutionary, modelled after mandolins and violins, with F-shaped holes rather than one round sound hole. Maybelle played the now-famous 1928 model for the majority of her career, and her L-5 is now kept at the Country Music Hall of Fame in Nashville, Tennessee.

After the Carter family split, Maybelle and her daughters toured during the 1950s and 1960s as Mother Maybelle and the Carter Sisters. Maybelle also briefly toured with former Carter family member, Sara Carter, during the 1960s folk music scene and made a historic appearance at the Newport Folk Festival. You can also hear Mother Maybelle featured on the 1971 Nitty Gritty Dirt Band's platinum-selling album, *Will the Circle Be Unbroken*. This classic album also features Roy Acuff, Junior Huskey and Doc Watson.

Though no one has made a movie or documentary on Mother Maybelle's life, you can see part of her story in the 2005 film *Walk The Line*.

# Merle Travis (1917–1983)

Virtually without peer as a guitarist and songwriter, Travis was such a unique stylist that he had an instrumental style ('Travis picking') named after him. Only Chet Atkins comes close to the influence that Travis had on guitarists and country music. Born in Rosewood, Kentucky, to a family of impoverished coal miners, Travis turned this experience, coupled with a phrase that Travis's father used to describe their lives, into the song 'Sixteen Tons'. As a songwriter, his originals, including 'Sixteen Tons', crossed over into other musical genres as popular standards in the hands of other artists. He was also influential in the development of rock-and-roll, and recorded a number of top-ten hits and novelty songs.

Travis's first instrument was a five-string banjo and he was lucky enough to live next door to both Ike Everly, later the father of Don and Phil (the Everly Brothers), and Mose Rager, who played in a unique three-finger guitar style that developed in that part of Kentucky.

Travis's repertory soon included blues, ragtime and popular tunes, although he paid the bills by working in the Civilian Conservation Corps as a teenager. His break came during a visit to his brother's home in Evansville, Indiana, in 1935, where his chance to entertain at a local dance resulted in membership of a couple of local bands and an appearance on a local radio station.

In 1937, he landed a permanent broadcasting gig at Cincinnati's WLW until World War II forced it to disband. As a member of the Drifting Pioneers, Travis acquired a national following, and he also began playing with Grandpa Jones and the Delmore Brothers in a gospel quartet called the Brown's Ferry Four. While touring with Jones, Travis visited a church in Cincinnati and heard the sermon that became the song 'That's All'.

Travis spent a short stint in the Marines, but he was quickly discharged and returned to Cincinnati. By early 1945 Travis was in Los Angeles, where he began making appearances in Charles Starrett's Western films and playing with Ray Whitley's Western swing band. In 1946, he released the topical song 'No Vacancy' – dealing with the displacement of returning veterans – along with 'Cincinnati Lou', and earned a double-sided hit. His next major project was a concept album, *Folk Songs of the Hills*, which was intended to compete with Burl Ives' successful folk recordings. The record, a set of four 78-rpm discs, was released in 1947, but it was considered a failure. However, it yielded several classics, among them the

Travis originals 'Sixteen Tons', 'Dark As a Dungeon', and 'Over by Number Nine'. It also introduced such standards as 'Nine Pound Hammer', and it became a unique document, depicting a beautiful all-acoustic solo guitar performance by this virtuoso. Using his thumb to stop the bottom two strings allowed him to create mobile upper chords that were teamed with jazzy voicings, open strings and rolling fast arpeggios. This style inspired generations of guitarists.

---

**WLW signed Travis to become a member of the show, *The Boone Country Jamboree*. Through WLW, Travis was exposed to several musicians with whom he formed a friendship and musical collaboration. The new friends wanted to make a record but WLW prohibited their musicians from making recordings, so they created a recording using the pseudonym 'The Sheppard Brothers'.**

---

Merle Travis's career went off the rails for a period due to drug and alcohol addiction but he was able to overcome this and returned to the stage in the 1970s, regularly appearing on country music television shows. In 1974 he recorded an album of duets with Chet Atkins, and followed this with a period of prolific output, recording several guitar solo albums, a blues album and a double LP that paid tribute to the legendary country fiddler Clayton McMichen, who had played with Travis in the 1930s.

He died of a heart attack in 1983 at his home in Tahlequah, Oklahoma. In 1992, the Four Legends Fountain was erected in Drakesboro, Kentucky honouring Merle Travis and three other pioneers of the Kentucky 'thumb-picking' style, Kennedy Jones, Ike Everly and Mose Rager.

# Arthel 'Doc' Watson (1923–)

Arguably, there have been three influential country folk guitar players in the 20th century: Merle Travis, Chet Atkins and Doc Watson, a brilliant flatpicking guitarist from Deep Gap, North Carolina.

Unlike Travis and Atkins, Watson was middle-aged before he gained any attention through the release of his first album, *The Doc Watson Family*, in 1963.

The record is a mixture of folk, country and bluegrass and was an influential record for guitar players in the early 1960s. His appearances at the Newport Folk Festivals in 1963 and 1964 stunned musicians, who were amazed to hear such virtuoso playing from someone from the backwoods. Performers of folk and country music alike – such as Ricky Skaggs, Vince Gill, Clarence White, Emmylou Harris and many others – acknowledge Watson's influence on them. Watson has provided a further service to country and folk music by sharing an almost encyclopedic knowledge of many traditional American songs.

While Merle Travis and Chet Atkins started on acoustic guitars and moved to electric, before Watson's 'discovery' during the folk revival in the early 1960s, he played electric in a local all-purpose band that performed current rock, swing, country – and, of course, folk music.

Watson was struck blind at an early age. When he was ten, his father gave him a homemade fretless banjo, which Doc played consistently for the next three years. Around the same time, he began attending the School for the Blind in Raleigh, North Carolina. At the age of 13, Doc began playing the guitar, and six months later Doc and his older brother Linney began performing on street corners, singing traditional numbers.

By his late teens, Watson had learned fingerpicking from his neighbour, Olin Miller. In 1941, Watson joined a band that had a regular radio programme in Lenoir, North Carolina. On this show he earned his nickname; one of the announcers referred to the guitarist as 'Doc' during the broadcast. For the next six years he played around North Carolina.

In 1947, he married Rosa Lee Carlton, the daughter of fiddler Gaither W Carlton. To pay the bills, he worked as a piano tuner. In 1953, Watson joined the supporting band of a local pianist and railway worker named Jack Williams, where he played electric guitar and performed a variety of music, from country to rock and pop. After staying with Jack for eight years, Watson joined the Clarence Ashley String Band.

From 1964 onwards, Watson recorded nearly one record a year throughout the decade. No sooner had interest in folk music waned than Watson was back in great demand because of the three-disc *Will the Circle Be Unbroken*, a watershed album in 1972 created by the Nitty Gritty Dirt Band, which featured Watson, Travis, Roy Acuff and a virtual Who's Who of country greats. Merle Watson, Doc's son and a serious talent in his own right, began appearing with his father regularly. The pair won two Grammys for traditional music, in 1973 and 1974.

Father and son played together for more than 15 years, until Merle died tragically on the family farm in 1985. Following his son's death, Doc Watson has continued with his appearances, showcasing his beautiful voice, his great instrumental talent, and his mastery of traditional material.

## Hank Williams (1923–1953)

Williams is considered the father of contemporary country music. He was a major star by the age of 25 and dead at the age of 29. He began recording in Nashville in 1946 with a line-up that featured electric and acoustic guitars, and he helped set the scene for the rock-and-roll revolution of the 1950s.

**Many artists from across the musical spectrum have paid homage to Hank Williams' talent by creating cover versions of his famous songs. Artists as varied as Al Green, Bob Dylan, Huey Lewis and the News, Martina McBride, the Grateful Dead, the Red Hot Chili Peppers, Norah Jones and Elvis Presley have all covered Hank's tunes.**

In four short years, he established the rules for all the country performers that followed him – and, in the process, much of popular music. Williams wrote a body of songs that hit the top-ten charts and became popular classics, including 'Your Cheating Heart', 'I'm So Lonesome I Could Cry', and 'Hey Good Lookin''. Williams' direct, emotional lyrics and vocals became the standard for most popular performers.

## Chet Atkins (1924–2001)

An asthma sufferer throughout his youth, Atkins was a sickly child from a humble background in Tennessee. When his parents separated when he was ten, Atkins moved to Georgia to live with his father, hoping the climate would be easier on his asthma.

His father was a music teacher and song leader with a number of travelling evangelists, and his brother Jimmy – 13 years Chet's senior – was himself an accomplished guitar player. Atkins' first instrument was a ukulele strung with wire from a screen door; he then graduated to an inexpensive Sears Silvertone. Atkins said that his childhood adversity was a significant motivator in driving him to be 'the greatest at what he did'.

A series of performances on local radio stations, as well as the popular Old Dominion Barn Dance (a Saturday-night country music and humour radio show, broadcast live from a theatre in Richmond, Virginia), ended poorly, because his sophisticated musicianship was at odds with the simple twangy 'hillbilly' guitar the producers wanted. His break came in 1947 with a gig with the legendary Carter family at the Grand Ole Opry, a weekly country music concert in Nashville, where his talents were finally appreciated. After that, his close association with the RCA record label in Nashville led to Atkins becoming a sought-after session player, working on records by some of the great pioneers of both country and rock-and-roll, including the Everly Brothers and Elvis Presley.

**Chet Atkins bought Elvis Presley's recording contract from Sam Phillips of Sun Records. This move would prove crucial to rock-and-roll history as Chet produced Elvis's music at RCA, and Sun Records was able to produce the music of Johnny Cash, Carl Perkins and Jerry Lee Lewis with the money it received from the Elvis buyout.**

Atkins joined RCA as a vice president and staff producer and almost single-handedly created the smooth sound that became known as the 'Nashville Sound', scoring major hits with nearly every country star of the era. On leaving RCA, Chet continued his highly successful career as a recording artist, signing with Columbia Records, where he remained until his death.

# Jimmy Bryant (1925–1980)

Jimmy Bryant was born Ivy J Bryant Jr on 5 March 1925, in Moultrie, Georgia. His father was a musician and made music important in Jimmy's life. Starting off playing fiddle, Bryant developed his gift for music rather quickly and became a local fixture with various bands performing at Saturday-night barn dances. Bryant was 18 years old when, in 1943, he was drafted into the US Army. He suffered a severe head injury while fighting in Germany. This injury caused Bryant to be hospitalized for several months, at which time he began to investigate the guitar and transferred all of his super-fast fiddle licks to the instrument. With that, the Jimmy Bryant guitar style was born.

Any guitarist coming up in the 1950s was easily inspired by Bryant's guitar playing. He always performed with confidence and a swagger that made his advanced techniques look very easy. He was the fastest player that anyone had ever heard. He was a clean player as well, playing every note with absolute precision.

The best way to hear the comprehensive work of all things Jimmy Bryant is a three-CD box set full of Bryant's best playing called *Frettin' Fingers; the Lightning Guitar of Jimmy Bryant*. Also worth mentioning are the recordings he did with Rockabilly Hall of Fame steel-guitar legend Speedy West. This duo played together on many sessions and soon began working and recording their own material. This was an explosive pair of musicians. Their melodic, fast guitar lines were so intertwined with each other that they created an exciting brand of music that no one had ever heard before. They recorded between 1950 and 1956. During this time they cut vinyl on a vast amount of material, including the now legendary 'Stratosphere Boogie'.

**Jimmy Bryant was the first endorser of the Fender Broadcaster model, later renamed the Telecaster. The Telecaster had a simple design and produced a revolutionary sound that forever changed the electric guitar industry; it was an ideal pairing with Bryant's innovative style.**

Jimmy Bryant was one of the early guitar heroes. He was a sharp dresser with a slick look. There's a classic photo with Bryant and his 'guitar car'. It is the epitome of all things hot guitar. He died from lung cancer in September 1980, aged 55.

# Hank Garland (1930–2004)

Walter 'Hank' Garland was born in Cowpens, South Carolina, on 11 November 1930. First inspired by the Carter Family, Hank heard Maybelle picking 'Wildwood Flower' when he was a young boy, and he dreamt that he was playing the guitar. Garland's father bought him a used steel-string when he was six, and Hank began taking guitar lessons. Hank burst onto the Nashville studio session scene in the late 1940s at the age of 14. He would eventually become one of the highest paid, most in-demand session guitarists of his day. He recorded his million-seller 'Sugarfoot Rag' aged just 16. He played guitar for some of the greatest performers in music history, including Hank Williams Sr., Elvis Presley, Roy Orbison, the Everly Brothers, Patsy Cline, Brenda Lee and Bobby Darin, as well as with jazz greats Charlie Parker and George Shearing, and is heard on hundreds of country-and-western records.

Hank Garland had a passion for jazz music. Because he could only play country in Nashville – and nothing else, Hank took trips to New York and recorded three jazz albums between 1958 and 1961. Hank could often be seen in New York playing at the Birdland Club.

It seems almost unbelievable, but Hank Garland's professional career lasted only 15 years. In 1961, at the age of 30, he nearly died in a violent car accident near Nashville. During his recovery, it was apparent that he had suffered severe brain damage, which had claimed most of his motor functions and coordination. It seemed that the dream of becoming the 'greatest guitarist in the world' was no longer a reality. After his recovery, he would leave Nashville behind, along with the historic sessions he recorded as a country and jazz sideman with Elvis Presley and numerous others.

Hank Garland was determined not to be defeated by this near fatal setback. He began relearning the guitar from the very beginning. Two years after the accident, he regained his command of the guitar and returned to Nashville 13 years later for a brief appearance at the 1976 Fan Fair Reunion Show. He played a rendition of his 'Sugarfoot Rag' and delighted the audience.

# Jerry Reed (1937–2008)

Jerry Reed Hubbard was born in Atlanta on 20 March 1937. 'The Guitar Man', as he was known in country music, was a singer-songwriter who has had a successful career as a soloist and an in-demand session guitarist. He was also a popular actor and appeared in the *Smokey and the Bandit* trilogy of movies as Burt Reynolds' sidekick. He cut his first record, 'If the Good Lord's Willing and the Creeks Don't Rise', at the age of 18. Gene Vincent covered his song 'Crazy Legs' in 1958, and with that Reed's popularity began to rise.

Jerry Reed's biggest successes came from famous artists covering his songs. Brenda Lee covered his 'That's All You Got to Do' in 1960; Elvis Presley covered 'Guitar Man' in 1967, as well as 'US Male'. Success continued for Reed as a popular session and tour guitarist. In 1962, his singles 'Goodnight Irene' and 'Hully Gully Guitar' caught the ear of Chet Atkins, who would eventually produce Reed's 1965 'If I Don't Live Up to It'. Reed first top-20 hit would come as an Elvis tribute record, 'Tupelo Mississippi Flash'.

Jerry Reed's biggest hit came in 1971 with the song 'When You're Hot, You're Hot', which was also the title track of his first solo album. He won a Grammy for this song in 1973. In that same year, Reed scored his second number-one single, 'Lord, Mr. Ford', from the album *Lord, Mr Ford*. Reed always considered himself more of a songwriter than a player. Truth be told, if you ever heard Jerry Reed play instrumental guitar, you would wonder how he could also write such great songs! Chet Atkins was Reed's primary producer and always thought Reed was a better fingerstyle player than he was.

**The most copied and played of Jerry Reed's instrumentals is 'The Claw'. The common problem with this piece is that guitarists tend to play it as fast as they can, which makes it sound less musical.**

Jerry Reed continued to release music throughout his career. In 1979, he released *Half & Half*, a record comprised of both vocal and instrumental selections. In 1980, Jerry released *Jerry Reed Sings Jim Croce*, a tribute to the late singer-songwriter. In 1982, Reed released the US chart-topping novelty hit 'She Got the Goldmine

(I Got the Shaft)', followed by 'The Bird', which peaked at number two. The 'Guitar Man' is a fixture in Nashville and can still be heard in films like Adam Sandler's *The Waterboy*. Reed released 'Let's Git It On' in 2006, before his death in September 2008 from emphysema.

# Don Rich (1941–1974)

Don Rich was a gifted guitarist, fiddler, singer and songwriter. His main success came from teaming up with Buck Owens and the group the Buckaroos. Rich and Owens play together at dances and on local television programme, in Tacoma, Washington with Don primarily playing fiddle. Don Rich was Buck Owens' 'pickin' buddy'. Don found his first success with the Buckaroos 1961 when they scored hits for Capitol Records entitled 'You're for Me' and 'Kickin' Our Hearts Around'. They also made a number of albums on their own, including *The Buckaroos Play the Hits*, an all-instrumental collection released in April 1971. Rich released his own album, entitled *Fiddlin' Man*, a few months later.

At this point, Don Rich was better known for his virtuoso ability on the guitar. But with national exposure on the television show Hee Haw, Rich became a celebrity on a show that also starred his boss and chief collaborator. Sadly, Rich was killed on 17 July 1974, en route to meet his family in Morro Bay, California, when his motorcycle struck a central reservation. Buck Owens spoke of Don Rich decades later in a television interview, where he said with tears in his eyes, 'Don was my picking buddy. I lost my friend and pickin' buddy.'

*Country Pickin'* is the first-ever compilation of the signature guitar style, fiddle work and vocal genius of the late Don Rich. This compilation includes 24 precise representations of the legendary Bakersfield sound. Featured on the compilation are classics like 'Buckaroo' and 'I'm Coming Back Home to Stay'.

# Deana Carter (1966–)

Deana Carter is the daughter of Fred Carter Jr, a renowned guitarist, singer and composer. Fred Carter is revered as one of Nashville's premier session guitarists. He recorded for Muddy Waters, The Band, Elvis Presley and Simon and Garfunkel. Deana had many contacts with musicians through her father. Though musicians, producers and record executives surrounded her throughout her life, Deana decided to go to college after an unsuccessful bid at stardom. At the age of 17, she entered the University of Tennessee to read rehabilitation therapy. After she graduated, she worked with recovering stroke and head-injury patients. She would eventually realize that her first love was music, and although she found the work she was doing rewarding and worthwhile, Deana decided to pursue the music career she abandoned earlier.

Deana Carter's first big break came when one of her demo tapes was heard by country legend Willie Nelson. Nelson invited her to take part in the 1994 Farm Aid VII concert, where she was the show's only female soloist. Deana Carter received a record deal with Capitol Records later that year thanks to that same demo tape. In 1996, Deana Carter's first Capitol release, *Did I Shave My Legs for This?* featured the hit single 'Strawberry Wine'. It became a number-one hit and won the CMA single of the year award in 1997. The album would eventually sell five million copies. Deana was successful with songs on soundtracks like Sandra Bullock's film Hope Floats and the animated feature Anastasia. In 1999, she won the 'Best Female Country Guitarist' at the Gibson Guitar Awards. She continues to perform and record, releasing a live album and six studio albums to date. Her 2007 album, *The Chain*, was a tribute to her father, after which she took a break from music to spend time with her son. In 2010 she signed a new recording contract with Warner Bros. Nashville.

# Chapter 13

# Folk Guitarists

Folk music is a loosely used term that refers to the music of the 1960s. Folk guitarists are usually defined as singer-songwriters (such as Bob Dylan, Joan Baéz and Judy Collins). The term is widely used by the media and music industry to include any acoustic music. There is contemporary folk music and traditional folk music. Contemporary songs include protest songs or songs about social issues. Traditional songs include regional references and stories about a culture and its people. Folk music can feature other acoustic instruments accompanied by acoustic guitars. This chapter introduces some of the most famous folk guitarists.

## Elizabeth Cotten (1895–1987)

Elizabeth Cotten started playing her older brother's banjo at eight years old and soon after began playing his guitar as well. Completely self-taught, she played her guitar left-handed and upside-down, causing her to play the bass lines with her fingers and the melody with her thumb. This style of playing became what is known as 'Cotten picking' or alternative-picking style of playing.

Elizabeth Cotten began doing domestic work at the age of 12, which was what her mother had done. She was married young, at the age of 15, to Frank Cotten and they had one daughter, Lillie. In 1940, she divorced Frank and moved in with Lillie and her husband. Cotten completely retired from guitar playing for 25 years, except for occasional church performances. It wasn't until she was in her 60s that she began recording and performing publicly.

**Elizabeth Cotten was discovered in her 60s by the pioneering folksinging Seeger family while she was working for them as a housekeeper. Her first recording, *Negro Folk Songs and Tunes* (later reissued as *Freight Train and Other North Carolina Folk Songs*) was produced by Mike Seeger in 1958 and is considered one of the greatest folk albums ever recorded.**

In 1984, Cotten received a Grammy Award for *Elizabeth Cotten Live!*, recorded when she was 90 years old, as well as a National Heritage Fellowship. In 1989, Cotten was one of 75 influential African-American women chosen to be included in the photo documentary *I Dream a World*. Elizabeth Cotten died on 29 June 1987, at age of 92 in Syracuse, New York.

## Pete Seeger (1919–)

Along with Woody Guthrie, singer-songwriter Pete Seeger is considered one of the pioneers of modern folk music. Seeger is synonymous with the folk boom of the late 1950s/early 1960s, helping to transform folk from an orally transmitted body of traditional songs found mainly among rural dwellers to mass-market entertainment, popular on university campuses and in New York coffee houses.

Born in New York, the son of Julliard musicologist Charles Seeger, one of the first researchers to investigate non-Western music, Pete Seeger was educated at a series of exclusive private schools, including Harvard, where he read sociology. He began playing banjo in his teens and developed an intense interest in folk music that only grew over time.

In 1938, he shocked his parents by dropping out of university to hitchhike across the United States, meeting many legendary folk musicians along the way, including Leadbelly and Woody Guthrie.

When he returned to New York in 1940, Seeger formed the Almanac Singers, a rotating cast of folk singers (at times including Woody Guthrie) that merged politically progressive lyrics with folk tunes. They performed mainly at union rallies, strikes and similar events. The Almanac Singers disbanded during World War II, when Seeger was drafted.

After serving in the military for several years, Seeger returned to New York in 1948 and formed the Weavers, the first mainstream American folk group. The Weavers scored several big hits in the late 1940s and early 1950s, including 1948's 'Goodnight Irene', which stayed at number one for weeks, setting a chart record not broken until the 1970s.

During the McCarthy-era Red Scare, the Weavers suffered boycotts because of their left-leaning views. This severely curtailed their success. However, in 1955, the group gave a legendary performance at Carnegie Hall, which set the stage for the urban folk boom of the late 1950s.

From 1958 onwards, Seeger opted for a solo career and he quickly became a star in his own right, known for songs such as 'If I Had a Hammer' (a hit for Peter, Paul and Mary), 'Where Have All the Flowers Gone', 'Turn! Turn! Turn!' (later popularized by the Byrds), 'Guantanamera', and, most famously, 'We Shall Overcome'. Seeger became a fixture at civil rights rallies, university campuses, labour strikes and anti-war protests, where audiences would often sing along so loudly that Seeger himself could hardly be heard.

In 1961, Seeger signed to Columbia Records, and his popularity grew even further over the next few years. Towards the end of the 1960s, Seeger shifted away from typical American folk, embracing African music, Latin-American folksongs and other forms of world music. He wrote several famous how-to books on acoustic guitar and banjo and became active in the nascent environmental movement, drawing attention to pollution of the Hudson River through boating trips. He later formed the activist group Clearwater, which teaches schoolchildren about water pollution.

# Woody Guthrie (1912–1967)

Born in Okemah, Oklahoma, Guthrie described the small frontier town in Okfuskee County like this: 'Okemah was one of the singiest, square dancingest, drinkingest, yellingest, preachingest, walkingest, talkingest, laughingest, cryingest, shootingest, fist fightingest, bleedingest, gamblingest, gun, club and razor carryingest of our ranch towns and farm towns, because it blossomed out into one of our first Oil Boom Towns.'

Guthrie's father, Charles, was a cowboy, land speculator and local politician. The family's financial and physical ruin and his mother's institutionalization due to Huntington's disease devastated Guthrie, creating a uniquely wry and rambling outlook on life.

A skinny, wiry man with a head of unruly curly hair, Guthrie was a keen observer of the world around him. In 1931, when Okemah's boomtown period went bust, Guthrie left for Texas. In 1933, in the panhandle town of Pampa, he married Mary Jennings, and together they had three children. The Great Depression and the Great Dust Storm of 1935 made it impossible to make a living. Driven by a search for a better life, Guthrie joined the westward migration of dust-bowl refugees known as Okies.

Without money and hungry, he hitchhiked, rode freight trains and even walked to California, developing a love for travelling on the open road – a practice he would repeat often. By the time he arrived in California, in 1937, he had experienced the intense hatred of Californians for the Okies and for other outsiders who were flooding the state.

Guthrie's identification with outsiders soon found its way into his songwriting, as evident in his Dust Bowl ballads, such as 'I Ain't Got No Home', 'Talking Dust Bowl Blues', and 'Tom Joad and Hard Travelin'. His 1937 radio broadcasts on KFVD, Los Angeles, and XELO (just over the border in Mexico) brought Guthrie wide public attention. It also gave him a platform from which he could develop his talent for controversial social commentary and criticism on topics ranging from corrupt politicians, lawyers and businessmen to praising the humanist principles of Jesus Christ, Pretty Boy Floyd and union organizers.

Never one to stay in one place for too long, Guthrie headed east for New York in 1939, where he was quickly embraced by leftist organizations, artists, writers, musicians and other intellectuals.

Meeting and mingling with artists such as Leadbelly, Cisco Houston, Burl Ives, Pete Seeger, Will Geer, Sony Terry, Brownie McGhee, Josh White, Millard Lampell, Bess Hawes, Sis Cunningham and others, Guthrie took to such social causes as union organizing, anti-fascism and strengthening the communist party. Generally, he fought for the things that he and his friends believed in the only way he knew how: through political songs of protest.

**In 1940, folklorist Alan Lomax recorded Guthrie for the US Library of Congress in a series of conversations and songs. The Almanac Singers, the politically radical singing group of the late 1940s, would later reform as the Weavers, the most commercially successful and influential folk music group of the late 1940s and early 1950s.**

Finally, disillusioned with New York's radio and entertainment industry, Guthrie headed down South. With the final dissolution of his first marriage, and despite Guthrie's constant travelling and performing, he nevertheless courted an already-married young Martha Graham dancer named Marjorie Mazia. This relationship provided Guthrie with a level of domestic stability and encouragement he had not previously known, enabling him to complete and publish his first novel, *Bound for Glory* (1943). A semi-autobiographical account of his Dust Bowl years, *Bound for Glory* received critical acclaim. Together, Guthrie and Marjorie had four children: Cathy, who died at age four, Arlo (who grew up to be a famous folk singer in his own right, with a major hit in the 1960s, 'Alice's Restaurant'), Joady and Nora.

An ardent anti-fascist, during World War II Guthrie served in both the Merchant Marines and the army, shipping out to sea on several occasions with his 'buddies' Cisco Houston and Jimmy Longhi.

In 1946, Guthrie settled in Coney Island, New York, with his wife and children.

Soon his behaviour and health began to deteriorate, becoming increasingly erratic and creating tensions in his personal and professional life. He moved to California, remarried for a third time, and then returned to New York. He was eventually diagnosed with Huntington's disease, the same neurodegenerative condition that had taken his mother from him. For the next 13 years he was in and out of hospitals. Finally, on 3 October 1967, at Creedmoor State Hospital in Queens, New York, Woody Guthrie died.

**The Smithsonian Institution and the Woody Guthrie Foundation and Archives have collaborated on a major travelling exhibition about Guthrie's life and legacy, allowing thousands of people to view for themselves Guthrie's artwork, writing and songs.**

Popular and folk musicians such as Bruce Springsteen, Billy Bragg, Wilco, Ani DiFranco and countless others continue to draw inspiration from Woody Guthrie, reinterpreting and reinvigorating his songs for new audiences.

# Odetta (1930–2008)

Born Odetta Holmes in Birmingham, Alabama, Odetta grew up in Los Angeles, California, and studied music at Los Angeles City College. As a teenager, Odetta's dream was to sing oratorio, but she felt that a black woman couldn't become an opera singer. She was classically trained in operatic performance from the age of 13, and by 1944 was working in musical theatre – her first professional experience – as an ensemble member with the Hollywood Turnabout Puppet Theatre. Odetta would remain there for four years, working alongside Elsa Lancaster. At the age of 19, in 1949, she joined the national touring company of the musical *Finian's Rainbow*.

While Odetta was on tour with *Finian's Rainbow*, she began mingling with a group of young balladeers in San Francisco. This chance meeting let Odetta to pursue her career in folk singing. She made her name by playing around the United States in all the big cities, including New York and San Francisco. In San Francisco she and Larry Mohr recorded the 1954 *Odetta and Larry* for Fantasy Records.

Soon afterwards, Odetta began a solo career. Her recordings include *Odetta Sings Ballads and Blues* (1956) and a live album recorded at the Gate of Horn in Chicago in 1957. *Odetta Sings Folk Songs* was one of 1963's bestselling folk albums. To really hear Odetta sing and speak on her style of singing, you can check out *Odetta: Exploring Life, Music and Song* by Homespun Video. Here you get to see and hear the legend perform in an intimate venue. Martin Scorsese's 2005 documentary, *No Direction Home*, highlights Odetta's influence on Bob Dylan.

Odetta performed what would be her final tour in the summer 2008 at the age of 77 but by the autumn her health went into decline. She was hoping to perform at the inauguration ceremony of President Barak Obama, in January 2009, but a month before this, she died of heart disease, ending an extraordinary life and career.

# Joan Baéz (1941–)

The definition of a folk guitarist and singer-songwriter, Joan Baéz is a soprano who has a three-octave singing range. Joan Chandos Baéz was born in Staten Island, New York. She is the daughter of Mexican physicist Albert Baéz (the co-inventor of the X-ray reflection microscope), and Joan Bridge (also known as Big Joan). Baéz grew up in New York and California, and when her father took a faculty position at the Massachusetts Institute of Technology (MIT), she attended Boston University and began to sing in coffee houses and small clubs. She was invited by Bob Gibson to attend the 1959 Newport Folk Festival, where she was a hit.

In 1960, her first album, *Joan Baéz*, came out on Vanguard Records. She performed with Bob Dylan early in her career, and they toured together in the 1970s.

Joan's father refused lucrative defence industry jobs during the height of the Cold War. Unlike his colleagues, Albert Baéz even refused to work on the Manhattan Project to build an atomic bomb at Los Alamos. This decision had a profound effect on Joan early in her life and influenced her in the future. She was also subjected to racial slurs and discrimination in her childhood because of her Mexican heritage and features. Joan Baéz became involved with a variety of social causes early in her career, including civil rights and non-violence. She was sometimes jailed for her protests.

Early in her career, Joan Baéz performed historical folk songs and unique covers of other artists. She slowly began adding political songs to her repertoire during the 1960s. Eventually, she would add country songs and more popular music, though always including many songs with political messages. One of her biggest hits, 'The Night They Drove Old Dixie Down' (from the 1971 Vanguard release *Blessed Are…*), was a folk ballad written by Robbie Robertson and first recorded by The Band in 1969. Baéz actually changed the lyrics! She changed the words 'there goes Robert E Lee' to 'there goes the Robert E Lee', changing the reference from the general to the steamboat. The song's story revolves around the Civil War.

---

**In 1967, the Daughters of the American Revolution denied Joan Baéz permission to perform at Constitution Hall, due to her anti-war activities. She retaliated by performing a free concert at the base of the Washington Monument before an estimated audience of 30,000.**

---

Joan Baéz continues to perform concerts around the world. Though she has been nominated for a Grammy award several times over, she has never won. In August 2001, Vanguard Records begin re-releasing Baéz's first 13 albums that she recorded with them between 1960 and 1971 as part of their Original Master series. Each reissue has been digitally restored, plus there are unreleased bonus songs and new and original artwork. A&M records reissued her first six records with them in 2003.

She remains politically active, using her music and personal appearances to support such causes as human rights, gay and lesbian rights, poverty, the anti-war in Iraq movement and the presidential campaign of Barak Obama. In 2011, Amnesty International honoured her with The Joan Baéz Award for Outstanding Inspirational Service in the Global Fight for Human Rights.

# Bob Dylan (1941–)

Born Robert Allen Zimmerman, Bob Dylan has been a major folk music figure for five decades. Some consider him to be the central figure of the folk movement in the 1960s. Influenced by the music of Woody Guthrie, his songs, such as 'Blowin' in the Wind' (1962) and 'The Times They Are a-Changin'' (1963), became anthems of the anti-war and civil rights movements. His studio album, *Modern Times*, released in 2006, became his first number-one album in the United States in 30 years, making him at the age of 65 the oldest living person to top the charts.

Dylan's on-stage instrumentation includes a guitar, keyboard and harmonica. His backing band is a constantly changing line-up and he has toured steadily since the late 1980s. He has performed with other major artists, such as Joan Baéz, Paul Simon, Eric Clapton, Tom Petty, Bruce Springsteen, Jack White, The Band, Mark Knopfler and the Foo Fighters. His songwriting remains his highest accomplishment, incorporating politics, social commentary, philosophy and literary influences. Jimi Hendrix covered 'All Along the Watchtower', making it a new rock classic.

Dylan has explored many traditions of American song, from folk and country/ blues to rock-and-roll and rockabilly, to Celtic balladry, jazz, swing, gospel and Broadway. With nearly 50 years of recording archives, Bob Dylan keeps making and performing great music for all generations and genres.

# Joni Mitchell (1943–)

Born Roberta Joan Anderson, Joni Mitchell is another legend of not only folk music, but of rock music as well. She is a Canadian singer-songwriter who recorded her first album at the age of 25 in New York. Relying purely on her voice and acoustic guitar playing, her first two albums, *Joni Mitchell (Song to a Seagull)* (Reprise, 1968) and *Clouds* (Reprise, 1969), are representations of the folk style of the 1960s. She came into her own style in the early 1970s with visual imagination, a unique sense of place and landscape, and an ability to attain a deep and personal lyric. The album *Blue* (Reprise, 1971) best illustrates her instrumental prowess on guitar, sense of harmonic command and profound lyric sense.

**Outside of the guitar and music in general, Joni Mitchell is a visual artist. She has either painted or photographed all the artwork for her album covers, an indication of her need for self-expression.**

In the albums *From Court and Spark* (Asylum, 1974) to *Mingus* (Asylum, 1979), Mitchell demonstrates her exploration of jazz harmony, which reached its peak on *Hejira* (Asylum, 1976). *Hejira* featured legendary guitarist Larry Coryell and fretless bassist Jaco Pastorius. Unfortunately, this deviation from her 'traditional' success caused Mitchell to become under-represented in rock journalism circles in relation to her output and critical rating. Like most recording artists in the 1980s (young and old), she shifted her sound to more synth pop and drum-machine soundscapes. Some critics have said her albums of the 1980s feature too much production, a problem for most popular music of the time.

As a guitarist, Mitchell has done amazing work with special guitar tunings (known as 'Joni's weird tunings'). Almost every song she composed on the guitar uses an open or non-standard tuning. The use of alternative tunings allows more varied and complex harmonies to be played on the guitar, without the need for difficult chord shapes. One of the most innovative uses of technology is Joni's use of the Roland VG-8 guitar system and a custom-made Parker Guitar strung with six open E strings. The VG-8 is programmed to receive the output of each string and change the pitch to any note the player desires. This system is perfect for Joni as she simply steps on one of the five pedals on the VG-8 and goes through her many different tunings without ever having to touch a tuning peg!

Like many artists from her generation, for a long time Joni felt the music industry had become a place she didn't want to visit. She was primarily working on her visual art and refused to tour or give a concert. However, in 2007 she released a new album, Shine, inspired by the war in Iraq, which reached number 36 in the UK album charts, and number 14 in the US – her highest chart position in 30 years – and earned her a Grammy for the track 'One Week Last Summer'. Mitchell is currently undergoing treatment for Morgellons Syndrome, a rare and unexplained skin disease.

## James Taylor (1948–)

Guitarist John Mayer praised James Taylor as the 'blueprint' for his inspiration. James Taylor is considered a confessional singer-songwriter. This style of writing explores the emotions involved in personal relationships and experiences that relate to personal loss. His second album, *Sweet Baby James* (1970), established him as a leading figure of the era. Pop classic 'Fire and Rain', and his other folk-ballad songs feature unexpected major sevenths and other jazz-derived chords. His subsequent albums since *Sweet Baby James* contain original songs as well as revivals of hits from the 1950s and 1960s, such as 'Handy Man' and 'Devoted to You'. 'Devoted to You' was one of a number of duets Taylor performed with his then wife, Carly Simon. His strength has remained the confessional mode of songwriting. You can hear it at its best on *That Lonesome Road* (1981), *Native Son* (1991), and *Jump up Behind Me* (1997). His *Greatest Hits album* (1976) is his bestselling album to date.

On 1 March 1971, James Taylor was featured on the cover of *Time* magazine. The magazine described Taylor as the forerunner of the singer-songwriter era. The featured article called Taylor, 'the man who best sums up the new sound of rock'.

James Taylor has won five Grammys, three of them for Best Male Pop Vocals. He was inducted into both the Rock and Roll Hall of Fame and the Songwriters Hall of Fame in 2000. He continues to tour regularly.

# Ani DiFranco (1970–)

Ani DiFranco was born in Buffalo, New York, and began guitar lessons at nine years of age. DiFranco also started her own record label, Righteous Babe Records, with $50 when she was 18 years old. She has never signed with a major label and has been the model for independent artists in their struggle to control their music.

Because Ani owns her own label, she allows herself a great deal of artistic freedom, including the ability to release records as much, and as often, as she wants, and to include controversial material and language. She has turned down attractive recording contracts. You can hear her views on this topic in her songs, most notably in 'The Million You Never Made'.

Ani DiFranco's guitar playing skills include rapid fingerpicking and use of alternative tunings. She also employs a complicated overhand 'slap' technique that gives her a very percussive sound. Her lyrics have also received praise for their sophistication and wordplay in general. Song content is important and filled with subtle irony as well as descriptive use of metaphors. DiFranco's music has been classified as folk rock and alternative rock, but she has collaborated with a wide range of artists including Prince and both Maceo and Corey Parker of James Brown fame. DiFranco has released more than 40 recordings since 1990, including live recordings and videos.

# Chapter 14

# Rock and Pop Guitarists

Rock-and-roll took the world by storm in many ways. It has an interesting mixture of diverse styles – gospel, boogie-woogie, jazz, pop and even Western swing. The 'twangy' sound of rock-and-roll comes straight out of country music, while its soul comes from rhythm-and-blues influences. In fact, some of the earlier rock guitar solos are clearly country riffs. The early beginnings of rock-and-roll guitar are the stuff of legend; here are some of the greatest players of the genre.

## Chuck Berry (1926–)

Hailed as the 'Father of Rock-and-Roll', Chuck Berry's distinctive guitar playing, songwriting and showmanship have influenced every rock-and-roll musician to follow him. He grew up singing in a Baptist church in St Louis, Missouri, and he absorbed influences as diverse as Robert Johnson, Charlie Christian and Muddy Waters. Adapting the concept of boogie-woogie piano to the guitar, his first big hit was 'Maybellene' in 1955. He then recorded a series of hits that defined rock, including 'Johnny B. Goode', 'No Particular Place to Go', 'Sweet Little Sixteen' and 'Roll Over Beethoven'. He was the first person to be inducted into the Rock and Roll Hall of Fame (in 1986) and is also a member of the Songwriters Hall of Fame.

Berry's song 'Johnny B. Goode' is included on the copper records aboard the *Voyager* space probes, launched into outer space in 1977 to reach out to the universe with the best of our culture. In 1985, Chuck Berry entered the Blues Foundation's Hall of Fame. Now in his 80s, he continues to perform once a month at the Blueberry Hill bar in his hometown of St Louis.

## Bo Diddley (1928–2008)

Bo Diddley was born Otha Elias Bates. He would get the legendary 'Bo Diddley' nickname growing up as a youth in the streets on the South Side of Chicago, although he claimed not to know what the name meant. After four decades of performing, touring and recording, Bo Diddley earned the unique distinction of sounding like no one but Bo Diddley. His playing had driving rhythms and a hard-edged guitar sound. Even his clothing style was unique, not to mention his very unusual rectangular Gretsch guitar. Bo was one of the few artists who straddled rock-and-roll, blues and rhythm-and-blues styles. His first major hit was *I'm a Man* in 1955 on Chess Records.

Before his music career took off, Bo Diddley had a variety of jobs while he was trying to support his family. One of his jobs was being a prizefighter, and the others included construction and labouring jobs. Whenever he could, he would do gigs with local musicians, and was eventually discovered by the Chess brothers. Bo Diddley's effect was so far-reaching in the Chicago rhythm-and-blues scene that even Muddy Waters recorded a few tunes similar to Bo's. Today, you can hear a lot of Bo Diddley's music in adverts for a myriad of products including cars, which only seems fitting for a man some called 'The Originator'.

In May 2007 Bo suffered a stroke following an energetic performance at a concert in Iowa. Three months later he suffered a heart attack. He died in June 2008 at his home in Florida.

# Scotty Moore (1931–)

Born Winfield Scott Moore III on 27 December 1931, Moore began playing the guitar at the age of eight by learning from family and friends. Scotty Moore enlisted in the navy in 1948 at the age of 16 (below the minimum age), and served in both Korea and China. When he was discharged in January 1952, he moved to Memphis and began working with local bands. In 1954, Scotty began working with Sam Phillips of Sun Records. One day, Sam asked Scotty to audition with a talented singer who was recommended by Sam's secretary. The singer was Elvis Presley. The first major record the two made was 'That's Alright Mama'. Scotty Moore would remain Elvis's guitarist for 14 years. The Elvis band (along with drummer DJ Fontana) would appear in movies as the Blue Moon Boys until 1958.

Though Elvis had many guitarists by his side throughout his career, Scotty Moore is the one who helped him originate that rockin' Memphis sound. Scotty was also Elvis's first manager when Elvis was signed to Sun Records. Scotty Moore appeared with Elvis for the last time in the historic NBC '68 comeback' special in 1968 at NBC's Burbank studios in California.

Scotty served as the head of studio operations for Sun Records in 1960. This experience led him to open a recording facility of his own in Nashville, called Music City Recorders. In 1964, he released the classic instrumental album *The Guitar That Changed the World*. At this point in his life, Scotty began to focus more on audio engineering and production but as a studio owner and freelancer. He engineered television shows for Opryland Productions, which featured artists like Johnny Cash, Carl Perkins and Jerry Lee Lewis (Sun Records alumni), Dolly Parton and Perry Como, to name but a few. He continued to work in this field and occasionally played and toured with Carl Perkins and other former band mates in the 1990s. In 2002, Scotty Moore received the Orville H Gibson Lifetime Achievement Award by Gibson Guitars. In addition to the award, Scotty received a brand-new Gibson Tal Farlow model guitar.

The Orville H Gibson Guitar Awards is an annual awards ceremony traditionally presented on the day before the Grammy awards. It recognizes guitar players and players of related fretted instruments for their artistic accomplishments and honours musicians who reflect the spirit of Orville H Gibson.

In December 2004 Scotty Moore was honoured by British stars including Eric Clapton, Mark Knopfler, Ron Wood, David Gilmour, Bill Wyman and Albert Lee who gathered at London's Abbey Road Studios for three days of tribute performances in front of an invited audience. Scotty participated in the event, which was filmed and eventually released on DVD. He is a true living legend.

# Frank Zappa (1940–1993)

While Jimi Hendrix was arguably the most talented guitar player ever, Zappa was probably the most sophisticated and imaginative composer of the 1960s rock scene.

Born in Baltimore, Maryland, Zappa grew up in California. Zappa first started playing drums, and his heightened percussive and rhythmic sense can be heard woven throughout his career. He joined a band called the Soul Giants in 1964. The following year they transformed themselves into the Mothers of Invention, and in 1966 they released their first album, *Freak Out*. The album introduced the intense and emotional world of rock-and-roll to Zappa's sardonic humour, penchant for creating pastiches of popular styles, and avant-garde musical experimentation.

From the start, Zappa tried to expand the musical language of rock by folding in modern classical and jazz-influenced harmony, odd time signatures, exotic instruments and studio techniques like editing, overdubbing and tape manipulation. He developed a way of playing the guitar in long, directional solos with effects, expanding organically with his rhythmic and melodic ideas. Zappa created highly innovative material that has both quality and depth.

Frank Zappa released 62 albums during his lifetime. Since his death from prostate cancer in 1993, the Zappa Family Trust has released a further 27 albums (to date) in his name.

# Steve Cropper (1941–)

Originally from Missouri, Steve Cropper moved with his family to Memphis when he was nine years old. The sounds he heard around him were gospel and early forms of rhythm and blues. Growing up in Missouri, Cropper heard mostly country music and nothing else. Moving to Memphis 'cured' his ears. His guitar heroes at that time were the usual lot – Chet Atkins, Chuck Berry, Tal Farlow and others. Having received his first mail-order guitar at the age of 14, Steve went to work learning the music he heard around him.

Steve Cropper has the distinction of being the co-writer of some of the most famous songs in rock-and-roll history: 'Sitting on the Dock of the Bay', 'Knock on Wood', and 'In the Midnight Hour'. He was a part of the famous Booker T & the MGs, the house band for Stax Records. One of the first commercially successful mixed-race bands of that era, Booker T & the MGs toured with artists on the Stax Records label, including legends like Otis Redding and Sam and Dave. Cropper's signature intro lick on Sam and Dave's 'Soul Man' is about as familiar to soul music fans as it is to rock fans. Cropper's legendary record 'Green Onions' can be heard in many feature films.

'Green Onions' was a B-side recording that was made when studio and Stax Records co-owner Jim Stewart pressed the record button while the band was playing, unbeknownst to them.

After Cropper's decade-long stint with Booker T & the MGs, he left Stax Records and started recording, writing and producing records for Jeff Beck, Jose Feliciano and Tower of Power. A huge break came when he and bassist Duck Dunn were asked to be in the backing band for the Blues Brothers with Dan Ackroyd and John Belushi. They recorded three albums and shot *The Blues Brothers* film in 1977. The group disbanded after John Belushi's death in 1982, but they reunited for the *Blues Brothers 2000* film, with John Goodman replacing John Belushi.

Steve Cropper remains an active session guitarist with numerous recording credits to his name. In 2003, *Rolling Stone* magazine readers voted him one of the Top 100 Guitar Players of all time. He has a signature guitar model, called the

'Cropper Classic', which is made by Peavey and is one of the most respected and coveted guitars available today.

# Jimi Hendrix (1942–1970)

One of the greatest – if not the greatest – rock guitarists of all time, Hendrix outshone his contemporaries, reinventing the sound and concept of playing the electric guitar. Born in Seattle, Washington, he was drawn to blues and rock through radio and records. He got his first guitar at the age of 12 and was playing with local bands by the time he was 16. After serving in Vietnam during the early 1960s, he returned to America and turned professional in 1962.

He was a sideman for a number of rhythm-and-blues artists, such as Little Richard, Ike and Tina Turner, and the Isley Brothers, but Hendrix felt his talents weren't being used to his best ability, so he broke out on his own. Hendrix moved to New York in 1965, playing in various bars and clubs, while hooking up with blues rocker John Hammond Jr. In 1966, Hendrix formed his first band, Jimmy James and the Blue Flames. While playing in Club Wha? in Greenwich Village one night, he was approached by the Animals' bass player, Chas Chandler, who convinced Hendrix to move to London.

## The Jimi Hendrix Experience

Hendrix arrived in London in September 1966, and Chandler became his manager and worked with him on his first solo gig. An extraordinary guitarist and spectacular showman, Hendrix was an immediate sensation. Bringing drummer Mitch Mitchell and bassist Noel Redding on board, the Jimi Hendrix Experience was born. The newly formed band's first live dates were played in France, and then they went into the studio.

Jimi Hendrix played left-handed, though he played a standard right-hand model Fender Stratocaster upside down, strung the traditional way and tuned down a semitone. Hendrix's main amplifiers were Marshall 100-watt models with two four-by-twelve cabinets, and he often used fuzz pedal, wah-wah, an Octavia and a Uni-vibe built or modified by engineer Roger Mayer.

The Experience incorporated rhythm-and-blues and soul, and moulded those sounds into what became the epitome of psychedelia, just becoming the signature fashion of the late 1960s.

Hendrix's debut single was 'Hey Joe'. During the session, Hendrix met Roger Mayer, an electronics engineer who had developed new sound effects for the guitar. These effects can be heard on the band's next single, 'Purple Haze'.

Hendrix exploded onto the scene with his debut album, *Are You Experienced?* (1967), which he followed up with *Axis: Bold As Love* later that same year. Both albums took Hendrix's guitar playing and songwriting to new levels. Each song put Hendrix into the UK top-ten, and they earned him a top spot at the Monterey Pop Festival in the United States later that year. Drawing on the rhythm-and-blues showmanship of his early years, Hendrix commanded everyone's attention when he played his guitar behind his back, with his teeth and over his head. One of his set's highlights was 'Wild Thing', when he smashed his guitar against amplifiers to generate atonal chords, before pouring lighter fluid over the instrument, setting it on fire and smashing it to pieces, stunning his audience.

## Experimentation

Everyone from music moguls to teenagers were taken aback by Hendrix's experimentation. He used distorted riffs, mind-blowing feedback and thumping wah-wah pedals to make his music speak to the crowd.

In 1969, he played at Woodstock with an extended line-up that included Billy Cox replacing Noel Redding on bass. The performance was electrifying and captured on film. It climaxed with an anti-Vietnam War version of 'The Star Spangled Banner', filled with screeching avant-garde notes and feedback, becoming a grotesque parody of the original.

Later Hendrix formed a new group called the Band of Gypsies. They recorded one album in 1970, named after the band, which is a live recording of their debut concert at the Filmore East in New York on 31 December 1970. Hendrix would record one more album before he died of an accidental drug overdose in 1970 at the age of 27: the double LP *Electric Ladyland*. During the five years or so that he was active in the studio, Hendrix experimented with funk, jazz and Mississippi Delta blues, but never released such an album. From these sessions, producers posthumously culled tracks and released them.

In July 1995, Al Hendrix, Jimi's father, gained control of his son's estate. With the help of Jimi's sister, Janie Hendrix-Wright, he has brought to fruition a video of the making of *Electric Ladyland*.

Jimi Hendrix is buried in Greenwood Memorial Cemetery in Renton, Washington, a suburb of Seattle.

# Jimmy Page (1944–)

With the formation of Deep Purple and Led Zeppelin in 1968, a style of heavy rock emerged that was a clear synthesis of blues, rock, classical guitar and jazz, although fuelled by driving high-powered amplification and effects. One of the key figures to emerge in this field was Jimmy Page. Born in the West London suburb of Heston, Page was performing and recording as a teenager in London in the late 1950s and early 1960s. He produced John Mayall's *I'm Your Witchdoctor* (1965), which featured Eric Clapton, and the following year he joined the Yardbirds. In mid-1968, when the quartet split over artistic differences, Page went on to form the New Yardbirds, a hard-rock group that fulfilled the remaining contractual obligations of the Yardbirds.

The New Yardbirds quickly changed their name to Led Zeppelin and became arguably the most popular hard-rock group of the 1970s, selling tens of millions of albums worldwide. Because of the success of Led Zeppelin, Page became widely acknowledged as one of the most talented guitarists in rock music. In addition to his guitar work, Page also produced Led Zeppelin's albums, developing and shaping the band's sound.

The band broke up in the early 1980s, and several years later Page recorded with a new quartet called The Firm, which released two top-30 albums in 1985 and 1986 before it disbanded. In 1988, Page released his solo debut, *Outrider*, on Geffen Records; the album featured appearances by former Led Zeppelin vocalist Robert Plant and drummer Jason Bonham, the son of Zeppelin drummer John Bonham.

**Jimmy Page is alleged to own in excess of 1,500 guitars. Page himself gave this rough estimate to a BBC Radio interviewer in 2005. Page's primary guitar is a 1959 Gibson Les Paul that he acquired in 1969 from Joe Walsh.**

During the 1990s, Page worked with former Whitesnake vocalist David Coverdale, and then reunited with Robert Plant for an *MTV Unplugged* special that showcased the pair performing old Led Zeppelin songs with a world music twist. Some of that material appeared on *1994's No Quarter*, which was supported by a world tour.

In 1999, Page teamed with the Black Crowes for a concert that led to a tour, and an album called *Jimmy Page and the Black Crowes Live at the Greek*, which has exclusive online distribution through Musicmaker.org.

Today, Page continues to record and perform. His autobiography, published in 2010 and titled *Jimmy Page by Jimmy Page*, is a 512-page limited-edition collector's item, bound in leather, wrapped in silk and autographed by the author, retailing at over £400.

# Jeff Beck (1944–)

Along with Jimi Hendrix and Eric Clapton, Beck is considered one of the great guitarists of his generation, renowned for his technical ability and versatility. Though he has not received the same sort of media attention as Clapton and Hendrix, he nevertheless has hundreds of thousands of fans worldwide.

Born in Wallington, in the London Borough of Sutton, Beck attended art school in London but spent most of his time performing with various local bands. A stint with the infamous Screaming Lord Sutch built up Beck's reputation and, in 1965, the Yardbirds asked him to replace departing guitarist, Eric Clapton.

Beck performed with the blues-rock group for about a year and a half, maintaining their hit streak with top-ten hits like 'Heart Full of Soul', while extending the group's rhythm-and-blues sound to a more Hendrix-like psychedelic territory, such as on 'Shapes of Things'.

By the end of 1966, Beck left the Yardbirds to create the Jeff Beck Group, working with Rod Stewart. They released their debut LP, *Truth*, in 1968, and were one of the first bands to establish the new kind of heavy metal sound that Led Zeppelin developed. In 1970, Rod Stewart and Ron Wood left and joined Small Faces. Beck reformed the group with vocalist Bobby Tench, bassist Clive Chaman, keyboardist Max Middleton and drummer Cozy Powell. In 1973, he formed a new trio with former Vanilla Fudge/Cactus members Tim Bogart (bass) and Carmine Appice (drums).

In 1975, Beck made a comeback with the acclaimed *Blow by Blow*, an instrumental jazz-fusion album produced by Beatles producer George Martin. For his follow-up album, *Wired*, Beck worked with ex-Mahavishnu Orchestra keyboardist Jan Hammer, repeating the success of *Blow by Blow*.

In 1985, the polished pop-rock album *Flash*, recorded with session musicians, became one of his most commercially successful albums, spawning the hit single 'People Get Ready' (sung by Rod Stewart) and the Grammy-winning instrumental 'Escape'.

After taking some time off and appearing on Mick Jagger's 1987 album *Primitive Cool*, Beck returned with an all-instrumental album, *Guitar Shop*, in 1989. It won a Grammy for Best Rock Instrumental and received widespread critical acclaim. In March 1999, Beck released his first album of original material in more than a decade, *Who Else!*, a collection of 11 new guitar compositions in styles ranging from techno to blues to traditional Irish, arranged and produced by Beck and Tony Hymas. *You Had It Coming* came out in 2001. More recently, his 2003 album, *Jeff*, won a Grammy and his 2010 album, *Emotion & Commotion*, was his highest-ever charting album in the UK.

# Eric Clapton (1945–)

Clapton is possibly the most prominent rock guitarist to have emerged from the UK since the 1960s. At an early stage, his style showed the influences of bluesmen like Big Bill Broonzy, Robert Johnson and Muddy Waters. His song 'After Midnight' is one of 500 songs that shaped rock-and-roll, according to the Rock and Roll Hall of Fame.

In 1963, Clapton joined the seminal rhythm-and-blues group the Yardbirds. Two years later he left the band because he felt that they had become too much of a pop group, making room for Jeff Beck and Jimmy Page, two more guitarists who would become superstars of the rock and blues scene.

Clapton went to California and joined John Mayall's Bluesbreakers. (Mick Fleetwood, John McVie and Peter Green, the nucleus of Fleetwood Mac, also played with Mayall.) A year later, Clapton returned to London to form Cream, with bass player Jack Bruce and drummer Ginger Baker.

Following the break-up of Cream in 1968, Clapton formed Blind Faith with his neighbour, Steve Winwood, and ex-Cream drummer Ginger Baker. Blind Faith didn't last long either, and Clapton's next public appearance was as a member of John Lennon's Plastic Ono Band at the Rock 'n' Roll Revival Show in Toronto.

In 1970, Clapton formed his own band, Derek and the Dominos, and fell in love with Pattie Harrison, the wife of his close friend George Harrison. In fact, it was Pattie who inspired Eric to write the classic song 'Layla'. (Clapton eventually married and later divorced Pattie.) Clapton retired from the music business for a period while he dealt with a drug problem.

---

**In 1973, Clapton's good friend, The Who's Pete Townshend, organized a concert to help Clapton celebrate beating his drug addition. In return, Clapton appeared as the Preacher in the 1975 film version of The Who's** *Tommy*.

---

In 1990, Clapton won a *Billboard* Music Award for Top Album Rock Artist, but he also lost several members of his road crew and his friend Stevie Ray Vaughan in a helicopter crash. In February 1991, Clapton won his first solo Grammy for Best Rock Vocal Male for 'Bad Love'. The following month, his four-year-old son was killed after falling from a 53rd-storey window. The single 'Tears in Heaven' expressed his grief at the tragedy. In 1993, Clapton took home six Grammys for his *Unplugged* album, on which the single featured. He continues to perform regularly.

# Robert Fripp (1946–)

Fripp has been in the vanguard of rock music for more than 30 years, exploring the no man's land where rock and experimental music meet. Born in Wimborne Minster, Dorset, he began his musical career in the 1960s with the League of Gentlemen, a group primarily known for backing visiting American pop stars during their visits to the UK. Later, with brothers Peter and Mike Giles, he formed the trio Giles, Giles and Fripp. They recorded one album, the odd *The Cheerful Insanity of Giles, Giles and Fripp*, in 1968.

Fripp's next band is arguably the most famous of his projects, King Crimson, in which he was joined by Mike Giles. Beginning with their debut album in 1969,

*In the Court of the Crimson King*, the band established themselves as one of the best in progressive rock, combining Hendrix-influenced rock with sophisticated composition and improvisation borrowed from jazz, classical and experimental music. For five years, King Crimson went through numerous personnel changes. Fripp broke up the band in 1974.

After the demise of Crimson, Fripp more fully embraced an on–off collaboration with former Roxy Music member and synthesizer whizz Brian Eno. Together, they recorded two albums of heavily layered, atmospheric electronic music, *No Pussyfooting* (1973) and *Evening Star* (1975), on which he used a system of endless tape loops dubbed 'Frippertronics' to create a harmonically dense thicket of accompaniment. The Frippertronics system became a signature sound on many of Fripp's subsequent solo records and signalled Fripp's presence on records on which he appeared as a guest artist, including albums by David Bowie, Peter Gabriel and Daryl Hall.

In 1979, Fripp came out with his first solo album, *Exposure*, whose hard edge acknowledged the dawning punk rock movement, but two years later, to everyone's surprise, Fripp reconstituted King Crimson, featuring former band mate Bill Bruford as drummer as well as newcomers Adrian Belew and Tony Levin. The new line-up recorded three albums – *Discipline*, *Three of a Perfect Pair* and *Beat* – before disbanding in 1984. For the rest of the decade, Fripp worked on various solo projects, using the name of his first group, the League of Gentlemen, for a series of albums and touring with a travelling guitar workshop, the League of Crafty Guitarists.

For a third time, King Crimson became a working band, releasing *Vrooom* (1994) and then *Thrak* (1995). The group remained active, recording and touring until 2008. Fripp also followed a parallel career as a solo performer, exploring electronic and experimental music such as the *Soundscape* series of albums in the mid-1990s, and *A Temple in the Clouds* (2000). More recently, he has worked with Microsoft recording sounds for their Window's Vista software, and has also enjoyed collaborations with artists as diverse as Porcupine Tree, Toyah Willcox (his wife), saxophonist Theo Travis and Judy Dyble (Fairport Convention).

# Nancy Wilson (1954–)

Nancy Wilson is the lead guitarist of the hard-rock band Heart. She joined her sister Ann, who was already in Heart, and the band became one of the hottest rock groups of the 1970s with hits like 'Crazy on You', 'Magic Man', and 'Barracuda'. Nancy can be heard playing guitar throughout the recordings and her technique is very tight. Her acoustic work (on an Ovation Balladeer early in her career) was always a showstopper at their concerts.

The two-girl sister attack was rare in rock-and-roll but very effective during this period. But it didn't garner them much success in the early 1980s. They had huge success in 1985 with a self-titled release on Capitol that launched four top-ten hits, including 'These Dreams', 'What about Love', and 'Never'. In 1999, Nancy's solo debut, *Live at McCabe's Guitar Shop*, was released after being recorded two years earlier at the Santa Monica, California, venue of the same name.

# Edward Van Halen (1955–)

Eddie (as he is best known) and his brother Alex were born in Holland. When both boys were young, the family immigrated to the United States and settled in Southern California. Both parents loved music, and both brothers began training in classical piano at the age of seven. But Eddie wanted to play rock-and-roll. The brothers each bought instruments that the other would end up playing. Eddie bought himself a drum kit, and Alex began taking flamenco guitar lessons. Alex would play Eddie's drums so much that he soon became the better drummer. So Eddie decided the guitar would be his instrument of choice. And what a choice it was.

Van Halen taught himself to play by listening to records and copying what he heard. Eric Clapton was his main influence, and in no time, Eddie was able to play every one of Clapton's solos. After school and a few bands, the Van Halen brothers eventually met David Lee Roth and Michael Anthony, and the four of them formed a band called Mammoth. The name didn't last long as there was another band using it, so they decided to use the last name of the brothers – Van Halen.

Ted Templeton, a Warner Bros. Records producer, caught Van Halen's act at a club one night and signed them immediately. When their self-titled album debuted, it featured a solo instrumental called 'Eruption'. That piece of music had guitarists scratching their heads for years. It was loud, artistic and beautiful all at once. The entire record is a guitar tour de force led by Eddie's guitar riffs and the singing of David Lee Roth. The signature guitar songs are long, but they are all worth learning. These songs include 'Jump', 'Mean Streets', 'Little Guitars', 'Runnin' with the Devil', 'Panama', 'Hot For Teacher' and many more.

---

**Van Halen is known for playing a guitar of his creation, which he called a 'Frankenstrat'. The guitar consisted of a Charvel Stratocaster-type body, a vintage Gibson pickup, a Fender tremolo bridge and a single volume control. The single volume control came to be because of Van Halen's lack of electrical knowledge – he didn't know how to wire multiple circuits and so made the simplest circuit he could.**

---

The very essence of a guitar god, Eddie Van Halen redefined rock guitar technique and changed the sound of the guitar in the early 1980s. He is one of the most-respected and best-loved guitar players of his generation, and is now mentioned among the greats like Eric Clapton and Jimi Hendrix. His fiery solos soon became known for tapping, a technique in which he tapped the fretboard with his playing fingers while making notes with his fingering hand. His talent and skill are beyond question.

# Chapter 15

# Using Amplifiers to Get Good Sound

Now that you have reached a comfort level with strumming, playing chords and single-note playing, you should start to think about the kind of sound you want to get out of your instrument. Sound is a personal thing and is heard in a different way by every musician. To get the best sound out of your guitar, you may want to consider getting an amplifier. You may feel that an amp is an unnecessary expense but its impressive effect on the quality of your guitar's sound may just change your mind.

# The History of the Amplifier

By 1930, anyone familiar with electricity knew that the movement of metal through a magnetic field caused a disturbance that could be translated into an electric current by a nearby coil of wire. Electrical generators and phonograph (record player) pickups already used this principle. The problem in building a guitar pickup was creating a practical way of turning a string's vibration into a current.

After months of trial and error, Hawaiian steel-guitar player George Beauchamp – who, with Adolph Rickenbacker, formed the Electro String Company in the early 1930s – developed a pickup that consisted of two horseshoe magnets. The strings passed through these and over a coil, which had six pole pieces concentrating the magnetic field under each string.

When the pickup seemed to work, Beauchamp enlisted Harry Watson, a skilled guitar maker for National Guitars, to make an electric Hawaiian guitar. It was nicknamed the Frying Pan.

Electro String had to overcome several obstacles, however. To begin with, 1931 was the worst year of the Great Depression, and no one had money to spend on newfangled guitars. Furthermore, only the most farsighted of musicians saw the potential, and the US Patent Office did not know if the Frying Pan was an electrical device or a musical instrument.

From the very beginning, Electro String developed and sold amplifiers. This is an obvious first step, really, because without an amplifier the new electric guitar would have been useless. The first production-model amp was designed and built by a Mr Van Nest at his Los Angeles radio shop.

Soon after, Beauchamp and Rickenbacker hired design engineer Ralph Robertson to work on amplifiers. He developed the new circuitry for a line that by 1941 included at least four models. Early Rickenbacker amps influenced, among others, Leo Fender, who by the early 1940s was repairing them at his radio shop in nearby Fullerton, California.

By today's standards, the amps were pretty meek. Their output was about 10 watts, which is low, and they used radio technology, vacuum tubes and small loudspeakers. However, as the popularity of the electric guitar grew, there was a corresponding demand for louder amps.

The breach was filled by Leo Fender. In 1949, he worked with his engineer, Don

Randall, to produce the first Super Amp model amplifier. With the Fender solid-bodied guitars (the Telecaster and Stratocaster) in general production, and the introduction of the Gibson Les Paul in 1952, the demand for amps went through the roof as the popularity of the solid body grew. Output rose to a reasonable 50 watts with 12-inch speakers – still the norm for guitar amps.

By the late 1950s, the British company Vox had produced the AC30, which is as much a classic amp today as the Fender Twin Reverb. The Vox was particularly popular with blues and rock musicians because it produced a warm tone, which musicians such as Jimi Hendrix, Jeff Beck and other heavy-metal rockers discovered could be overdriven to create the fuzzy, distorted effect that has come to define the early 1960s rock guitar sound.

Splitting up a combo amp into individual components came about during the rock era of the 1960s. The amp became known as the 'head' and the speakers became known as the 'stack'. You could get more powerful amps and much bigger speakers this way, and by combining various amps and speaker combinations, musicians could produce more volume.

As the 1960s wore on, and rock bands played bigger and bigger venues, power and volume once more became a problem. This was solved when the British engineer Jim Marshall produced a 100-watt amp connected to a stack of four 12-inch speakers. Pretty soon the Marshall stack was the norm for rock concerts.

By the 1970s, the vacuum-tube technology of the 1930s was finally being replaced by cheaper and more predictable solid-state transistors, although musicians complained about the coldness of the sound compared to the warmth of the tube amp. It was popular among those who liked a thinner, cleaner sound.

The transistors' brittle sound was offset by the wider frequency range and the ability to play cleanly (without distorting) at higher volumes. Different tubes could produce different sounds, but they needed to be replaced periodically because they came loose or burned out.

By the 1980s, amplifier makers went back to creating a valve sound, often creating hybrid models that featured tube preamps and solid-state power amplifiers, getting the best of both worlds. Today, a traditional guitar amp combines an amplifier and a loudspeaker in one unit, called a combo. They are compact and relatively easy to transport.

# Understanding Amplifiers

Combo amps (and amps in general) come in a variety of sizes and shapes, but certain functions are common to most models. These are: input sockets, individual channel volume controls and tone controls, plus a master volume control.

There are two basic stages in producing a sound through a combo amp: the preamp, which controls the input volume and tone, and the power amp, which controls the overall volume. Most of the tone colours are created during the preamp stage.

### Input Socket

The input socket takes the signal from the guitar and sends it through the cord that connects the guitar to the amp via a jack socket. If there is more than one input socket, other instruments, such as a second guitar or a microphone can be fed into the amp at the same time through these other input sockets.

### Volume and Tone Controls

The channel input volume control allows the player to adjust the volume on the amp. It usually boosts the signal from the guitar and passes that signal along to the tone controls.

Channel tone controls can often be as simple as bass and treble controls. More sophisticated models such as the Mesa Boogie can feature a full-blown graphic equalizer. Basically, the controls split the signal into two or more channels, allowing for precise programming of the sound.

Output volume is the final stage of the process. The signal from the preamp passes through the power amplifier and is controlled by a master volume knob that controls the signal to the loudspeaker. The master volume controls the volume of the total output to the speakers, regardless of how many input channels are being used.

### Other Controls

More sophisticated models have controls that affect distortion, reverb and tremolo. Speakers come in a wide range of sizes and can be linked together to produce different kinds and volume of sound. Basically, a loudspeaker is the opposite of a microphone. When a string creates a disturbance in the magnetic field around the pickup, the final adjusted signal (having passed through preamp and power amp) is passed to a voice coil, connected to a large diaphragm, often made out of cardboard or some other responsive and flexible material. The coil receives the signal, transmutes that into a magnetic field of its own, and causes the diaphragm and cone to vibrate. The vibration disturbs the surrounding air and recreates the sound waves that were originally generated by striking the guitar string.

Most guitar amp loudspeakers are rated by their impedance factor, which varies from 8 to 16 ohms. (Impedance is an electrical term. Measured in ohms, it is the total opposition to the flow of the alternating current in a circuit.) It's important that amp output and speaker impedance are matched up. Too high a rating and the overall volume of the combo will be reduced. Standard 12-inch speakers can be connected together in pairs or quads (though 10-inch and 15-inch are also common now), although the way they are connected will affect the overall sound output.

## Getting Started

It's a good idea to begin with a small practice amp that can deliver a good signal at 6 or 12 watts. In general, what you pay for in an amp is power, not features, so practice amps can be quite cheap. It's also worth bearing in mind that you can often plug your guitar into the auxiliary or tape jack of a home stereo unit. If the unit doesn't have a suitable jack plug socket, go to a local electronics shop and tell the salespeople what you want to do. They can usually find you an adapter that will allow you to plug the guitar jack into a phono plug that will work on the stereo unit.

Before you plug in, however, make sure the volume is right down on the stereo unit, or you'll risk blowing out the speakers. You can even connect small practice amps, with no speakers, to headphones. That way, you can get a range of effects – such as distortion, EQs and compression – without disturbing anyone else.

**FIGURE 15-1:**

TECH 21 TRADEMARK

30 COMBO AMP

# Effects

Electronic effects allow you to produce quite a range of tones and colours. Some new combo amps have effects built into them, but most of the time nearly all of the effects you want to produce will have to be created by interposing an effects unit of some sort between the guitar and the amp. The jack plug that would normally be inserted into the amp is inserted in the 'in' socket of the effects unit, and another lead connects the 'out' socket of the effects unit to the amp. Most effects units are powered by nine-volt batteries, although they also have a wall-socket transformer. A transformer that's not created for the unit can hum, damage the foot pedal or even not work. We'll look at some the most commonly used effects now.

## Reverb

This is a natural effect that gives the impression that the sound is bouncing off walls and ceilings. Modern units allow you to programme the parameters of the sound, such as the size and shape of the imaginary room. Reverb is often used to breathe life into dead sound and is perhaps the most common effect used in a recording studio.

## Delay

Like reverb, delay gives the sense of sound bounced off a faraway object. You can create different effects depending on the length of the delay, which is measured in milliseconds (500 milliseconds = half a second).

## Echo

When the delay is long enough that the repeated signal can be heard as a distinct sound in its own right, then you have an echo. You can control the speed of the echo and get sounds that range from the early days of 1950s rock-and-roll to the experiments of Robert Fripp or Queen's Brian May.

## Phase and Flange

Phasing takes place when the same signal sounds as though it is being played back from two different sources at the same time. When the two signals are slightly out of sync – that is, when the peaks of the sound wave of one signal are overlaid on the valleys of the second signal – you get a sweeping sound called phase cancellation that sounds a little like a revolving Leslie speaker for a Hammond organ, popular in the 1970s. If the delay is more dramatic, then the sweeping sound becomes known as flanging.

## Chorus

By adding variations in pitch to a delayed signal, it's possible to create the sound of a doubled signal, as if a six-string guitar has become a twelve-string, in a crude analogy.

## Pitch Shifting

With pitch shifting, the signal is digitally sampled – that is, a piece of a recorded track is digitally copied and then fed into a loop to be played endlessly. Then it is replayed at a different speed, which changes the original pitch to a new pitch. Units often have a range of an octave above and an octave below the original note. If, for example, you set the unit to play sixths, then every sound that goes into the unit will be played a major sixth higher.

## Distortion

The best known of all effects, distorted sound can be created in a number of different ways. The volume of the signal is boosted to the point of distortion in a preamp then the distorted signal is amplified by the power amp.

## Compression

Often used in conjunction with other effects, compression makes the guitar notes sustain for a longer period, giving them more body, although it smoothes out the overall dynamics of a note.

## Wah-Wah

Wah-wah is a sound popularized in the 1960s and 1970s by Frank Zappa and Jimi Hendrix. A foot pedal controls a filter similar to a guitar's tone control, causing an almost vocal-like quality on occasion. The rhythm guitar sound in the original version of the film *Shaft*, for example, is a typical wah-wah funk sound.

## Tremolo

Tremolo is another effect that has a dated 1950s retro sound. Solid-body guitars used to have tremolo arms that could be manually activated. Now it primarily comes in a pedal unit, and it sounds as though you're playing through a slowly moving fan. However, tremolo arms are standard equipment on Fender Stratocasters even today.

## Volume Pedal

The volume pedal can be set so that you can alternate, at the flick of a switch, between playing lead guitar and rhythm guitar. The pedal instantly raises or lowers the volume of the amplifier.

### Combining Effects

Effects pedals can be combined, linking them together. However, the exact sequence of effects used can change the sound, depending on whether a particular effect is placed before or after another. If you use more than one effect, it's probably worthwhile considering buying a switching foot pedal unit that will help you control which effect you want to dominate your sound, and in what order you want the effects to be.

A modern solution to this problem has been the development of a multiple-effects pedal, which can be programmed to remember a particular sound, or sequence of sounds, and also does away with a suitcase full of effects pedals littering the floor before you like mouse traps.

A word of caution: effects will not make you play better or help you disguise mistakes. If you can't play well acoustically, you won't play better with a bunch of tricks loaded onto your guitar. Choose your effects with some taste. They can date you, and they can interfere with the tracking of the guitar signal, making it seem as though you are constantly playing out of sequence – that is, with 'bad' time – from the other members of the group.

Always carry a good supply of batteries if you don't have a transformer, and really practise with the effect at home before you decide to use it on a gig or recording.

## Bringing Technique, Amplification and Effects Together

Let's take a look at some effects on different styles of music. The music is specific to the effect being used. When you decide on the effect you want to purchase, try these examples. You'll be very pleased!

### Delayed Eighth Notes

The delayed eighth note is a lot of fun to play with. Commonly used by guitarist The Edge of U2, this effect is simple to set. First you get a delay unit and set the feedback (how many repeats you want) on '1'. Figure 15-2 shows a C scale to a D minor sounding scale played as eighth notes. The result of using an eighth note delay is seen below with the notes in parenthesis. Give it a try – you'll be playing for hours.

**FIGURE 15-2:** DELAYED EIGHTH NOTES

## Wah-Wah Style

This is simply fun. Using a wah-wah pedal (popularized by Jimi Hendrix), play the example shown in Figure 15-3. The fun comes in when you play the first chord, then you mute the remaining chords while moving the wah-wah pedal up and down. You'll probably notice your mouth moving along as well. Don't worry, it's not habit-forming.

**FIGURE 15-3:** WAH-WAH STYLE

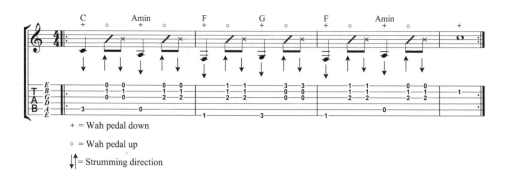

+ = Wah pedal down

○ = Wah pedal up

↕ = Strumming direction

# Intermediate to Advanced Playing Techniques

Now we'll look at all the scale shape techniques you have mastered from Chapter 8 and apply effects to them. These scale shapes are called sequences. To make them more fun to play, use the effect listed on each scale shown in Figures 15-4 to 15-7. As you get more proficient, you can also increase your speed. You are going for accuracy, but remember to enjoy the sound of the effect too.

**FIGURE 15-4:** C MAJOR SEQUENCE WITH EFFECTS

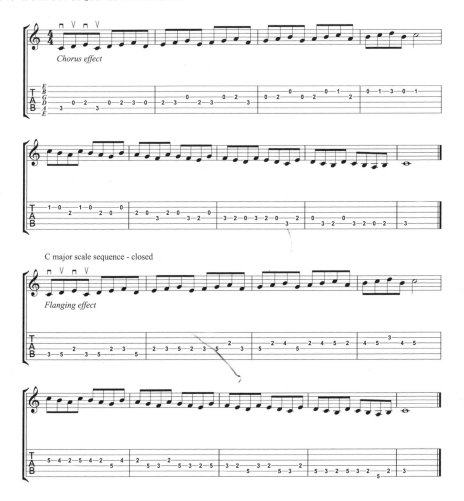

**FIGURE 15-5:** G MAJOR SEQUENCE WITH EFFECTS

**FIGURE 15-6:** C MAJOR SEQUENCE II WITH EFFECTS

C major scale sequence - closed

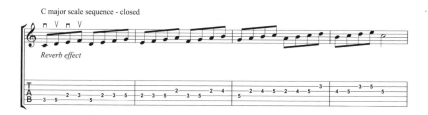

**FIGURE 15-7:** G MAJOR SEQUENCE II WITH EFFECTS

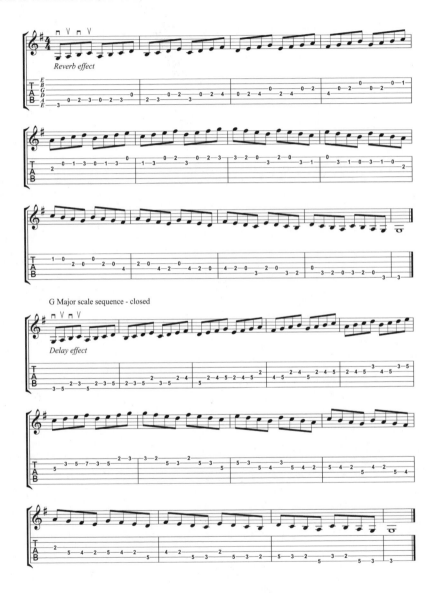

# Chapter 16

# Buying a Second Instrument

You have purchased your first guitar and because of this book, you have begun to get better acquainted with the inner workings of the instrument and you're feeling like a future guitar hero. Now you're ready to get a second guitar! Perhaps you started off with an acoustic guitar and now the electric is talking in your ear. Or, maybe you started with an electric and the idea of playing acoustic guitar has become an interesting future prospect.

# Hints on Instrument Purchases

Choosing and buying a guitar is a fairly important step in learning how to play. The absolutely best thing you can do is to read more magazines, like *Total Guitar*, *Guitar & Bass* and *Acoustic Magazine*, to name but a few. Reading these magazines over a period of a few months will give you a better overall look at what's out there before you purchase your second instrument. Take along a friend or ask a guitar teacher to help you. While this won't always be possible, it will still be a helpful step.

Regardless of how well you've done your homework, you should never buy a new instrument (whether it's your first, second or third) on your first visit to a music shop. Test lots of different types of guitars and visit lots of music shops more than once before you make a decision on your second instrument. Coming up with a plan now that defines your ideas about music doesn't mean you can't change your mind later on. This isn't do or die, here. It's just a place to start. To begin, you'll want to consider issues such as type, expense, appearance, construction, neck and action, which are discussed later in this chapter.

## How to Do Research

Doing research is really the key to buying any instrument. Research includes doing price comparisons between different types of guitars and then comparing shop prices. You may take the time to go guitar shop hopping – always more fun with a friend. You will also want to consider some online shopping comparisons. Once again, the music magazines are always your best starting point for your research. They have product reviews in every issue, and these reviews are always very informative when it comes to details, playability and price value.

You can also use the old tried-and-tested method of simply asking people you know and see how they pick their instruments and why they chose a certain manufacturer. Sometimes a person who is asked kindly about his or her choice of musical instrument will be more than pleased to share information on their pride and joy.

## Buying from a Shop

When you go to a music shop, be very clear and focused on your objective. Sometimes salespeople can be pushy and overbearing, which can be a turn-off.

Bring your research materials – price comparisons and product reviews with you. (You know the old expression, 'forewarned is forearmed'.) Often, salespeople in music shops work on commission, meaning that they make their salary based on the retail value of products they sell. So they may tend to be pushier than a salesperson who has no direct profit from your purchase. Sometimes a commissioned salesperson can make shopping uncomfortable, but don't let it bother you. Kindly let them know you are looking to purchase a second instrument, that you are interested in a certain type of guitar, and that you are 'just looking'.

---

**Many people have difficulty bringing up the subject of getting a discount with a salesperson. Ask the salesperson to give you the price, including VAT and case, for the guitar. When he gives you the final quote ask, 'Now what can you do for me to get that price a little lower?' You might have to use a little bit of pressure, but it's something you'll get used to doing.**

---

It is also possible to get distracted by the show-off players who come in all the time and play the guitars all day without buying anything. This frustrates salespeople as well, so be alert to the vibe in the shop. Now that you are playing guitar a little more regularly, be prepared to test the different types of instruments and their sounds. As you become a more experienced player, physical differences and tonalities are going to be more apparent to you.

## Buying on the Internet

One word: eBay! What eBay has done for guitar buying is amazing. eBay has allowed shops to sell guitars online to people around the world that their local clientele wouldn't necessarily be interested in. This is a great deal for you, the second guitar purchaser. When a shop is clearing out its stock, you have the opportunity to get a great deal on an instrument you really want to buy with limited funds. In addition to eBay, many of the larger chains have websites. Even some guitar manufacturers allow you to buy directly from them online. For example, Carvin, a musical instrument and pro audio company that has been around for more than 60 years, only sells direct to the consumer and continues to do it successfully.

But is it a good idea to buy a guitar through mail order or over the internet? Some people may say 'not really'. If you are someone who needs to test-drive the instrument and make sure that you're comfortable with it and that it works, then continue to do so. Everyone has a different way of doing things. The main objective is to get a second instrument in the way you feel most comfortable.

---

**Are there different size options for younger people, whose hands are still growing, or for adults with small hands?** Yes. If you have smaller hands, you might be more comfortable playing a smaller instrument. Besides full size, guitars also come in half-size and three-quarter-size versions with shorter necks (which means less finger stretching) and smaller bodies, which are easier to reach around. Both steel-string and nylon-string guitars come in these sizes.

---

## Types of Guitars

By this time, you will have decided which style of music you are beginning to gravitate towards. With that in mind, remember there are three types of guitar to consider: classical, acoustic (and acoustic-electric) steel-string, or solid-body electric. What you buy largely depends on the kind of music you are listening to and learning to play.

If you've decided you want to learn to play a number of styles, you should always have either a classical or folk (acoustic) guitar in your guitar arsenal. A classical guitar uses nylon strings, which are a little easier on your left-hand fingertips (assuming you're right-handed), though the neck is a little broader than a folk guitar. A folk guitar has steel strings, which are a little tougher on your fingertips at first, but it has a narrower neck. Most styles of music incorporate an acoustic guitar, so having an acoustic or classical guitar is always a good choice.

There are lots of different types of guitars built for the many different kinds of music you can play. If you go into a music shop and say you're looking for a guitar to play Eric Clapton-like rock blues, the salesperson will show you a solid-bodied electric like the Fender Stratocaster or a Gibson Les Paul. Say that you want to play jazz guitar like Emily Remler or Johnny Smith, and the salesperson will bring you an F-hole, hollow-bodied guitar like the Gibson ES-175 or a lesser-name brand guitar of similar quality.

For blues and rhythm-and-blues, there are several axes that will do the job, such as the Gibson ES-335 or ES-355. If your second instrument is for acoustic music, go for a Takamine or a Walden guitar for the mid-priced quality purchase, and a Martin, Taylor or an Ovation at the higher end. If you want to play classical or flamenco, start on a nylon-string guitar from the aforementioned acoustic manufacturers.

The kind of acoustic guitar you buy depends a lot on the kind of music you want to play. Here are some styles of playing and the best guitar(s) to play them on:

- **Rock/alternative rock** Six-string steel, twelve-string steel.
- **Funk** Six-string steel.
- **Folk** Six-string steel, twelve-string steel, classical.
- **Fingerpicking style** Six-string steel, twelve-string steel, classical.
- **Blues** Six-string steel, twelve-string steel, resonator.
- **Jazz** Six-string steel, twelve-string steel, classical.
- **Brazilian** Classical.
- **Flamenco** Classical.
- **Bluegrass** Six-string steel, twelve-string steel, resonator.
- **Flatpicking style** Six-string steel.
- **Country** Six-string steel, twelve-string steel.
- **Classical** Classical.
- **Slide** Six-string steel, resonator.

The truth is, though, that you can play anything on any kind of guitar. What counts is not the kind of guitar you have, but what's in your head. The best advice is to keep it simple. Remember, even rockers like Jimi Hendrix, Chuck Berry and Steve Vai played acoustic guitar as well as they could play electric.

## Expense

First things first: money. Buying cheap is not necessarily the best idea, though you don't have to spend thousands of pounds on an instrument and equipment either. Don't put yourself into debt, but be aware that you should think in terms of spending at least £120 to £200. You could easily spend £600 or more if you're not careful.

---

**Call a music shop, or check out manufacturer catalogues for models of instruments and prices. For example, a Gibson Les Paul sells for approximately £1500. A Fender Stratocaster costs around £600, and a decent factory-made nylon-string classical guitar can be bought for as little as £200 or thereabouts.**

---

The more expensive the guitar is, the better (and more seductive) it seems to be. You need to try to balance the 'new toy' syndrome with a realistic understanding of what you can afford, and what you need to learn to play well. Play a really expensive guitar and compare it to a much cheaper model. What differences do you notice? Unless you are working as a musician and you're buying yourself a new tool of the trade, don't spend too much. It won't be worth it.

## Used or Second-Hand Instruments

Is it a good idea to buy a guitar used or second-hand? Certainly. While a new guitar has to be broken in and can take up to six months to 'wake up', a used guitar in good condition is 'alive' and could be a bargain. You can expect to pay as much as 40 percent less than list price for a used guitar (unless it's a classic of some sort), depending on where you get it. Compare the prices in music shops, pawnbrokers and newspaper ads, and gather as much knowledge and information as you can.

## Aesthetics/Appearance

A green guitar does not inherently play better than a red or yellow one. Of course, what your new 'partner' looks like is important in terms of your desire to spend a lot of time with it. Still, never buy a guitar on looks alone. There may be a lot of guitars from the 1980s with really fancy graphics on them. This was a direct result of the dawning of the MTV era. These particular instruments may be more fun to look at than they are to play.

# Listening for a New Sound

Remember to tap the top and back of the instrument gently to make sure nothing rattles. (You're listening for loose bracing struts inside.) Look inside the sound hole for glue spills and other signs of sloppy workmanship. Check that all the pieces of wood join together smoothly and that there are no gaps between pieces.

An acoustic guitar's sound is principally made by the top – the back and sides reflect and amplify the sound. So a solid-wood acoustic guitar is preferable to a laminated-wood guitar (where the manufacturer presses together layers of inexpensive wood and covers the top layer with veneer). However, solid-wood guitars can be very expensive, and laminated-wood guitars can be pretty good. They are sometimes stronger than solid-wood guitars; the lamination process results in a stronger (though less acoustically responsive) wood.

With electric guitars, make sure that knobs, wires and other metal parts are secure and rattle-free. Strum the open strings strongly and listen for rattles. A solid-body guitar is basically an electric instrument with no real loud acoustic sound. Some people will try and tell you that the wood an electric guitar is made from is irrelevant, and that it is all in the electronics. Not true! You should also make sure the pickups and wiring are in good working order. There should be no hum or shorts, and the volume and tone controls should all work without crackles and other noises.

---

An extremely important subject to discuss with your salesperson is the shop's returns policy. You should have the right to return your instrument for any reason, no questions asked, for at least a week after your purchase date, for a full refund (possibly less the ubiquitous 'restocking fee') or an exchange. Make sure you clearly understand the returns policy that will apply to your purchase.

---

As when you checked out your first guitar, listen to how long the note will sustain. Fret a note and play it. Don't use an open string and don't move the string, just keep fretting the note until it fades away. Why bother with this? Well, a good sustain period is four seconds or more, which means the guitar will be good for playing fusion and rock. It also means the guitar is in good order. If the sustain is less than four seconds, then it's a questionable instrument and you should think twice about buying it.

Bear in mind, however, that this doesn't necessarily make it a bad instrument. There could be a number of reasons that the sustain is not longer. If the guitar is otherwise a bargain, a guitar repairer might be able to fix this problem easily. Have a professional check out the instrument before you make a final decision. The lack of sustain could be something as simple as a bridge that is out of alignment, a nut that needs to be filed properly, or old or low-quality strings.

## Neck

Pick up the guitar by the head and peer down the neck to make sure it's not warped. Does the guitar have a truss rod? Most guitars now come with them, but make sure. Does the neck bolt on? You can usually see where the neck is attached at the heel with a heel plate, under which are four or five bolts. Fender-style guitars have bolt-on necks. Is the neck glued on? Classical guitars and the Gibson Les Paul have glued necks. It looks as though the neck and the body are made from one piece of wood.

Run your fingers along the edge of the neck to make sure the fret wire doesn't need filing or reseating. The fret wire should be seated well on the fingerboard, and the ends should not be loose or feel jagged. Do you prefer a neck made from ebony, rosewood or maple? Cheaper guitars use mahogany or plywood stained black or rust red. The more expensive guitars with the better fingerboards are worth the money. Are the notes at the bottom of the neck in tune? Are they as easy to play as the notes at the top of the fingerboard? Do any of the notes have a buzzing sound even though you're stopping them properly? Is the intonation accurate? Do the notes on the twelfth fret correspond to the harmonics at the same place? The notes may have different tonal qualities, but they should have the same pitch. Pay attention to the third and sixth strings in particular. On a guitar that's not set up well, or has a problem, these strings may be hard to keep in tune.

If you don't trust your own knowledge or ears, enlist the help of an experienced guitarist. It's vital that you don't buy something that's going to be really hard to play.

## Action

The instrument's action, or playability, is determined by the setting of the string over and between the nut (at the bottom of the guitar) and the bridge (just before the tuning heads). Setting and adjusting these two things is a real art. The strings shouldn't be so low that the notes buzz when they are played, nor so high that the notes need a lot of physical strength to hold down. As you are purchasing your second guitar, make sure you understand that this new instrument will feel different. Acoustic guitar action is always higher than a solid-body guitar action. If the notes are hard to play or out of tune, get someone in the shop to adjust the instrument. If they can't – or won't – fix the instrument, don't buy it.

# The Importance of a Good Case

Now that you have decided on your new second guitar, please make sure it has a good strong case. The temptation is always to buy a soft gig bag. Going back and forth from gig to gig or rehearsal may be practical with a gig bag, but a hard-shell case is always a better way to go when it comes to storing the instrument when you're not playing it. This is especially true for acoustic guitars. Hard-shell acoustic guitar cases are made out of plywood. Their strength comes in three-ply and the stronger (and heavier) five-ply cases. The five-ply cases usually have an arched top lid for added strength. There are also cases manufactured using an injection-moulding process and special fibreglass polymers. These cases are usually black and lightweight, but very sturdy. They may sometimes be less expensive than the wood cases because they can be churned out more quickly in the manufacturing process.

In addition to a guitar case, you may need these other guitar accessories: a guitar strap, extra strings, extra picks, capo (a device that allows you to change the key of your guitar by clamping down certain strings), slide (for a slide guitar), humidifier, guitar stand and a guitar maintenance kit that includes guitar polish, polishing cloths and special cleaning fluids for the fingerboard and strings.

All hard-shell cases have a liner inside of them called high pile and low pile. This is the fuzzy velvet-feeling material that protects the surface of the instrument. Under the pile is foam that helps protect the instrument from shocks. A good case should have at least four latches to lock the case lid securely with the body. The handle on the case should be strong as well. If you purchase a five-ply case, make sure the handle is not a soft one. It should be strong enough to keep the guitar balanced.

## Closing the Deal

You've picked your instrument. Now your mission is to bring that guitar home for the lowest possible price! Note that this changes your relationship with your salesperson from teammate to adversary because his mission is to sell it to you for as much money as possible. Your mantra will be 'Never pay list price'. Many people assume that if the price tag on the guitar says £399, that's the price they'll be expected to pay. This is not true – music shops expect to sell you the guitar for less than list price. Many shops show both the list price and their own price on the tag in an effort to impress you in advance with the discount you'll be getting. Whatever the price tag says, remember that your salesperson has the power to significantly reduce the price of your guitar from the list price. The trick is to get him or her to do that for you. To make that happen, remember these tips:

- Keep your salesperson on a need-to-know basis. If you tell him that you're in love with this guitar and have to have it right now, you've tipped your hand and your discount will be smaller as a result.
- Keep it casual. Mention to your salesperson that you've seen a lot of nice guitars in other shops around town. Also, try out a few other guitars besides the one you've got your eye on, including some that are cheaper so your salesperson will be happy when you 'gravitate' towards your beloved selection. And don't appear to be in any hurry to buy a guitar today.
- Know if the price you're being quoted includes a case. If so, ask if the case is a hard-shell case or a soft gig bag. This is a significant difference because a hard-shell case sells for around £60, and a gig bag sells for around £20, on average.

- Never, ever pay list price for a guitar! No music shop today could stay in business if it sold its instruments for list price when 30-percent discounts are commonplace.

## Quick Tips for Buying a Second Guitar

You're about to walk into a guitar shop and haven't done much research (though this is not recommended!). You wonder what points are crucial when it comes to buying a good-quality instrument. The following list summarizes the main features you will need to know when shopping. Bring this page with you, and make sure you have covered all the points listed before you invest your hard-earned money in a new guitar:

- Step up the instrument quality when possible, but don't overspend.
- Enjoy your instrument. Learn how to play it. It will feel different in your hands than your current instrument.
- Get an experienced guitar technician to check the fingerboard for potential warping. The intonation and electronics should also be looked at.
- Make sure the action is set the way you like it. Look at the distance between the nut and the bridge. A low action means the strings are closer to the frets, so your fingers don't have to work as hard to press the strings to the fingerboard. Listen for buzzes and rattles. Once again, a guitar technician is best suited for these procedures.
- Check the tuning heads. If they turn too easily, the strings may slip, making the guitar difficult to keep in tune.
- Check for noise. With the guitar plugged in, stand it close to an amplifier and listen. Whistling or feedback might suggest the pickups aren't well isolated, and it could be a problem playing the guitar at high volume. Make sure the amplifier in the shop is not masking faults with the guitar you're playing.

# Chapter 17

# The 21st-Century Guitar

Guitar design is always evolving. But it is far behind in design evolution compared to the advancements of electronic synthesizers and electronics in general. Guitars are designed ergonomically first, then secondly for sonic beauty. The use of different woods and building methods plays a part in the ongoing design of the guitar. In the past few decades, there has been a movement to find alternative building materials to protect natural resources. Materials such as aluminum, plastic and graphite composites have been used to build excellent-sounding instruments.

# New Guitar Designs

It's hard to believe now, but even the standard Fender Stratocaster or Gibson Les Paul were once considered radical new guitar designs. Today, anything that doesn't resemble these two instruments is considered radical. With acoustics, any guitar that had a 'cutaway' was considered an abomination. Ovation Guitars solved many problems for the performing guitar back in the 1960s with its 'electro-acoustic' instrument the Balladeer. Today, almost all production acoustic guitars are electro-acoustic.

**Ovation guitars received great advertising exposure in America by giving a guitar to Glen Campbell in the late 1960s. Glen Campbell had a television show called _The Glen Campbell Goodtime Hour_. Every week, Glen and his Ovation Balladeer were seen in millions of homes around the country. Glen Campbell also played guitar on the Beach Boys'** _Pet Sounds_ **album.**

## The Handle by Peter Solomon

The Handle guitar, shown in Figure 17-1, was designed by Peter Solomon for Jim Reed Guitars. The materials are made from carbon fibre, developed for the aerospace industry, and are used in F1 racing cars among other things. The Handle is constructed of ultra-lightweight material and is incredibly resistant. It won't bend or buckle under high temperatures or humidity, and it is said that the carbon fibre offers a much wider harmonic range than wood. The entire guitar is hollow, creating a resonance chamber similar to that of a semi-acoustic guitar. The only wood used is ebony for the fretboard. You can read more about this instrument at www.xoxaudiotools.com.

**FIGURE 17-1:**

THE HANDLE GUITAR

## Phifer Design and Concepts by Woody Phifer

Woody Phifer has been building and repairing guitars for over a quarter of a century. His approach to guitar building centres on the traditions of the masters, as the sample in Figure 17-2 shows. His multi-ply binding adds elegance to the body, neck, headstock and recessed panels. The hand-built wooden bridge is fully adjustable. The bridge and solid brass tailpiece are recessed into the body. The shape is designed with the human body in mind. The offset cutaways offer greater access to the fretboard. The visually striking body design is balanced in a standing or seated playing position. Amazingly, the guitar weighs in at under 7lb! The other new design concept worth mentioning is that the bodies are constructed with a new multi-wood composition. You can read more about Phifer Design and Concepts at www.phiferdesigns.com.

**FIGURE 17-2:**

WOODY PHIFER PRO SERIES

## Floyd Rose Guitars

In 1977, Floyd Rose introduced the Floyd Rose locking tremolo bridge. The 'Floyd Rose', as it would come to be known as, revolutionized the guitar industry. Jump ahead 25 plus years, and Floyd has introducedthe quickest way to change strings on a guitar with the Floyd Rose Speedloader series, shown in Figure 17-3. The Speedloader series incorporates a radical advancement in guitar bridge and string design. The Speedloader series consists of a tremolo or fixed bridge and a special nut (see Figure 17-3). The integrated Speedloader bridge and Speedloader string design allows a complete set of strings to be changed in less than one minute by eliminating the need for tuning keys, wrenches, string stretching or major retuning! The neck weight of the guitar is lighter because of the absence of string tuners at the headstock. The special strings are calibrated to their actual pitch for instant loading and tuning, which is great for onstage use. You can read more about the Floyd Rose Speedloader series and their new titanium ultimate locking tremolo at www.floydrose.com.

**FIGURE 17-3:**

FLOYD ROSE SPEEDLOADER

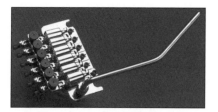

## Born to Rock Design F4c Aluminum Guitar

The F4c line, shown in Figure 17-4, was invented by a guitar player whose friend complained that no one could make a guitar with a neck that stayed straight. Intrigued by this problem, the guitar player realized that the harder you pull a string, the straighter it gets. If the guitar strings position the neck, rather than the neck trying to position the strings, then the neck stays straight. This is the logic behind the Born to Rock design concept. Suspending the neck on pivots allows the strings to position the neck. A string under tension defines a straight line. As the strings are straight, so is the neck.

In a conventional guitar, the rigidity of the neck is usually the solution to prevent it from warping. As the strings pull the neck forwards, a truss rod is put in the neck to keep the neck as straight as possible.

The neck, bridge and pickups are a floating unit suspended from the headstock and body by pivoting joints. String tension is handled from the headstock to the body by a lightweight, hollow aluminum tube. This tube does not have to be heavy or tremendously rigid because it is designed to bend as it takes up the string tension. Check out this unique instrument at www.borntorock.com.

**FIGURE 17-4:**

THE BORN TO ROCK F4C GUITAR

## RainSong Graphite Acoustic Guitars

RainSongs, shown in Figure 17-5, are the only graphite acoustic guitars in the world. The body, neck and soundboard are all made out of 100-percent pure graphite. The company developed its own manufacturing process, called Projection Tuned Layering. The combination of graphite construction and Projection Tuned Layering eliminate the need for bracing by providing uniform stiffness across the soundboard. That's right – RainSongs are made entirely without braces!

International trade in Brazilian rosewood has been banned for some decades. The only imports that are allowed for use of guitar building are from already cut tree stumps or pieces that were cut before the ban and stored for future use.

RainSong guitars are also impervious to humidity and temperature changes. This means the guitar can survive travel and changes in the environment. The guitars come in both electro-acoustic and standard acoustic models with no electronics. More on RainSong guitars can be found at www.rainsong.com.

**FIGURE 17-5:**

THE RAINSONG GUITAR

# Radical New Effects

Effects used to be simple. Using a chorus, delay, flanger or distortion was the norm. Today, effects are more digital than ever! Combining one effect with another by morphing the two sounds is the standard these days. Pedal boards took over in the 1980s and they haven't looked back. In fact, while some pedal boards have got bigger, others have got smaller but have more features. Technology has taken over the guitar effects and pedal world.

## Korg Pandora PX4

Expanding on the popular Pandora series, this multi-effects unit also has a built-in headphone amp. It is small and very portable. It has the standard classic guitar effects and simulated amplifier sounds. Also built in is a metronome. Another great feature in this box are the rhythm patterns with bass drums. It's excellent for practising.

## M-Audio Black Box

The Black Box, shown in Figure 17-6, features an array of unique effects that automatically beat-sync to your song tempo or the included drum patterns. Clearly, it's the next step in creating the future songwriter in you. The Black Box quickly allows you to access intricate delay lines, randomized filters, pulsing feedback effects and countless other modern digital effects.

The Black Box was developed by M-Audio and Roger Linn Design. The design is based on Roger Linn's Adrenelinn II effects box. The Black Box is also a USB audio interface for computer-based recording. The Black Box features 40 accurate amp models of many of the greatest guitar amps ever built. The unit also contains more than 120 unique effects, many of which beat-sync to the internal drum patterns or to an external sequencer (hardware or computer based). One hundred built-in drum patterns with tap tempo make it easy to try out different grooves and tempos. A built-in microphone preamp is also included for recording and processing vocals and acoustic instruments.

**FIGURE 17-6:**

THE M-AUDIO BLACK BOX

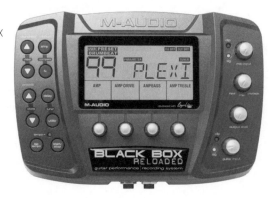

# Software Amplifiers

The current trend in guitar amplification is the use of virtual guitar amplification. These virtual amps emulate the sound of vintage and modern amplifiers. What is amazing about these products is their sonic possibilities and flexibility. They weren't readily accepted by the masses early on, especially by the purist community. In addition, the computer processing speeds that are needed to run these applications are high, so not everyone could enjoy their features.

---

When recording direct to disk, latency becomes an issue. Latency is the result of the time it takes for the signal from the guitar to pass through the A/D converter inside the audio interface, to the computer and the audio buffer setting in the software, and then to come back through the D/A converters. That journey causes a delay between the time when the guitarist hits a note and when the computer outputs the sound.

---

Today, however, computers are faster (aren't they always getting faster?) and software programmers are taking advantage of the faster processing power available to them. There are many of these products today and we'll take a look at them in all price ranges so that you can make your own informed decisions.

## FreeAmp2

Let's begin this section with something that is actually free! FreeAmp2, from Fretted Synth Audio (shown in Figure 17-7), is an amazing little hidden gem on the web. All of the software on this site is free, and there is quite a selection to choose from. The software is only used as a VST plug-in for your host application. With more than 128 presets, FreeAmp2 even contains a built-in guitar synth – also for free. You can choose from seven different amps types and EQs. There are six different speaker types, plus bypass and adjustable-by-the-mic placement. Check out the site at http://rekkerd.org/fretted-synth/

**FIGURE 17-7:**

FREEAMP2

## Alien Connections ReValver

ReValver is an effect plug-in for Windows (98 to XP), with more than 50 chainable sub-modules specially designed for guitar sounds. It has the distinction of being one of the first guitar-amp simulation plug-ins to be introduced to the market. The virtual racks you see are called modules. Each module represents a different virtual component, such as a preamp, a power amp, a speaker cabinet, a chorus, a flanger, an autowah, a delay, and so forth. Revalver is a user-configurable system. You can define the system by selecting signal-modelling amp modules. There are, however, certain restrictions concerning how the modules must be used and in what order. A maximum of 16 modules can be connected at any given time. You can read more about ReValver at www.alienconnections.com.

## IK Multimedia Amplitube 2

IK Multimedia's AmpliTube 2 offers more than 1200 different combinations of preamp, EQ and speaker configurations. It is compatible on both Mac and Windows machines and requires a fast processer to run well. AmpliTube contains Preamp and EQ models, as well as Power-Amp and Cabinet models.

In addition to the standard stomp-and-rack effects modelling, there are microphone models and a very detailed tuner. You can download additional presets at www.amplitube.com. The presets will help you get started with AmpliTube. There is also a standalone version of AmpliTube called AmpliTube Live, which as you can tell by the name is primarily for live stage use. You can read more about this product at www.ikmultimedia.com.

## Nomad Factory Rock Amp Legends v1.8

Nomad Factory's Rock Amp Legends pays tribute to the early days of rock guitar amps. Developed with the help of former Aerosmith guitarist Jimmy Crespo, this plug-in will make the classic rock-and-roll purist very happy. Rock Amp Legends looks like a Marshall amp, and it sounds like one with classic lead and modern lead simulations. At the time of this writing, parameters in Rock Amp Legends responded to sequencer automation under all supported plug-in formats except for Audio Units. You can read more about Nomad Factory Rock Amp Legends and their other creative music software at www.nomadfactory.com.

## Native Instruments Guitar Rig 2

Guitar Rig 2 is guitar amp modelling at its best (see Figure 17-8). This program runs as either a standalone application or a plug-in on both Mac and PC platforms. Guitar Rig's components may be arranged in any order. It also offers two digital-recording components called Tape Decks that are great for learning old and new licks and practising to drum loops as well as songs. Guitar Rig comes with Rig Kontrol 2, a fully programmable outboard pedal with four footswitches and an expression pedal. Rig Kontrol 2 also functions as a preamp. This allows laptop users to use Guitar Rig as an effects pedal for live performance. The amp models are of very high quality. Guitar Rig can appear to be a little on the pricey side, but it gives you a programmable pedal board interface and a great piece of software. For more details on Guitar Rig 2, visit www.native-instruments.com.

**FIGURE 17-8:**

GUITAR RIG 2

# USB Guitars

The newest trend to hit the modern day guitar is the introduction of USB-equipped guitars that plug directly into the computer's USB port. This technology eliminates the need for the guitarist to use a soundcard to get audio into their recording program. You can now plug your guitar into the computer the same way you plug in a digital camera or external hard drive. These new guitars differ in price and quality, but their application is breaking new ground in the way you can record your newfound guitar skills.

### iGuitar

The Brian Moore Guitar Company was the first company to introduce the USB concept with its iGuitar (shown in Figure 17-9). The design principle was to just plug the iGuitar into the USB port on any computer (PC or Mac) and get direct access to any of your favourite computer-based recording program or guitar effects program. The attraction for the guitarist is irresistible!

The benefits to using it are many. First, the signal from the guitar is what is referred to as a line level signal. This means that there is no need for an external

**FIGURE 17-9:**

BRIAN MOORE iGUITAR

audio-interface preamp. The second benefit is that there is no special software driver needed for the guitar to work with the computer. This is known as being class compliant. The third benefit is that the guitar is bus powered. This means there is no need to use a battery or A/C power supply. The Brian Moore Guitar is also a high-end instrument with many other features, such as a piezo pickup system for acoustic guitar sounds, and it is MIDI capable. But these features make for a high-end price. As there are many models to choose from, you may want to look at the company's website, at www.brianmooreguitars.com.

## Behringer iAXE393 USB-Guitar

The Behringer iAXE393 USB-Guitar (shown in Figure 17-10) is a high-quality electric guitar that comes with a maple neck and three single-coil pickups with five-way switching. A built-in connector allows you to connect your headphones straight to your guitar so you can jam with your favourite music already in your computer. This guitar also comes with Native Instruments' Guitar Combos Behringer Edition software pack, which features their exclusive Tapedeck and Metronome racks. The Behringer iAXE393 USB-Guitar comes packaged with additional multi-track recording and editing software so you can record your music on the spot. You can jam with MP3, WAV, AIFF and OGG songs or backing tracks on your PC or Mac. For more details visit www.behringer.com.

**FIGURE 17-10:**

BEHRINGER IAXE393
USB-GUITAR

## M-Audio JamLab Personal Guitar System

JamLab (shown in Figure 17-11) is a compact interface that connects to your computer via a USB connection, and features a 1/4-inch input for your guitar and 1/8-inch headphone/line output. The total package includes the GT Player Express software with guitar amp simulations and virtual effects boxes for EQ, chorus, reverb and more. The GT Player Express software can also play standard audio files (WAV, MP3 etc.), and can even slow them down, which is perfect for practising and easy learning. You also get the 'Best Of' WAV drum loops from the M-Audio ProSessions Sound and Loops Library. You simply load the loops into GT Player Express in any order for an instant custom drum machine to jam with. It's an excellent all-purpose portable solution. For further information go to www.m-audio.com.

## ESI USB JamMate UG-1

The ESI USB JamMate UG-1 is another USB-based electric guitar that plugs into your computer or laptop. This guitar uses a proprietary audio technology driver called USB Instrument Manager. This driver and manager will allow the JamMate USB instruments to play along with other JamMate USB instruments, like bass and drums, powered by ESI. The UG-1 guitar also comes with a built-in headphone amp, and it functions as a standard electric guitar. It is compatible with Windows XP and Mac OS X and comes packaged with Amplitube Live amp simulator software. Check it out at www.jammate.ir.

**FIGURE 17-11:**

M-AUDIO JAMLAB
USB AUDIO INTERFACE

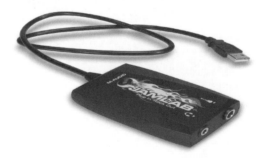

# USB Cables and Other Hardware

Recently added to the USB market are USB guitar cables. These cables feature a 1/4-inch jack for the guitar on one end, and a class-compliant USB connector for the computer on the other end. The beauty of these new cables is that they allow you to use any guitar you like! For those of you who are really comfortable with your existing guitar, and don't want to spend a lot of money (yet) for a special guitar to plug into a computer, these cables are the answer.

## The SoundTech LightSnake

The LightSnake cable (shown in Figure 17-12) is a USB cable for guitars or other musical instruments. The LightSnake instrument cable is essentially a sound card on a cable, and you can use this cable to record audio directly into your computer. The quarter-inch mono plug of the LightSnake cable plugs into your instrument and then connects the USB end to one of your computer's USB ports. This is a true USB plug-and-play connection. No additional drivers are needed for supported operating systems (Win 98 SE, Win 2000, Win XP, and Mac OS 9/OS X). The LightSnake features SoundTech's patented 'Live when Lit' technology cable ends that glow when connected properly and flash to indicate when sound is being transmitted. You can learn more about the technology at www.soundtech.com.

**FIGURE 17-12:**

SOUNDTECH LIGHTSNAKE
USB CABLE

## IK Multimedia StealthPlug

This specialized cable is designed to work primarily with the IK Multimedia's AmpliTube line for live playing, recording or practising anywhere at any time. Though the StealthPlug is large, it is feature-rich, with onboard volume controls and headphone. The StealthPlug requires software installation to work with the computer. You can find more info regarding the StealthPlug and other IK Multimedia guitar software at www.amplitube.com.

### DVForge GuitarPlug

The DVForge GuitarPlug is a small USB audio adapter for Mac OS X users that plugs into the output jack of an electric guitar, bass or dynamic microphone cable and converts the analog signal output to a high-quality USB audio signal. The GuitarPlug is cylindrical, 2.3- by 0.7-inches in size, USB bus powered, has an on-off switch, and a blue LED power indicator. It converts mono analog audio to 16-bit, 48KHz better than CD-quality digital USB audio, and is a class-compliant, plug-and-play device. This is the only Mac-specific product of the three cables described in this section.

# Digital Lessons

When it comes to learning on your own, there are many ways to do this. Guitar lessons on DVD are great because of the instant subject access they provide. Companies such as Homespun and Hotlicks have recently converted their video catalogs to DVD.

Another source of digital learning are multimedia CD-ROM hybrids like eMedia (www.emediamusic.com). eMedia produces the bestselling *Guitar Method Vol. 1* and *Intermediate Guitar Method* guitar instruction software. They also produce *Bass Method*, which is the first comprehensive multimedia bass tutorial. This method of digital learning brings the computer into the mix, but it requires that you install eMedia's software.

Lately, the online instructional market has begun to explode with companies like Workshop Live (www.workshoplive.com) and Truefire (www.truefire.com). These websites have some of the most comprehensive videos of great players. Do yourself a favour and investigate these sites. They can only help your playing and give you better comprehension of the instrument.

# Chapter 18

# How to Choose a Teacher

Choosing the right teacher should be done with a very well thought-out approach. You must feel comfortable in a variety of ways with the instructor you select. Keep in mind that you will most likely see this person once a week for a few months or more, and you will be learning in an environment that may be smaller than you're accustomed to. It may be the first time you have one-on-one instruction on an instrument that you actually like. The idea is to find someone who can teach you properly and someone you can respect and learn from.

# Location

One of the most important things to consider when looking for a teacher is where he or she is located. Is the teacher located next door or in the next town or city? There are important factors to consider when it comes to travelling. Sure, it looks cool to carry your guitar case everywhere when you are learning, but if you have a heavy hard-shell case, it can become daunting. You should always consider the distance that needs to be travelled to support your newfound interest. It doesn't make too much sense to travel 45 minutes to an hour for a 30-minute lesson. Guitar teachers are very easy to find, strangely enough! Good guitar teachers, like everything else, are harder to discover.

Some music shops offer guitar lessons, which is the norm. In this situation, you are going somewhere familiar, perhaps where you bought your instrument, and are surrounded by guitars and equipment you may one day want to buy. It also helps that you see other people learning from the same person. That's a good thing. Who knows? Maybe one day you'll work at that same music shop and give lessons.

**Music shops sometimes offer different methods of paying for your lessons. Some payments are based on weekly, bi-weekly or monthly schedules. Make sure you pick a payment schedule that best suits your funds availability. It is also important to ask how catch-up lessons are handled in case of an absence.**

If you find yourself travelling to a teacher with a private teaching studio, it's a good idea to get someone to accompany you on your first visit. When you're by yourself, you don't always pick up on everything in your surroundings. A second pair of eyes is always good and helps you with feeling comfortable with meeting someone new. Now, you shouldn't bring your favourite guitar-playing friend and try to get a two-for-one deal, but you should consider bringing someone for a second opinion.

The size of the room you learn in is very important. What if you are tall? The chairs may be too low to sit in comfortably. Physical obstacles are usually the reason that students discontinue guitar lessons. Being in a cramped room in close quarters with another person may not be suitable for learning. Always visit the location and examine all aspects of the learning environment.

# Group Lessons or One-on-One?

The environment you put yourself in to learn music is very important. You will find yourself in a group lesson or one-on-one with a private teacher. Both have definite advantages and drawbacks. The group setting in a classroom affords you an outlet for healthy competition (and inspiration), where you can measure your standing in relation to the progress of other students. You also learn to function with fellow guitarists and other musicians in an ensemble manner, and you will develop an awareness of how to blend in with others, which is important. This awareness will also help when it is time to start 'the band' (more on this subject later). Dynamics, chord accompaniment and when to play can often be learned more easily in a classroom or group setting.

**Most class instructors 'teach to the mean', which means they teach the average overall level of the class rather than the most advanced or least proficient. Depending on how far you've developed, this can be to your advantage or disadvantage.**

Each class takes on its own personality and pace, requiring the instructor to adapt his or her teaching approach accordingly. A class can and should be fun, stimulating and challenging. Even though a teacher you're considering studying with may not be a performer in front of the classroom, he or she should keep things moving and have enough enthusiasm for the subject to keep those who would fall behind awake.

Some teachers criticize students in a classroom setting. Though this is not a preferred method, in some cases and with some students this approach can create a positive learning experience. There are disadvantages to this approach as well, such as disillusioning the student. But the pressure to learn quickly is a reality for the professional musician. The earlier you get it in your system, the easier it will be to accept the negative comments of others in the future. If you feel this isn't the best environment for you, then private lessons are the best solution. This affords you the luxury of having an instructor teach you at your own pace.

**Certain people don't work well in the classroom. Competition can ruin enthusiasm for more sensitive students, and large groups may cause even more discomfort. It's often harder for a person to concentrate in a class, and specific problems can't be addressed if they're too complex.**

### The Good Player, Bad Teacher Trap

There are teachers who are just amazing players. They play at performing venues and always impress the crowd. But sometimes money gets a little tight, so they teach to make a few extra pounds. You may have heard of students who have taken lessons from these players. The teacher gives them chords to play while the teacher just jams over the chord progression – for the entire lesson!

If your potential teacher is a great player, but can't communicate a well thought-out lesson for you, you need to reconsider your choice. He may have forgotten what it's like to struggle from one simple open chord to another. The instructor you choose must be able to recognize the level of your ability and take you to the next level on a regular basis. Find a teacher who makes you comfortable.

## Filtering Out Recommendations

You may know people who are currently taking lessons – ask them for some recommendations. Everyone has different interests. The rock lover may adore his rocker teacher, but you are interested in jazz. The folk guitar player loves her mellow '1960s was the greatest decade ever' teacher, but you want to learn funk guitar. Look for a serious teacher, never one who wants to make a clone out of you by refusing to allow for your differences in musical taste and goals. Many famous players started with teachers who knew of the style they were interested in but had the training and musical background to help them progress in the music of their choice. If 'do it the way I do' is your instructor's solution for educating you, you might be better off seeking another teacher who's more diverse and open-minded. Find someone who's compatible with the way you want to learn.

---

A good guitar instructor can show you things in a matter of weeks that it might take you a year to figure out on your own. It's important that you trust your teacher and that you admire his or her ability on the guitar for this relationship to work. So if after a few weeks you're not getting that feeling from the first one you choose, look for a new one.

---

# University External Programmes

Some universities with a school of music have an external guitar programme that you can sign up for. These programmes are usually given through the continuing education division. The benefits of these programmes are that they are attached to the university, and certificates are usually awarded after each term. For someone preparing for university, this kind of programme can be very beneficial. Some schools offer some kind of preparatory credit that looks quite nice on university applications. Note that some courses are taught by students (as well as faculty) of the school. Fear not – these student teachers are usually working towards a music education degree and are beginning to work in their field.

The external university learning option is good in many ways. The prices may vary depending on the prestige of the institution, but you get a focused learning experience from either a top student or one of the tutors of the school. Going forwards, if you are looking at a university where you can learn more guitar and music in general, this is a good way to start.

# Auditioning a Potential Instructor

Here are some key points you will want to consider when auditioning a teacher:

- Always seek a teacher who can adapt to your own learning talents.
- Ask the teacher how he or she will go about helping you overcome any confusion you may have.

- Make sure the teacher uses lesson plans, schedules and progress reports. These are important.
- The ultimate goal of a teacher is to help you teach yourself to learn. Trust your instincts and be sure you have high standards when considering any decision about a teacher.

## Researching Reputation

It is important to know the lesson reputation of your instructor. You should do some research and find out what the instructor teaches. The following are essential for learning in any guitar lesson:

- **Music theory** In order to explain basic to advanced musical ideas, fundamentals have to be established.
- **Ear training** Being tone deaf is not an option! You must be able to discriminate between high and low tones. This skill takes time to learn and develop, and a good teacher must have efficient methods on hand to guide you through.
- **Sight-reading** Reading music is a skill. It must be practised and gradually developed.
- **Transcription** The ability to transcribe guitar licks and teach you how to do it is essential. Find yourself a teacher who has transcribed a good amount of guitar solos to begin to teach you improvisation, in addition to phrasing and dynamics.
- **Improvisation** Improvisation can be taught and it must be explained thoroughly. Today's guitarist needs to know how to improvise as many styles as he or she can learn.

A good teacher can help the confused new musician focus on a goal and stick to it. It's up to you, the student, to eventually settle on an instructor. All players are students of music, and no one can ever know quite enough.

# Hourly Rates and Catch-Up Lessons

When it comes to the expense of taking lessons, evaluate what you can actually afford. That cool teacher you've heard amazing things about will probably cost you anywhere between £15 and £30 an hour. You are paying for an expert to assist you in learning a new skill. The instructor should get his or her requested rate, as long as your research backs it up. The lesson goals and expectations should be clearly printed and handed to you, the student. You should understand the rules regarding punctuality and lateness. Most importantly, what are the rules regarding absences and catch-up lessons? Make sure this information is on the printout. While it may be OK in some instances to have a verbal agreement or understanding, having a clearly printed syllabus will make you feel like you're in the right place with the right teacher.

# Lesson Plan or Curriculum

It would be most helpful to monitor your progress as the lessons go on throughout the weeks, months and years. Make your goals clear to your instructor, and have regular discussions to make sure you are both on the right track. The best way to do this is to have a notebook or journal to monitor all of your practice hours, homework assignments and future projects if any. Years later, you'll be very impressed at how far you have come in your playing skills. It will also show your instructor how serious you are about guitar playing. It may sound like a tedious task to keep records of all the material you have learned, but the reward is the self-realization that you have become a better musician as well as a guitarist.

# Performing Opportunities

Performing in public is the best testament to how far you have come as a guitarist. Some schools require performance in an end-of-term concert. You should never shy away from these events, which help shape your character and performance skills. The more you perform in public, the more you get used to it. When the clapping gets louder and longer, the smile on your face becomes wider and wider. Once the word gets around that you are becoming a great player, you will have a lot to be proud of. Guaranteed.

# Chapter 19

# Listening and Playing with Friends

You have learned a lot of important information in this book. Now comes the added bonus that comes with learning guitar: listening to and playing guitar music just for pleasure. There are many elements to listening to music, including song structure, loud or soft qualities, instrumentation and so on. Now that you're an experienced player, you'll be able to make sense of all of it and then play what you've learned with friends. There is nothing better than playing music with a pal. This chapter introduces you to playing with others and possibly forming your first band.

## Understanding Sound Placement

The human brain can distinguish only up to four sounds at once – at best. As you are listening to the environment around you, you are focusing in and out on different sounds. This is why certain music sounds different to you the more you listen to it. Because of many different factors, you begin to notice that there is a certain effect on a voice that you never noticed before. Maybe that's because you now understand how a reverb or echo sounds on a voice, and you can hear it clearly in the mix.

**As an experiment, stand in front of a building with your eyes closed. Listen to all the sounds around you and try to identify them. Do the experiment again but this time, try to discern certain sounds in a smaller space.**

When listening to recorded music, especially on a CD or an MP3 player, the music produces the exact same waveform every time you hear it. What you hear is determined by the placement of microphones during the recording process. Different genres of music use specific miking techniques that shape the way listeners hear that music. When you listen on headphones or on loudspeakers, you are hearing a basic stereo reproduction of the music. This is also known as binaural listening.

Listen to British music recordings from the 1960s. They have a certain flatness to them because they were recorded to have the music played back on mono 45rpm records. They were not necessarily mixed for stereo. But when you hear Jimi Hendrix's *Are You Experienced?*, not only does it sound loud, but the drums, guitar and vocals are clearly placed in opposite sides of the stereo spectrum. This almost mimics the way people focus on the music they hear. This recording technique was also due to the limited amount of recording tracks available at that time. *Are You Experienced?* was recorded on a four-track machine. Amazing!

# The Guitar in the Mix

When the guitar is heard on a recording, it has many places it can appear in the mix. Here are some of them:

- Fully panned left or right to isolate it from the band.
- Right in the middle of the mix.
- In panning positions referred to in clock-hand terms, such as 10 o'clock or 2 o'clock.
- In the middle (used in solo guitar, with either reverb or minimal delay to make the placement feel more spacious).

The best place to start listening to recorded guitar music is classical guitar. It may seem simple in the beginning, but the set-ups used to make those gorgeous recordings take many hours of preparation and trial and error. Next, move on to smaller band music like trios and work your way up to full-scale jazz and big bands that feature a guitarist. Any recordings by Bucky Pizzarelli will do just fine. After you have listened to an assortment of music, you will then have a better understanding of how the guitar fits into the recording and mixing process.

The best way to get started on listening to music is with the Chesky Records *Various Artists – Gold Stereo and Surround Sound Set-up Discs*. This disc was designed to help music stereo equipment enthusiasts improve every aspect of their stereo system and entertainment centre's performance.

# Playing Along

Once you have a handle on playing chords and are able to switch from one chord to another, you should consider playing along to your favourite CDs. There are numerous songbooks on the market that feature the music of some popular artists and that have detailed transcriptions of the group's songs. Sometimes when you try to figure out the chords yourself, you get them wrong and then keep playing the song incorrectly. Try and search for your favourite artist's songbook and start from there. In time you be able to pick out the chord changes yourself.

# Brief Introduction to Improvisation

Improvisation requires an open mind. It is an opportunity for self-expression. Perhaps you like the solo on an Eric Clapton record and you want to play along. Jamming with Eric Clapton is a dream for most guitarists, but millions do it every day by jamming along with a recording. When you improvise, you are making up solos and phrases as you go along. So how do you begin to learn that skill?

The beginning of improvisation begins with the pentatonic scale. There are two types: major and minor. The major pentatonic scale is the same as a major scale, only the fourth and seventh notes are removed. Figure 19-1 shows the C major pentatonic scale. The A minor pentatonic scale is shown in Figure 19-2. Try playing the scale in Figure 19-3. Do not concern yourself with which notes to play, just run up and down the scale. Try to make it familiar and easy.

**FIGURE 19-1:** C MAJOR PENTATONIC

**FIGURE 19-2:** A MINOR PENTATONIC

**FIGURE 19-3:** MAJOR AND MINOR PENTATONIC SCALES SHAPES

# Learning Songs with a Friend

Depending where you are in life, the genre of songs you learn will differ. Some will enjoy learning those classic songs from the 1960s, while others will enjoy 1970s rock music. But before you get started on your new career as the guitarist in a highly sought-after cover band, you and a friend should get started on some simple duets. They are fun, melodic and you can begin giving concerts immediately.

## Playing Duets

The first tune you will start with is 'Old Joe Clark', shown in Figure 19-4. This is a traditional bluegrass tune. As bluegrass music is played fast, my advice is to learn the tune first, then gradually speed up. On the repeats, you and the other guitarist should switch parts. Start making beautiful music together! You would normally play acoustic guitar for these songs, but if you feel the need to rock out, then please, by all means do so.

**FIGURE 19-4:**

OLD JOE CLARK

Figure 19-5 shows another bluegrass number 'Mississippi Sawyer', followed by Figure 19-6, which shows 'My Country 'Tis of Thee'.

**FIGURE 19-5:**

MISSISSIPPI

SAWYER

**FIGURE 19-6:** MY COUNTRY 'TIS OF THEE

# Starting Your First Band

Going from simple duets to a band is a huge step. You are more comfortable with your newfound skill, and you have a friend who shares your enthusiasm about the guitar. What's the next step? Start a band! Wait! Before you do the inevitable, you need to consider a few things first.

## Who Will Be in the Band?

OK, you have your first band member or partner in the band, so who else will join the band that will change the sound of music forever? Always remember to consider other people's time schedules and other commitments. Also bear in mind the skill level of the other potential band member – whether it's higher or lower than yours. Personality conflicts are always an issue when it comes to group activities (especially in rock music, not so much in classical guitar), so make sure you invite people you get along with in general.

FIGURE 19-7:

TWO FRIENDS PLAYING
THE GUITAR TOGETHER

## Who Will Play What?

You have designated yourself as the guitarist, and you maybe even have a second guitarist. Now you need a bassist and a drummer to have a complete band. Even though your little brother may be an awesome clarinet player in the school orchestra, that instrument may not be suitable for this situation. Perhaps you could use a keyboard player to play some cool electric piano or synthesizer parts in some songs. Hey – it was good enough for The Beatles. Also, who will be singing? That's a very important thing to consider. You will be playing songs, so it's a good idea to have a singer (a good one, if possible, to start out with). Maybe you'll give it a try yourself.

## What Kind of Music Will You Play?

Once you have assembled your future legendary band formation, you all have to agree on the genre of music you will be playing. You may be thinking rock, someone else may want to play blues, and the drummer may want to play polka (which is a lot of fun to play, by the way). Your band may become something special with all those interesting combinations, but the music may not be exactly what you had in mind after you started reading this book and became motivated to shoot for stardom. Make sure everyone involved with the band is on the same page when it comes to the genre of music you will be playing.

## Where Will You Practise?

Everyone knows that some of the best bands have come from the garage. If you live in a house and have an empty enough garage, then this will be a great place to start. The next option in the house is the cellar or basement. Of course, remember the biggest annoyance when it comes to practising in the house is noise! The advantage to practising in the basement is that the volume from practising with a full band (guitars, bass and drums to start) will become muffled due the physical structure of the property. Keep in mind, the sound of the band will still be heard, just in a diminished capacity. Do your best to be considerate to others who share the same living space that you decide to rehearse in.

Consider a rehearsal space in a facility nearby. These facilities usually charge anywhere from £5 to £15 an hour depending on the size of the room. The advantage here, of course, is that you get a room specifically designed for band rehearsal. A good facility will have soundproofed walls and, in some cases, a stage platform for you to practise addressing your future legions of fans. A good PA (public address) system is important for hearing vocals and overall sound levels of the band. Once the band chips in to pay for the rehearsal time, everyone involved tends to take the rehearsal more seriously.

Playing music with friends and even family is an activity that never gets boring. It lasts as long as your love of music and continued love for learning new songs as well as rediscovering old ones. Plus, you just may inspire someone to learn a new instrument – like the guitar.

## APPENDIX A
# Glossary

# A

### ACCENT
A dynamic effect that places an emphasis on a note or chord.

### ACCIDENTALS
Symbols in written music to raise (♯ = sharpen) or lower (♭ = flatten) notes by semitones. A double flat (♭(♭)) lowers the pitch by a tone. A natural (♮) cancels the accidental alteration.

### ACOUSTIC GUITAR
A hollow-bodied guitar that does not require electronic amplification.

### ACTION
The strings' playability along the neck. Action is affected by the strings' distance from the neck, the neck straightness and the string gauge.

### ACTIVE PICKUPS
Pickups that use a battery going directly to the pickup to boost the sound.

### ALTERED CHORD
A chord or scale in which one or more of the notes is changed to a note not normally associated with that scale.

### ARCH-TOP
A guitar, often an acoustic, with a curved top (soundboard) and F-holes similar to a violin's.

### ARPEGGIO
Literally, 'like a harp' – that is, playing the notes of a chord one after the other rather than together. Also known as a broken chord.

### ARTICULATION
The characteristics of attack and decay of single or groups of notes. For example, 'staccato' and 'legato' are types of articulations.

### ARTIFICIAL HARMONICS
Harmonics produced by fingering a note on the frets and lightly touching the string a fourth higher.

### ATONAL
Not part of the tonal system of major and minor keys; in no key at all.

### ATTACK
The characteristics of the beginning of a sound.

### AUGMENTED
Intervals increased by a semitone are known as augmented intervals. The augmented chord is a major chord with the fifth raised a semitone. (See also Diminished.)

# B

### BEBOP, HARD BOP
A style of jazz that emerged in the 1940s, using fast melodic lines over adventurous extended harmonies. The terms 'bop' and 'bebop' are interchangeable, and 'hard bop' usually refers to the 1950s blues-influenced variant.

**BINDING**

Thin strips of wood or plastic that seal the edges of the guitar body.

**BLUES**

An African-American style of music that uses a scale including flattened thirds, fifths and sevenths, known as the 'blue notes' in a scale. A blues style has a predominantly twelve-bar form.

**BODY**

The main part of the guitar, to which the bridge and neck are attached. On acoustic guitars and some electrics, the body serves as a resonating chamber.

**BOOGIE-WOOGIE**

A style of blues and jazz with a repetitive, rhythmic bass figure derived from early jazz piano playing.

**BOSSA NOVA**

A Brazilian rhythmic style of jazz and popular music widespread in Europe and the United States in the 1960s.

**BOTTLENECK GUITAR**

A technique using a metal bar or tube rather than the fingers of the left hand to play notes and chords, and to slide from one to another.

**BRACES**

Interior wooden strips that strengthen a hollow-bodied guitar. Brace size and configuration partly determine a guitar's tone.

**BREAK**

In jazz, a short solo passage without accompaniment that usually occurs at the end of a phrase.

**BRIDGE**

The structure that holds the saddle (or saddles), over which strings pass on the guitar body. Most bridges can be adjusted to raise or lower string height, changing the guitar's action and intonation.

# C

**CAPO**

A spring-loaded, adjustable clamp that becomes in effect a moveable nut. It fits over the neck and covers all the strings at a given fret, raising the pitch of the strings and allowing a singer or flamenco player to play in a different key and still use open-string chords and fingering.

**CHAMBER MUSIC**

Music for small groups of players (usually no more than nine).

**CHANGES**

The sequence of chords used as a basis for improvisation in jazz.

**CHOKING**

Damping the strings of the guitar to give short staccato chords.

**CHORDS**

Any combination of three notes played together, usually based on the triad formed by the first, third and fifth notes of the scale.

For example, the chord of C major consists of C (the root of the chord), F and G. Chords can be in root position – that is, with the root as the bass note – or various inversions using other notes in the chord as the bass.

### CHORD SUBSTITUTIONS
In jazz, alternatives to the conventionally used chords in a sequence.

### CHORUS
On an electric guitar, simulates the effect of more than one instrument playing the same note.

### CHROMATIC
Chromatic notes are those that fall outside the notes of the key a piece of music is in. The chromatic scale is a twelve-note scale moving in semitones.

### CLASSICAL
The term 'classical' is used loosely to describe art music to distinguish it from folk, jazz, rock, pop and so forth, but more precisely it refers to the period of music from around 1750 to 1830.

### COMPING
Jazz jargon for 'accompanying'.

### COMPRESSION
On an electric guitar, boosts the volume of quieter notes and reduces that of louder ones, evening out the sound of fast passages.

### COUNTERPOINT, CONTRAPUNTAL
The combination of two or more melodic lines played at the same time, within the same harmonic framework.

### COUNTRY (AND WESTERN)
Popular rural music originally from the Southern and Western United States that began with the Carter family.

### CUTAWAY
An indented area of the body that allows the guitarist's fretting hand to access notes higher up the neck.

# D

### DELAY (ECHO)
On an electric guitar, delay mimics the echo effect by playing a delayed copy of the original sound.

### DETUNING
Intentionally putting one or more of the strings out of tune for a specific effect.

### DIATONIC
Using the notes of the major scale.

### DIMINISHED
Intervals decreased in size by a semitone are known as diminished intervals. The diminished chord is based on intervals of a minor third, and the so-called diminished scale consists of alternating tones and semitones.

### DISTORTION
Change of tone quality, with a harsh sound, achieved by overdriving an amplifier, or the use of a distortion pedal, fuzz box or overdriver.

**DOUBLE STOPPING**

Forming a chord by stopping two or more strings with the left hand on the frets.

**DREADNOUGHT**

A large-bodied, steel-strung acoustic guitar.

**DRONE STRINGS**

Strings not intended to be played with the fingers but tuned to vibrate in sympathy with the main instrument's strings. Usually found on sitars.

# E

**ECHO**

An acoustic phenomenon in which a sound is heard repeated from a distance because of its reflection off a surface.

**EFFECTS**

Numerous special effects are possible on a modern electric guitar, including chorus, compression, delay, distortion, enhancer, expander, flanger, fuzz, harmonizer, Leslie, octave divider, overdrive, panning, preamp, reverb, tremolo, vibrato, volume pedal and wah-wah (see separate listings for each).

**ENHANCER**

On an electric guitar, a device to improve sound definition.

**EXPANDER**

The opposite of compressor, increasing the range of volume on an electric guitar.

# F

**F-HOLES**

Violin-style F-shaped sound holes, usually found in pairs.

**FEEDBACK**

The loud whine produced by a microphone or pickup receiving and amplifying its own signal from a loudspeaker.

**FILL**

In jazz and rock, a short melodic figure played by an accompanying instrument between phrases.

**FINGERPICKING**

Right-hand technique in which the strings are plucked by individual fingers.

**FLAMENCO**

A Spanish style of playing, singing and dancing. Forms of flamenco include alegrias, buierias, fandangos, farrucas, ganadinas, malaguena, seguidillas, siguiryas, soleas and tarantas, and the guitar often interjects falsetas (melodic improvised interludes) into these forms. Techniques in flamenco guitar playing include alzapua (up-and-down strokes with the thumbnail), apagado (left-hand damping), golpe (tapping on the body of the guitar), picado (fingerstyle) and rasqueado (strumming by unfurling the fingers across the strings).

**FLANGER**

On an electric guitar, a chorus-type effect, using a delayed signal with a slight pitch variation.

**FLAT-TOP**
A guitar whose soundboard, or top, is flat.

**FRETBOARD**
The wooden strip, usually of hardwood, attached at the top of the neck and into which the frets are set. Also called the fingerboard.

**FRETS**
Metal wires set into the fretboard at precise distances, allowing the strings to sound the correct pitches along the neck.

**FOLK**
The music of rural cultures, usually passed down orally. The word 'folk' is also used to describe composed music in the style of true folk music, particularly after the folk revival of the 1950s.

**FREE JAZZ**
A jazz style of the 1960s, which is freely improvised without reference to a specific tune or harmonic sequence.

**FUNK**
A term applied to some African-American music styles, particularly those with complex syncopated eighth and sixteenth notes.

**FUSION**
A jazz-rock fusion, but also any form of crossover from one style to another.

**FUZZ**
On an electric guitar, a form of distortion operated by a fuzz pedal.

# G

**GIG BAG**
A portable padded bag made either of canvas, nylon or leather that you can use as an alternative to a hard case.

**GLISSANDO**
A slide from one note to another.

**GRACE NOTES**
Short notes played just before the main note of a tune as an ornament.

**GROOVE**
A repeated rhythmic pattern in jazz and rock.

**GUITAR SYNTHESIZER**
Guitars with built-in electronics that send MIDI trigger information to external synthesizers, drum machines and so on.

**GUITTARÓN**
A large Mexican guitar with four or five strings. Primarily used in a mariachi band.

# H

**HABAFIERA**
A Cuban dance, or its rhythm.

**HAMMER-ON**
Notes played by hammering the string with the fingers of the left hand, rather than plucking with the right hand.

**HARMONICS**
Notes with an ethereal tone higher than the pitch of the string, produced by lightly touching the string at certain points.

**HARMONIZER**
On an electric guitar, a chorus-type effect adding a sound in harmony with the original signal.

**HEAD**
In jazz, the statement of the tune before and after the improvised solos.

**HEADSTOCK**
The structure at the end of the neck of the guitar that holds the tuning machines.

# I

**INTERVAL**
The distance between two notes. For example, C to G is a fifth (that is, five notes of the scale); C to E is a third (three notes); and C to C is an octave (eight notes).

**INTONATION**
The degree to which pitch is accurately produced in performance. It is also a system of tuning.

**INVERSION**
See chords.

# J

**JAMMING**
A term used when musicians get together to play and improvise music.

**JAZZ**
African-American in origin, characterized by the use of improvisation, 'blue notes' and syncopated rhythms.

# K

**KEY SIGNATURE**
An arrangement of sharps and flats (or lack thereof) at the beginning of each staff line.

# L

**LATIN**
Music of Latin-American origin, including dance rhythms such as the habañera, samba, rumba, bossa nova and so on.

**LEGATO**
Smoothly, not staccato.

**LESLIE**
The Leslie cabinet, originally for use with electronic organs, contains a rotating speaker, giving a swirling effect to music played on an electric guitar.

**LICKS**
In jazz and rock, short, almost clichéd, phrases inserted into a solo.

**LUTE**
A plucked-string instrument with an oblong, rounded body and a short fretted neck.

# M

**MACHINE HEAD**
See Tuning peg.

**MICROTONE**
Interval of less than a semitone.

**MIDI**
Musical instrument digital interface. An electronic protocol that allows musical

instruments such as electric guitars and synthesizers to communicate with sequencers, effects boxes, computers and so on.

### MINIMALISM

A movement in music from the 1960s using static harmonies, repeated patterns and a minimum of material.

### MODES

Scales using the notes of the diatonic scale, other than the major and minor scales. The modes, such as Dorian, Phrygian and Aeolian, originated in medieval music, but were adopted by jazz players in the 1950s.

### MODULATE

Move from one key to another.

# N

### NECK

The long structure that runs from the body to the headstock, and onto which the fretboard is attached. Necks have a longitudinal curve that can be adjusted by means of the truss rod. The width, shape and curvature of the neck largely determine a guitar's playability.

### NOTATION

Any means of writing down music.

### NUT

The notched fitting – usually of bone, ivory, ebony, metal or plastic – that guides the strings from the fretboard to the tuning pegs.

# O

### OCTAVE

An interval eight diatonic scale degrees above a note. Two notes an octave apart share the same letter name.

### OCTAVE DIVIDER

A stomp box pedal used on an electric guitar, an early form of harmonizer, adding a sound an octave above or below the original signal.

### OPEN TUNING

Tuning the strings of the guitar to a specific chord, rather than the conventional E-A-D-G-B-E. There are also other non-conventional tunings, such as D-A-D-G-A-D.

### OVERDRIVE

On an electric guitar, a form of distortion.

### OVERDUBS

Parts added to a recording after the original take.

# P

### PANNING

On an electric guitar, moving the source of the sound within the stereo field.

### PARTIAL CHORDS

Chords not using all the strings of the guitar.

### PASSING CHORDS

Chords used 'in passing' from one harmony to another, not part of the main harmonic sequence.

**PEDAL POINT**
A repeated bass note that supports a sequence of changing harmonies.

**PEDAL STEEL GUITAR**
An electric zither, used primarily in country music.

**PENTATONIC**
A scale of five notes, rather than the more usual seven.

**PHASING**
On an electric guitar, playing two identical sounds slightly out of phase with one another.

**PICK OR PLECTRUM**
Object used for striking the guitar strings, usually made from plastic.

**PICKGUARD**
A protective plate on the body of the guitar that protects the top from being scratched by a pick or fingers.

**PICKUP**
The device on electric guitars that picks up and transmits the sound of the strings to the amplifier.

**PICKUP SWITCH**
Allows pickups to be turned on individually or in various combinations.

**POTENTIOMETER (POT)**
A variable resistor used for an electric guitar's volume and tone controls. Amplifiers also have pots.

**PREAMP**
With an electric guitar, the preamplifier can be used as a form of tone control, or to boost the signal.

**PULL-OFF**
A note played by pulling the string with the fingers of the left hand.

# R

**RAGA**
A scale used in Indian music. There are hundreds of different ragas, many using microtones.

**RAGTIME**
An African-American style of music, a precursor to jazz.

**REGGAE**
A style of Jamaican popular music. A combination of American rhythm-and-blues and African music.

**REVERB**
On an electric guitar, this mimics the echo effect, either by a built-in spring reverb or a digital electronic emulation.

**RHYTHM-AND-BLUES**
African-American pop music originating in the late 1940s, the precursor to rock-and-roll.

**RIFF**
In jazz and rock, a short, repeated melodic phrase.

**ROCK, ROCK-AND-ROLL**

Rock-and-roll evolved in the 1950s from rhythm-and-blues, and in its 1960s form became known simply as rock.

**RUBATO**

Not strictly in tempo – played freely and expressively.

**RUMBA (RHUMBA)**

Afro-Cuban dance.

# S

**SADDLE**

The fitting that guides the strings over the bridge. Most electric guitars have individual saddles for each string. These can be adjusted to change a string's length and thus intonation.

**SCALES**

A series of ascending or descending notes in a specific key, the basis for compositions in the tonal system.

**SEGUE**

Moving without a break to the next movement, section or number.

**SEMITONE**

A half-step, or halftone. The smallest interval in the diatonic scale – for example, the distance between E and F, or B and C.

**SLIDE**

A style of guitar-playing using bottleneck, where notes and chords slide from one to another.

**SOLID BODY**

A guitar whose body is made from a solid piece of wood or is a solid lamination. Most electrics are solid bodies; some are semi-hollow.

**SOUNDBOARD**

The resonating top of an acoustic guitar.

**SOUND HOLE**

A hole (or holes) in the top of a guitar through which sound is emitted.

**STACCATO**

Detached. Staccato notes or chords are short and clipped, not smoothly moving to the next.

**STRAIGHT EIGHTS**

In jazz, playing 'straight eights' means playing exactly on the beat, whereas 'swing' indicates that the rhythm should be interpreted more freely. (See also Swing.)

**STRING-BENDING**

Using the fingers of the left hand to pull a string to one side, 'bending' the pitch of the note.

**STRINGS**

The cords that are plucked to cause vibrations that produce a guitar's sound. Most guitar strings are solid wire or thin wire wrapped around a solid core; classical guitars have nylon and metal-wound nylon strings. A string's thickness (gauge) depends on its position on the guitar and the relative thickness of the entire six-string set.

**SWAP FOURS**

In jazz, when soloists alternate improvisations with one another every four bars.

**SWING**

A style of jazz of the 1940s, mainly for big bands. Also an instruction to play rhythms freely. (See also Straight eights.)

**SYNCOPATION**

Shifting the accent of a melody off the main beat of the bar – a characteristic of jazz and much rock and pop music.

# T

**TABLATURE**

Musical notation using letters, numbers or diagrams to indicate pitch.

**TAILPIECE**

The device that holds the strings' ball ends.

**TEMPO**

The underlying speed of a piece of music.

**TIMBRE**

The tone quality of a sound.

**TONAL, TONALITY**

Relating to the system of major and minor keys.

**TONE (WHOLE TONE)**

An interval of two semitones – for example the distance between C and D, or F and G.

**TREMOLO**

On an electric guitar, small and rapid variation in the volume of a note.

**TRILL**

Rapid alternation between one note and the note above.

**TRUSS ROD**

A metal rod that runs through the length of the neck, increasing its strength and allowing adjustment of the longitudinal curve.

**TRUSS ROD ADJUSTING NUT**

The part of the truss rod system that can be tightened or loosened to alter rod tension.

**TUNING PEGS, TUNING MACHINES**

Devices set into the headstock that anchor strings and allow them to be tuned. Each tuning machine consists of a post, a geared mechanism and a tuning key.

**TURNAROUND**

In jazz, the harmony under the last phrase of a tune, taking the music back to the beginning for its repeat.

# U

**UNISON**

On exactly the same note. For example, on a twelve-string guitar, the pairs of strings are tuned in unison – that is, to the same note. In jazz, the tune of the head is often played by several instruments in unison.

# V

**VAMPS, VAMPING**

Repeated accompanying figure in jazz and popular music before the melody begins.

**VARIATION**

Technique used to modify a musical idea after it is first heard.

**VIBRATO**

On an electric guitar, small and rapid variation in the pitch of a note.

**VIHUELA**

A stringed instrument of medieval and Renaissance Spain.

**VOICING**

The spacing of the notes in a chord.

**VOLUME PEDAL**

Means of altering the volume of sound for an electric guitar, useful in creating the 'fade-in' effect or as a 'swell' pedal.

# W

**WAH-WAH**

With an electric guitar, the wah-wah pedal controls the relative bass and treble response of a sound. Fully down it has a high treble tone; fully up it emphasizes the bass. The characteristic 'wah-wah' sound is achieved by rocking the pedal back and forth.

**WHOLE-TONE SCALE**

A six-note augmented scale formed entirely of intervals of a whole tone, such as C-D-E-F#-G#-A#.

# Z

**ZITHER**

A stringed instrument in which the strings run the entire length of the instrument.

# APPENDIX B
# Websites for the Guitar

True Fire – custom guitar videos and CD-ROM instruction.
*www.truefire.com*

Workshop Live – video streaming of guitar lessons.
*www.workshoplive.com*

Acoustic magazine – the UK's only magazine dedicated to the acoustic world.
*www.acousticmagazine.com*

Fingerstyle Guitar – the magazine site for all things fingerstyle guitar.
*www.fingerstyleguitar.com*

Guitar Tricks – site for learning the little subtleties of guitar playing.
*www.guitartricks.com*

Total Guitar magazine – news, lessons, buyers' guides, competitions and more.
*www.musicradar.com*

Play Guitar magazine – excellent site for beginners.
*www.playguitarmagazine.com*

Just Jazz Guitar – online version of the American magazine.
*www.justjazzguitar.com*

Guitar at About.com – the place to find guitar lessons and daily MP3s. One of the best general sites for beginners.
*www.guitar.about.com*

Guitar chord dictionary – a free online resource.
*www.emediamusic.com/freetools/chord.html*

GuitarSite.com – home of Guitar News Weekly and the 2000 Guitars Database.
*www.guitarsite.com*

Guitar Player magazine – the original US guitar magazine with great features and historical references.
*www.guitarplayer.com*

Guitar World magazine – great magazine for all types of rock guitar music.
*www.guitarworld.com*

Jazz Guitar Online – jazz guitar lessons, transcriptions and licks.
*www.jazzguitar.be*

Harmony Central – the number-one online community for musicians.
*www.harmony-central.com*

Tappistry – site dedicated to the art of two-handed touchstyle guitar playing.
*www.tappistry.org*

## APPENDIX C
# Guitar Tricks

### Hammer-On
This is used a lot in rock, blues and folk playing. Fret a note with your first finger, say D at the fifth fret, String 5. Now, while the note is still ringing, 'hammer down' your finger on E at the seventh fret, String 5, and keep it there.

### Pull-Off
This is really a hammer-on in reverse. You need to have both fingers on the fret. Play the note E, as before, then pull off your finger so the D will sound clearly.

### Trill
If you rapidly combine both techniques above, you get a trick often used in rock-and-roll that may sound familiar, called a trill.

### String Bends
A lot of rock guitarists and blues guitarists use a string bend. If you pull or push the string, once you've fretted the note, you can actually bend it almost to the note on the next fret. It's the same sort of technique as using a mechanical tremolo arm. It generally works best if you use thin-gauge strings.

### Double-String Bends
A rock and blues cliché, but effective on occasion if the spirit moves you. The trick is to have both fingers in place ahead of time. Here, you play the D, on the seventh fret of String 3, bending it until you've reached the pitch of E, and – while still sounding the bent note – play E on an adjacent string (fifth fret, String 2), letting the two notes ring together.

### Vibrato
This just means deliberately invoking a 'wowwow' kind of effect. All you do is rock your finger back and forth on the note as you fret it. The more exaggerated the movement of your hand, the broader will be the 'vib'.

### Slide
This is simple. Slide your finger from one fret to another while the note is still ringing.

## APPENDIX D
# More Advanced Chord Shapes and Scales

**FIGURE APP1:** MAJOR SCALE FINGERINGS (TWO OCTAVES)

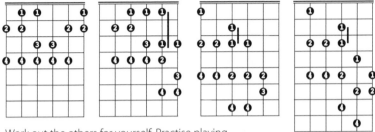

Work out the others for yourself. Practise playing through the cycle of fourths.

**FIGURE APP2:** MINOR SCALE FINGERINGS

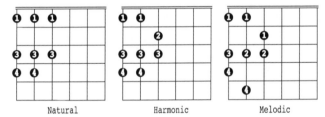

Natural          Harmonic          Melodic

Work these out in two octaves

**FIGURE APP3(A):** PENTATONIC SCALES

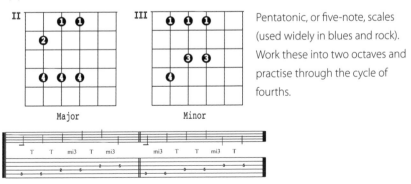

Major          Minor

Pentatonic, or five-note, scales (used widely in blues and rock). Work these into two octaves and practise through the cycle of fourths.

**FIGURE APP3(B):**

AUGMENTED SCALE

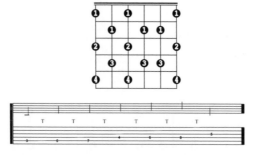

Augmented scale (or whole tone scale). As the name suggests, it moves in whole tones only.

**FIGURE APP3(C):**

DIMINISHED SCALES
There are two different types of scales, as shown above.

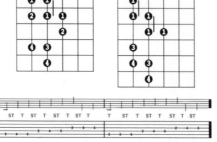

Work out in two octaves and play through the keys.

**FIGURE APP3(D):** BASIC SEVENTH CHORD SHAPES

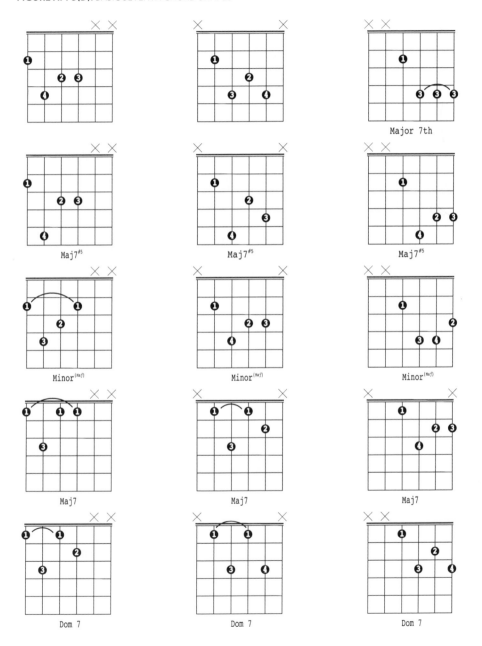

**FIGURE APP3(E):** BASIC SEVENTH CHORD SHAPES

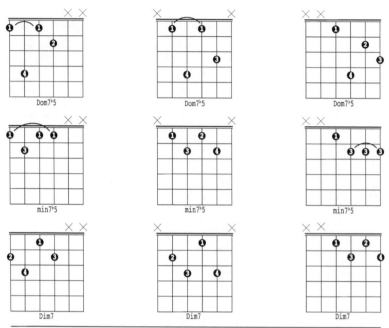

Diminished chords can take their name from any note in the chord.

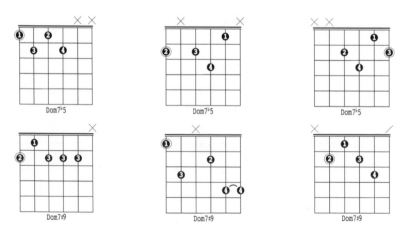

Can take its name from any note in the chord.

**FIGURE APP4:**

O LITTLE TOWN OF

BETHLEHEM

# O Little Town of Bethlehem

(Arranged by J. Wilkins)

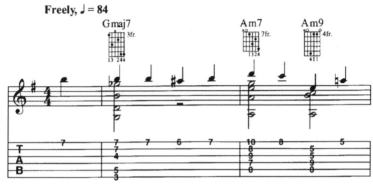

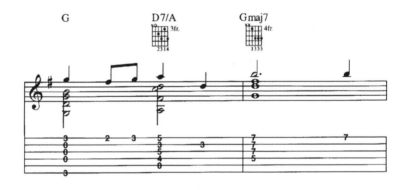

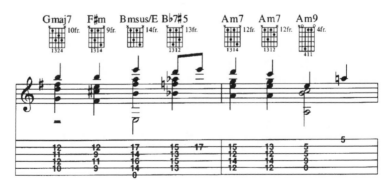

**FIGURE APP4:**

O LITTLE TOWN

OF BETHLEHEM

(*continued*)

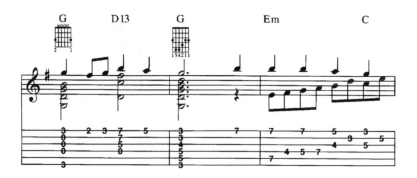

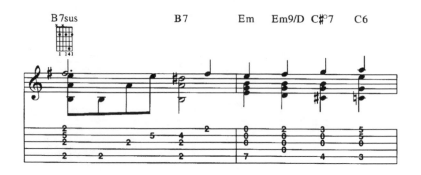

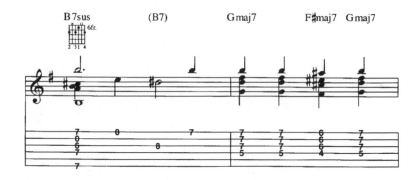

**FIGURE APP4:**

O LITTLE TOWN

OF BETHLEHEM

(*continued*)

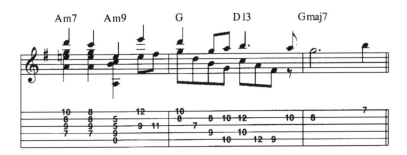

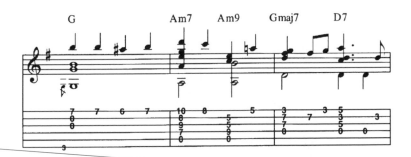

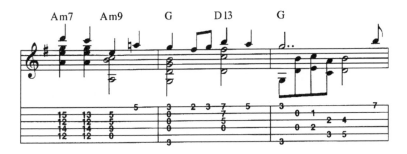

**FIGURE APP4:**

O LITTLE TOWN

OF BETHLEHEM

(*continued*)

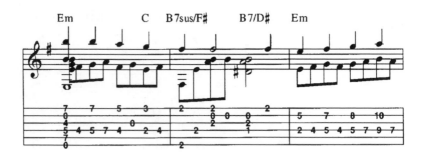

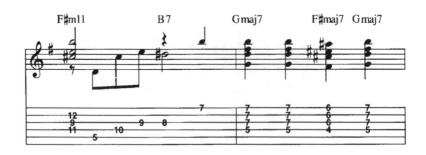

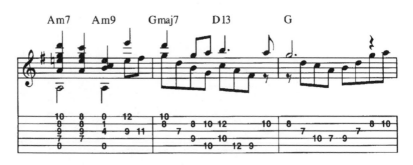

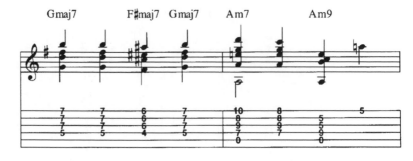

**FIGURE APP4:**

O LITTLE TOWN

OF BETHLEHEM

(continued)

**FIGURE APP4:**

O LITTLE TOWN

OF BETHLEHEM

(continued)

# Index

## Picture Credits

Line art by Ernie Jackson.
Photos by Evan Copp.
Model: Anthony Babino.

Figure 15-1 courtesy of Thomas Libis.
Figure 17-1 courtesy of Thomas Libis.
Figure 17-2 courtesy of Michael Tamborrino.
Figure 17-3 courtesy of Floyd Rose Marketing.
Figure 17-4 courtesy of www.borntorock.com.
Figure 17-5 courtesy of Rainsong Guitars.
Figure 17-6 courtesy of M-Audio USA.
Figure 17-7 courtesy of Fretted Synth Audio.
Figure 17-8 courtesy of Native Instruments, Inc.
Figure 17-9 courtesy of Brian Moore Guitars.
Fig 17-10 courtesy of BEHRINGER USA Inc.
Figure 17-11 courtesy of M-Audio USA.
Figure 17-12 courtesy of SoundTech Professional Audio.
Figure 19-7 models: Michael Puglia and Anthony Babino.

Guitars used for recording: Soloway Guitars, Godin Guitars. Software used for recording: Cubase SX3, Guitar Rig 2, Tech 21 XDI.

## Acknowledgments

Severe thanks go out to Ms. Lisa Laing. The editor extraordinaire.